ADVANCED EDUCATIONAL PSYCHOLOGY

ADVANCED EDUCATIONAL PSYCHOLOGY

Dr. M.S. Talawar
M.A., M.Ed., Ph.D.
Professor in Education &
Director –UGC-Academic Staff College,
Bangalore University, Bangalore

Dr. V.A. Benakanal
M.A., M.Ed., M.Phil., Ph.D.

CENTRUM PRESS
NEW DELHI-110002 (INDIA)

CENTRUM PRESS
H.O.: 4360/4, Ansari Road, Daryaganj,
New Delhi-110 002 (India)
Ph.: 23278000, 23261597
B.O.: No. 1015, Ist Main Road, BSK IIIrd Stage
IIIrd Phase, IIIrd Block,
Bangalore - 560 085 (India)
Tel.: 080-41723429
Visit us at: www.centrumpress.com

Advanced Educational Psychology

First Edition, 2009

PRINTED IN INDIA

Printed at Balaji Offset, Delhi

Contents

Preface

Educational psychology is the study of how humans learn in educational settings, the effectiveness of educational interventions, the psychology of teaching, and the social psychology of schools as organizations. Although the terms "educational psychology" and "school psychology" are often used interchangeably, In the US researchers and theorists are likely to be identified as educational psychologists, whereas practitioners in schools or school-related settings are identified as school psychologists. In the UK, however, this distinction is not made and the generic term for practitioners is "Educational Psychologist."

Educational psychology is concerned with how students learn and develop, often focusing on subgroups such as gifted children and those subject to specific disabilities. The subject Educational Psychology is now-a-days becoming more and more popular. In comparison to other subjects of study, more and more students are opting for it at the senior secondary stage and degree level. Even in the most prestigious competitive examinations like the IAS and the allied examinations or the Provincial Civil Service examinations the number of students opting Psychology, for the preliminary and mains in increasing every year.

The reason for its popularity lies well behind its body of knowledge which is quite interesting and its wide use and applications in almost all the walks and spheres of human life. Educational psychology can in part be understood through its relationship with other disciplines. It is informed primarily by psychology, bearing a relationship to that discipline analogous to the relationship between medicine and biology and also between Engineering and Physics. Educational psychology in turn informs a wide range of specialties within educational studies, including instructional design, educational technology, curriculum development, organizational learning, special education and classroom management.

Author

Unit I

Educational Psychology for the New Millennium

MEANING OF MODERN PSYCHOLOGY - STUDY OF PSYCHOLOGY: STRUCTURALISM

Psychology (Greek: lit. "study of the mind", from psykhç "breath, spirit, soul"; and *--logia* "study of") is an academic and applied discipline involving the scientific study of human mental functions and behaviour. Occasionally, in addition or opposition to employing the scientific method, it also relies on symbolic interpretation and critical analysis, although these traditions have tended to be less pronounced than in other social sciences such as sociology. Psychologists study such phenomena as perception, cognition, emotion, personality, behaviour and interpersonal relationships. Some, especially depth psychologists, also study the unconscious mind. Psychological knowledge is applied to various spheres of human activity, including issues related to everyday life—such as family, education and employment—and to the treatment of mental health problems.

Psychologists attempt to understand the role of mental functions in individual and social behaviour, while also exploring the underlying physiological and neurological processes. Psychology includes many sub-fields of study and applications concerned with such areas as human development, sports, health, industry, media and law. Psychology incorporates research from the natural sciences, social sciences and humanities. A person who studies or practices psychology is called a psychologist. The word "psychology" is the combination of two terms - study (ology) and soul (psyche), or mind. The derivation of the word from Latin gives it this clear and obvious meaning:

THE STUDY OF THE SOUL OR MIND

This meaning has been altered over the years until today, this is not what the word means at all. The subject of psychology, as studied in colleges and universities, currently has very little to do with the mind, and absolutely nothing to do with the soul or spirit. It is important to understand that words and ideas are supposed to refer to something. "The large tree in the front yard" refers to an actual thing that can be seen, touched and experienced. "The man walking his little dog last night at sunset" refers to an actual event that can be seen, observed and experienced. The realm of mind is an actual realm that can be experienced, and at one time there were words that accurately referred to this realm.

Let's see what a few dictionaries have to say and how a word could alter and lose its true and actual meaning.

"Psyche" is defined as:

- The spirit or soul.
- The human mind.
- In psychoanalysis, the mind functioning as the centre of thought, emotion, and behaviour.

And defining "soul", we have:

- The spiritual or immortal elements in a person.
- A person's mental or moral or emotional nature.

Most of us would agree we have a "psyche" per the above definitions in the sense of mind, thought, and emotions. Most would also agree they have a "soul" per the second definition above relating to man's mental, moral or emotional nature. We might all have different notions about what these ultimately are, but few could sanely disagree they exist. The derivation of "psyche" comes from Latin and the Greek *psukhe* - breath, life, soul. To get a better "feel" for this term try to think of it as the invisible animating principle or entity that occupies, interacts with and directs the physical body.

We are not dealing with opinions or beliefs here. This is simply what the words and terms mean. Get clear on this first and understand what the words and terms mean, before you start getting into the opinions of others on the subject. If you choose to decide the "mind" refers to nothing real after understanding what the words and definitions mean, despite the fact that almost 10,000 years of thinking men have seriously and carefully looked into this subject, and after no real investigation on your own part, then that's your decision.

Also, realise you will be basing this decision on "thinking" and "reason", both of which are only subsidiary to and *part* of any one mind, and neglecting to use a greater aspect of your mind - your personal awareness and direct observation. Basing a decision on what other people say about a mind involves only *concepts* and *ideas* about a mind. Observation involves *experiencing the mind itself* - your own mind. When it comes to minds there is only one mind any of us can directly observe or experience and that mind is our own. If you want to learn about minds, the only place to start is with your own. You cannot directly observe or experience the mind of another person, at least not without some extrasensory ability such as telepathy.

Originally, and for thousands of years, the subject of psychology involved the study of the human spirit, soul or mind. This involves things and functions not obviously visible to the physical senses. You can't see a mind with one's eyes. You can't "feel" a thought with one's hands. You can't place an emotion on a scale and weigh it. You can't detect imagination, even with sophisticated electronic detection devices. Just because some scientist's electronic device measures various electronic pulses or signals when you are asked to imagine something does not at all mean that they are "measuring imagination". What they are measuring is some brain reaction that occurs *when* you initiate an act of imagination.

There *is* a relationship between the mind and the brain, but this relationship is almost completely unknown and not understood. The same is true for any chemical reactions or events that occur concurrent with imagination, thoughts or feelings. There *is* some relationship, but it is poorly understood. In fact, the entire framework of the relationship is poorly conceived. Modern "scientific" fields, since they haven't been able to study or detect these things with the physical senses or laboratory measuring devices have taken a drastic leap and declared that these things therefore don't exist. They have therefore asserted that these things don't deserve recognition, and should be ignored in any "legitimate" study of man, the mind, and human behaviour. John Watson, a typical behavioral psychologist had this to say:

The extent to which most of us are shot through with a savage background is almost unbelievable.... One example of such a religious concept is that every individual has a soul *which is separate and distinct from the body.... No one has ever touched a soul, or seen one in a test tube, or has in any way come into relationship with it as he has with the other objects of his daily experience ....*

The behaviorist asks: Why don't we make what we can observe *the real field of psychology? Let us limit ourselves to things that can be observed, and formulate laws concerning only those things. Now what can we observe? We can observe* behaviour - *what the organism does or says. And let us point out at once: that* saying *is doing - that is,* behaving... - John Watson, behaviorist

Strangely, the study of the mind has come into the peculiar position of being a study that denies the mind! That's like biology denying the existence of biological organisms, but going on pretending to still be the science of biological organisms while actually dealing with something else entirely. A subject can't exist if it denies the very basis of its own existence by definition. That is the state of modern western psychology and psychiatry. Mmmm? They can't and shouldn't exist, but they do. The entire structure of these subjects as they currently exist is a sham.

Let's take a closer look at this. We each are quite aware we have a mind, emotions, and thoughts, even if we are not so clear or sure about the "soul" and "spirit". We know we are aware and possess self-awareness, but what the nature, qualities and potentials are of awareness is largely anybody's guess. We each know we possess consciousness. In fact, we are aware of our own consciousness as much or more than anything else, yet modern "science" ignores and even denies it. But the truth, despite what "science" or "professionals" say, is that the mind exists to and for each of us as an obvious and observable fact of direct experience. A quick look can tell us many obvious things.

I doubt any of us would suggest we don't have a mind, awareness, thoughts or feelings even though none of these things can be detected or perceived with the physical senses or "scientific" measuring gadgets. No third party observer can directly observe or detect *any* of these things. *We don't immediately run off and deny their existence,* and we correctly assume others have similar minds, thoughts, feelings and emotions. They do. Modern psychologists and psychiatrists, for all practical purposes, completely deny every aspect of the invisible world known to you as your mind. It *is* invisible to physical detection, but it *does* exist. In fact, it very much exists, but it is not made up of anything physical. While the mind deals with and relates to some subtle forms of energy, in the end it cannot be understood within the framework of matter or energy. Of course, any card-carrying materialist naturally hates that idea with a passion. To them, "if I can't measure it then it doesn't exist".

There is constant activity within each of our "invisible worlds". We are each in some way constantly analyzing problems, entertaining thoughts of tomorrow's occurrences, recalling yesterday's failures, wallowing in the sadness of a loss, concentrating on the creation of a musical composition, or day-dreaming. There are ever changing feelings and emotions about everything we experience, and an endless parade of judgments and commentary about what we see. Actually, for many of us, we have *too much* mind. It goes on and on and never seems to stop. It is a constant source of images, memories and ideas intruding themselves upon our awareness. Most of us can't control any of this and simply accept as inevitable this continual parade of images and ideas appearing across the landscape of our mind.

In a very real manner *all problems* with any mind, such as things psychiatry calls "depression", "anxiety", "compulsive disorder", "Attention Deficit Disorder" (ADD or ADHD), and even "suicidal ideation", are ultimately and solely *uncontrollable aspects of one's own mind that intrude upon the person's awareness*. It's not that these things don't exist in some way, but they don't exist in the way psychiatry understands and claims to solve them. A better way to handle these problems would be to assist the person to *increase control over the content of their own mind*. There are many ways to do this, although they have never been all pulled together, adequately investigated, codified and organized into a straight-forward workable compilation of methods. Modern "science" has simply discarded the notion of the mind, and from that point on, never bothered to investigate it closely with the aim to understand, solve or improve it.

First, this invisible world *is* totally real. It is *not* imaginary or a hallucination. My invisible world isn't directly real to you, and your invisible world isn't directly real to me, but they are *each real nonetheless*. The person who wants to argue this fact is simply a fool, dull, unable to comfortably observe his *own* mind (because it is possibly filled with degraded and nasty things), and probably addicted to the objects of physical sensation and perception to the exclusion of anything else (a modern materialist).

Second, this "invisible" world of mind involves many different aspects, functions and potentials. Imagination, attention, intellect, awareness, intention, reason, wills, responsibility, memory, and many other things exist in each of us. They are a vital and important part of us. Some people might venture to say some of these things ARE us. There is much to each of these areas and a short essay cannot begin to even scratch the surface of their nature, functioning, possible development and capabilities. But they definitely *do exist* and deserve recognition and attention. Any subject calling itself "psychology" would have to address *these things* in detail. The failure of modern psychology and psychiatry to do so is glaringly apparent. These subjects now only address behaviour, physiology, genetics and biochemistry, and the mind is of no real concern. *That* is a very sad comment on the current state of "modern psychology".

Members of the educational establishment write the dictionaries, and the educational establishment is entrenched in modern psychological theories. Let's return to the correct definition of the word. Adhering to the strict definition of the word, psychology would involve the study of man's invisible world as described above, and nothing else. By definition this is what the study would deal with.

This is not an opinion or bias. This is according to exactly what the word means and nothing else. Of course, relations to behaviour could be studied, and relations to brain activity could be studied, but the subject in itself, by definition is or should be the study of the mind or soul. A more correct name for the modern subjects of psychology and psychiatry would be "people control" because that's what they actually are. They are subjects involving how to alter thoughts, attitudes and behaviour. The intention is to control people. That in a nutshell is the purpose of behaviorism. Naturally governments and totalitarians love the subject. They also fund it in large way.

STUDY OF THE MIND

What would a study of the mind entail? It would investigate the nature, functioning, and potentials of man's inner and invisible mental activity. This would encompass such things as awareness, attention, intention, imagination and concentration. It would develop techniques for any individual to first, become aware of these functions, and to also strengthen and expand their use and control of these functions. It would also investigate the *actual source* of the problems anyone experiences with their own mind. Again, these things do exist, can be observed by anyone caring to examine *their own mind,* and involve a tremendous uncharted area of possible exploration, investigation, codification and summarizing. Freudian psychology and psychotherapy, despite all its faults, at least recognized and partially examined this realm.

For a subject calling itself the "science of the mind" to omit all this is a huge failure of modern psychology. It's actually absurd and would be laughable if the results of what they do weren't so insidious. It is equally laughable that many of these overly-educated boobs talk together as if they are the absolute pinnacle of truth about the subject of psychology. Sadly, too many others accept their claims and treat them as if they actually deserve respect, support and admiration. They don't. This has nothing to do with mysticism, spiritualism (communicating with the dead), astral travel, OBE (out-of-body experiences), or psychic phenomena. It's not that these don't or can't exist, but a serious and scientific examination of the mind need not involve or explain these things.

It might eventually, but it isn't necessary. The point is you *do have a mind*. It is more *you* than anything else. You can take away your possessions, your family, your friends, your job, your arms, your legs, your torso, your ears, your nose, your jaw, your skull, and the one thing that remains, which always remains, and which is closest to your basic identity, is your *mind*. This is the invisible space and activity you are aware of every second of every day and that most people experience as existing "in their head". This realm has been grossly ignored by modern psychological studies and theories to our continual detriment and harm. Some of this may be hard for some readers to understand or accept because an actual study and involvement with the mind isn't done at all under the current subject of psychology.

It's strangely absent from most modern concepts of Man. This concept has been largely eradicated from the "modern world view". Notions of the mind and related ideas about it have been falsely equated to "religion", "spiritualism" or "mysticism". We each have a mind. You know it, and I know it. We each experience it and its many various aspects as mentioned above. This is very simple and straightforward. Modern psychology, due to absurd notions, flawed presumptions, intellectual dullness, observational weakness, blatant prejudice, and tremendous financial concerns ignores the mind completely, and *instead* concentrates on physiology, and analyzing and controlling animal behaviour and responses to environmental factors. It's not that you don't have a body and use it to play your part in life. You do. There *is* physiology, and the environment *does* effect each and every one of us. But the current subject *pretends* to be a study of the mind and Man, and having failed completely at that has abandoned and finally denied the very existence of Man's mind. Worse, it pretends to be the *final word on the subject*, all the while attacking and suppressing any honest study or subject that deals with the actual field of the mind.

Modern psychology and psychiatry claim validity by posturing as "science". They claim to "study Man as an object of investigative science". They fail at this because any *legitimate* science should and would take into account *all* aspects of the subject it deals with. A valid science would not choose to omit a major body of data from its analysis, which is what they have done with the mind. Dealing with, examining, and limiting observations to a specific *smaller* realm of data, while ignoring a very large area of other data, which it finds inconvenient because it fails to conform to their pet theories, is exactly what has been done by the modern fields of psychology and psychiatry. Failing to take the *entire* subject matter into account has resulted in incorrect theories, faulty observations, flawed basic assumptions, and unworkable results.

Considering that every decent, creative, and wonderful thing in existence in the physical world started as an *idea* in the invisible and unobservable *mind* of someone should make this denial of the mind by "modern science" a major cause for alarm. This is doubly true when one also considers that every problem in society largely has its source in actual problems with an individual mind. Education and the environment may heavily influence problems with crime, violence, abuse, and sexual deviancy, but ultimately the final basic source of these problem areas resides in the individual minds of people.

THE HARMFUL RESULTS OF DENYING THE MIND

When the mind is denied, so ultimately is every good and decent thing that emanate from it including creativity, self-determinism, responsibility, morality, reason, and a value of life itself. The current decadent notion of man without a mind or inner personality, considered only as an animal or a biological organism has been institutionalized into the theories and practices of modern civilization in the media, sociology, education, government, economics, health, and of course, psychology and psychiatry.

This has had disastrous consequences in the form of increasing crime, divorce, violence, and decreasing levels of education, morality, personal responsibility, social stability and sanity. Simply, when the source of life itself for the individual and society is denied, oppressive practices parading as "science" surface and the quality of life and sanity rapidly deteriorates. This is the exact condition of modern western civilization. Psychiatric lobotomy, electric shock treatment, psychoactive drugs, behavioral manipulation, mass population control, and social development instead of intellectual education in the schools serve as a few examples.

It has become popular in modern society for people to toss off, giggle about, ridicule and flippantly criticize any alternative subject of the mind (i.e. yoga, meditation, ritual magic, Rosicrucianism, Scientology, etc.) It is *in vogue* to consider these weird and unusual. And true enough, some of them *are* weird. But the only really weird and unusual thing is that modern man is so dull and heavily indoctrinated that he is almost completely incapable of a) looking at anything fairly, b) getting involved in it more than superficially, c) examining it in some detail, d) remaining honest about what he observes and e) deciding for himself based upon accurate personal observations. This reduction in mental and observational ability is also a result of modern educational practices. These practices are direct descendants of modern psychological theories that view man as a "social organism", and tend to ignore his intellectual and cognitive abilities and development (i.e. aspects of a mind).

A leading psychological text begins by very carefully saying that today the word "psychology" does not refer to the mind or soul, and "has to be studied by its own history", since it no longer refers to the soul, or even to the mind. The

Diagnostic and Statistical Manual (DSM-IV), the psychiatric bible of "mental disorders" states,

Although this volume is titled the Diagnostic and Statistical Manual of Mental Disorders, the term mental disorder unfortunately implies a distinction between "mental" disorders and "physical" disorders that is a reductionistic anachronism of mind/body dualism.

They readily admit ignoring the "mind" as a thing of itself to be studied or understood. The current subject is spiritually bankrupt and all that emanates from it denies life, and everything positive about humanity. The logical conclusion of modern psychological theory is that man is an animal to be genetically bred, controlled, herded, and placed into suitable environments. This is the approach of the modern social planner and behavioral controller. These are the guys who governments fund, support and listen to. Is it any wonder things aren't going so well on planet Earth?

Mr. P.D. Ouspensky says it well:

To begin with I must say that practically never in history has psychology stood at so low a level *as at the present time. It has lost all touch with its* origin *and its* meaning *so that now it is even difficult to define the term "psychology": that is, to say what psychology is and what it studies. And this is so in spite of the facts that never in history have there been so many psychological theories and so many psychological writings.* - The Psychology of Man's Possible Evolution, 1950

He also adds that psychology may be the "oldest science and unfortunately, in its most essential features *a forgotten science.*" A brief look at history is in order so the reader can understand more of what a true subject of psychology might entail.

For thousands of years psychology existed under the name of philosophy. The Hindu *Vedas* contain the oldest record of man's examination of mind and spirit. In India all forms of *Yoga*, which are essentially psychology, are described as one of the six systems of philosophy. *Sufi teachings*, which again are chiefly psychological, are regarded as partly religious and partly metaphysical. In more modern times some version of these systems, still largely following in this same vein, can be found the subjects of Rosicrucianism, New Thought, Science of Mind, visualization techniques, practical magick, and Scientology.

If you found yourself flinching or reacting negatively to the mention of any of these subjects, such as Yoga, Rosicrucianism, Scientology, or any of the many other alternative approaches to the mind and reality, realise this is not necessarily because there is anything actually strange or weird about these subjects. It is often largely because modern psychology, psychiatry and affiliated proponents of modern materialistic "science" have successfully applied black PR to them to such a large degree. In fact, they have covertly attacked these subjects for most of this century. An intelligent and objective look into any of these fields, although sometimes initially confusing largely due to the newness of the subject and difference in approach to reality will result in a widened understanding of yourself (and Man in general). Granted, you do need to and in fact you MUST weed out some of the nonsense often added to these subjects.

Once you do take an honest look though it should become very obvious that modern western psychology has little to do with that incredible universe that exists a few inches behind your forehead. It must be mentioned that over time most of these subjects and fields (i.e. Scientology, Rosicrucianism, Transcendental Meditation, etc) have most definitely suffered from some combination of a) gross alterations introduced by self-appointed leaders following internal power struggles, b) manipulation of views and information by the more influential members, c) the sad tendency of some of the not-too-bright members to dictate changes not part of the original information, and d) the use of the subject and field to exert thought control and behavioral manipulation on its members. These faults are observably true and easily seen in the recent history of Scientology, though these faults exist in all to some degree. Lastly though, don't throw out the baby with the bathwater. While these all have serious flaws, don't use that as an excuse to dismiss everything about them outright without any serious examination. It takes careful and serious examination to separate the valuable from the invaluable - and there is often much of both to be found.

The mind *has* been examined, studied, drilled and "expanded", at times to the point of excruciating detail within many fields (i.e. Tibetan Buddhist Yogic practices). This is not to say that due to language barriers and the passage of time, that the information has not been lost to minor or major degrees or that these studies weren't without many errors, serious flaws, biases and differing opinions to start with. The point is not whether any of these are perfect studies (none are) or whether any of them have completed the task of researching the mind (none have), but that the *possibility for such a study most surely exists,* has been done before in various ways and to differing degrees, and that *modern psychology (and psychiatry) has nothing to do with this field.*

PSYCHOANALYSIS

From the 1890s until his death in 1939, the Austrian physician Sigmund Freud developed a method of psychotherapy known as psychoanalysis. Freud's understanding of the mind was largely based on interpretive methods, introspection and clinical observations, and was focused in particular on resolving unconscious conflict, mental distress and psychopathology. Freud's theories became very well-known, largely because they tackled subjects such as sexuality, repression, and the unconscious mind as general aspects of psychological development. These were largely considered taboo subjects at the time, and Freud provided a catalyst for them to be openly discussed in polite society. While Freud is perhaps best known for his tripartite model of the mind, consisting of the id, ego, and superego, and his theories about the Oedipus complex, his most lasting legacy may be not the content of his theories but his clinical innovations, such as the method of free association and a clinical interest in dreams.

Freud had a significant influence on Swiss psychiatrist Carl Jung, whose analytical psychology became an alternative form of depth psychology. Other well-known psychoanalytic thinkers of the mid-twentieth century included Sigmund Freud's daughter, psychoanalyst Anna Freud; German-American psychologist Erik Erickson, Austrian-British psychoanalyst Melanie Klein, English psychoanalyst and physician D. W. Winnicott, German psychologist Karen Horney, German-born psychologist and philosopher Erich Fromm, and English psychiatrist John Bowlby. Contemporary psychoanalysis comprises diverse schools of thought, including ego psychology, object relations, interpersonal, Lacanian, and relational psychoanalysis. Modification of Jung's theories has led to the archetypal and process-oriented schools of psychological thought.

Austrian-British philosopher Karl Popper argued that Freud's psychoanalytic theories were presented in untestable form. Psychology departments in American universities today are scientifically oriented, and Freudian theory has been marginalized, being regarded instead as a "desiccated and dead" historical artifact, according to a recent APA study. Recently, however, South African neuroscientist Mark Solms and other researchers in the emerging field of neuro-psychoanalysis have argued for Freud's theories, pointing out brain structures relating to Freudian concepts such as libido, drives, the unconscious, and repression.

STRUCTURALISM

Structuralism is an approach to the human sciences that attempts to analyze a specific field (for instance, mythology) as a complex system of interrelated parts. It began in linguistics with the work of Ferdinand de Saussure (1857-1913). But many French intellectuals perceived it to have a wider application, and the model was soon modified and applied to other fields, such as anthropology, psychoanalysis, literary theory and architecture. This ushered in the dawn of structuralism as not just a method, but also an intellectual movement that came to take existentialism's pedestal in 1960s France.

Structuralism enjoyed little popularity, and its general stance of antihumanism was in sheer opposition to the Sartrean existentialism that preceded it. But in the 1970s, it came under internal fire from critics who accused it of being too rigid and ahistorical. However, many of structuralism's theorists, from Michel Foucault to Jacques Lacan, continue to assert an influence on continental philosophy, and many of the fundamental assumptions of its critics, that is, of adherents of poststructuralism, are but a continuation of structuralism.

Structuralism isn't only applied within literary theory. There are also structuralist theories that exist within philosophy of science, anthropology and in sociology. According to Alison Assiter, there are four common ideas regarding structuralism that form an 'intellectual trend'. Firstly, the structure is what determines the position of each element of a whole. Secondly, structuralists believe that every system has a structure. Thirdly, structuralists are interested in 'structural' laws that deal with coexistence rather than changes. And finally structures are the 'real things' that lie beneath the surface or the appearance of meaning.

Structuralism appeared in academia in the second half of the 20th century, and grew to become one of the most popular approaches in academic fields concerned with the analysis of language, culture, and society. The work of Ferdinand de Saussure concerning linguistics is generally considered to be a starting point of structuralism. The term "structuralism" itself appeared in the works of French anthropologist Claude Lévi-Strauss, and gave rise, in France, to the "structuralist movement," which spurred the work of such thinkers as Louis Althusser, the psychoanalyst Jacques Lacan, as well as the structural Marxism of Nicos Poulantzas. Almost all members of this so-called movement denied that they were part of it[*citation needed*]. Structuralism is closely related to semiotics. Post-structuralism attempted to distinguish itself from the simple use of the structural method. Deconstruction was an attempt to break with structuralistic thought. Some intellectuals like Julia Kristeva, for example, took structuralism (and Russian formalism) for a starting point to later become prominent post-structuralists. Structuralism has had varying degrees of influence in the social sciences: a great deal in the field of sociology.

STRUCTURALISM IN LINGUISTICS

Structuralism states that human culture is to be understood as a system of signs. Robert Scholes defined structuralism as a reaction to modernist alienation and despair. Structuralists attempted to develop a semiology (system of signs). Ferdinand de Saussure was the originator of the 20th century structuralism, and evidence of this can be found in *Course in General Linguistics*, written by Saussure's colleagues after his death and based on student notes, where he focused not on the use of language (*parole*, or speech), but rather on the underlying system of language (*langue*) and called his theory *semiology*. However, the discovery of the underlying system had to be done via examination of the *parole* (speech).

As such, Structural Linguistics are actually an early form of *corpus linguistics* (quantification). This approach focused on examining how the elements of language related to each other in the present, that is, 'synchronically' rather than 'diachronically'. Finally, he argued that linguistic signs were composed of two parts, a signifier (the *sound pattern* of a word, either in mental projection — as when we silently recite lines from a poem to ourselves — or in actual, physical realization as part of a speech act) and a signified (the concept or *meaning* of the word). This was quite different from previous approaches which focused on the relationship between words and things in the world that they designate.

Key notions in Structural Linguistics are the notions of paradigm, syntagm and value, though these notions were not yet fully developed in Saussure's thought. A structural paradigm is actually a class of linguistic units (lexemes, morphemes or even constructions) which are possible in a certain position in a given linguistic environment (like a given sentence), which is the syntagm. The different functional role of each of these members of the paradigm is called value (*valeur* in French). Structuralist criticism relates the literary text to a larger overarching structure which may be a particular genre, a range of intertextual connections, a model of a universal narrative structure or a notion of the narrative being a system of recurrent patterns or motifs.

Saussure's *Course* influenced many linguists between World War I and WWII. In America, for instance, Leonard Bloomfield developed his own version of structural linguistics, as did Louis Hjelmslev in Denmark and Alf Sommerfelt in Norway. In France Antoine Meillet and Émile Benveniste would continue Saussure's program. Most importantly, however, members of the Prague School of linguistics such as Roman Jakobson and Nikolai Trubetzkoy conducted research that would be greatly influential. The clearest and most important example of Prague School structuralism lies in phonemics. Rather than simply compiling a list of which sounds occur in a language, the Prague School sought to examine how they were related.

They determined that the inventory of sounds in a language could be analyzed in terms of a series of contrasts. Thus in English the sounds /p/ and /b/ represent distinct phonemes because there are cases (minimal pairs) where the contrast between the two is the only difference between two distinct words (e.g. 'pat' and 'bat'). Analyzing sounds in terms of contrastive features also opens up comparative scope — it makes clear, for instance, that the difficulty Japanese speakers have differentiating /r/ and /l/ in English is because these sounds are not contrastive in Japanese. While this approach is now standard in linguistics, it was revolutionary at the time. Phonology would become the paradigmatic basis for structuralism in a number of different fields.

STRUCTURALISM IN ANTHROPOLOGY AND SOCIOLOGY

According to structural theory in anthropology and social anthropology, meaning is produced and reproduced within a culture through various practices, phenomena and activities which serve as systems of signification. A structuralist studies activities as diverse as food preparation and serving rituals, religious rites, games, literary and non-literary texts, and other forms of entertainment to discover the deep structures by which meaning is produced and reproduced within a culture. For example, an early and prominent practitioner of structuralism, anthropologist and ethnographer Claude Lévi-Strauss in the 1950s, analyzed cultural phenomena including mythology, kinship (the Alliance theory and the incest taboo), and food preparation. In addition to these studies, he produced more linguistically-focused writings where he applied Saussure's distinction between *langue* and *parole* in his search for the fundamental mental structures of the human mind, arguing that the structures that form the "deep grammar" of society originate in the mind and operate in us unconsciously. Levi-Strauss was inspired by information theory and mathematics.

Another concept was borrowed from the Prague school of linguistics, where Roman Jakobson and others analysed sounds based on the presence or absence of certain features (such as voiceless vs. voiced). Levi-Strauss included this in his conceptualization of the universal structures of the mind, which he held to operate based on pairs of binary oppositions such as hot-cold, male-female, culture-nature, cooked-raw, or marriageable vs. tabooed women. A third influence came from Marcel Mauss, who had written on gift exchange systems. Based on Mauss, for instance, Lévi-Strauss argued that kinship systems are based on the exchange of women between groups (a position known as 'alliance theory') as opposed to the 'descent' based theory described by Edward Evans-Pritchard and Meyer Fortes.

While replacing Marcel Mauss at his *Ecole Pratique des Hautes Etudes* chair, Lévi-Strauss' writing became widely popular in the 1960s and 1970s and gave rise to the term "structuralism" itself. In Britain authors such as Rodney Needham and Edmund Leach were highly influenced by structuralism. Authors such as Maurice Godelier and Emmanuel Terray combined Marxism with structural anthropology in France. In the United States, authors such as Marshall Sahlins and James Boon built on structuralism to provide their own analysis of human society. Structural anthropology fell out of favour in the early 1980s for a number of reasons. D'Andrade (1995) suggests that structuralism in anthropology was eventually abandoned because it made unverifiable assumptions about the universal structures of the human mind. Authors such as Eric Wolf argued that political economy and colonialism should be more at the forefront of anthropology. More generally, criticisms of structuralism by Pierre Bourdieu led to a concern with how cultural and social structures were changed by human agency and practice, a trend which Sherry Ortner has referred to as 'practice theory'.

Some anthropological theorists, however, while finding considerable fault with Lévi-Strauss's version of structuralism, did not turn away from a fundamental structural basis for human culture. The Biogenetic Structuralism group for instance argued that some kind of structural foundation for culture must exist because all humans inherit the same system of brain structures. They proposed a kind of Neuroanthropology which would lay the foundations for a more complete scientific account of cultural similarity and variation by requiring an integration of cultural anthropology and neuroscience—a programme also embraced by such theorists as Victor Turner.

STRUCTURALISM IN LITERARY THEORY AND LITERARY CRITICISM

In literary theory, structuralism is an approach to analyzing the narrative material by examining the underlying invariant structure, which is based on the linguistic sign system of Ferdinand de Saussure. The structuralists claim that there must be a structure in every text, which explains why it is easier for experienced readers than for non-experienced readers to interpret a text. Hence, they say that everything that is written seems to be governed by specific rules, a "grammar of literature", that one learns in educational institutions and that are to be unmasked. A potential problem of structuralist interpretation is that it can be highly reductive, as scholar Catherine Belsey puts it, "the structuralist danger of collapsing all difference".

An example of such a reading might be if a student concludes the authors of *West Side Story* did not write anything "really" new, because their work has the same structure as

Shakespeare's Romeo and Juliet. In both texts a girl and a boy fall in love (a "formula" with a symbolic operator between them would be "Boy + Girl") despite the fact that they belong to two groups that hate each other ("Boy's Group - Girl's Group" or "Opposing forces") and conflict is resolved by their death. Structuralist readings best focus on how the structures of the single text resolve inherent narrative tensions. If a structuralist reading focuses on multiple texts, there must be some way in which those texts unify themselves into a coherent system.

The versatility of structuralism is such that a literary critic could make the same claim about a story of two *friendly* families ("Boy's Family + Girl's Family") that arrange a marriage between their children despite the fact that the children hate each other ("Boy - Girl") and then the children commit suicide to escape the arranged marriage; the justification is that the second story's structure is an 'inversion' of the first story's structure: the relationship between the values of love and the two pairs of parties involved have been reversed.

Structuralistic literary criticism argues that the "novelty value of a literary text" can lie only in new structure, rather than in the specifics of character development and voice in which that structure is expressed. One branch of literary structuralism, like Freudianism, Marxism, and transformational grammar, posits both a deep and a surface structure. In Freudianism and Marxism the deep structure is a story, in Freud's case the battle, ultimately, between the life and death instincts, and in Marx, the conflicts between classes that are rooted in the economic "base."

Literary structuralism often follows the lead of Vladimir Propp and Claude Levi-Strauss in seeking out basic deep elements in stories and myths, which are combined in various ways to produce the many versions of the ur-story or ur-myth. As in Freud and Marx, but in contrast to transformational grammar, these basic elements are meaning-bearing. There is considerable similarity between structural literary theory and Northrop Frye's archetypal criticism, which is also indebted to the anthropological study of myths. Some critics have also tried to apply the theory to individual works, but the effort to find unique structures in individual literary works runs counter to the structuralist programme and have an affinity with New Criticism. The other branch of literary structuralism is semiotics, and it is based on the work of Ferdinand de Saussure.

STRUCTURALISM AFTER WORLD WAR II

Throughout the 1940s and 1950s, existentialism like that propounded by Jean-Paul Sartre was the dominant mood. Structuralism surged to prominence in France after WWII and particularly in the 1960s. The initial popularity of structuralism in France led it to spread across the globe. The social sciences were particularly influenced. Structuralism rejected the concept of human freedom and choice and focused instead on the way that human behaviour is determined by various structures.

The most important initial work on this score was Claude Lévi-Strauss's 1949 volume *Elementary Structures of Kinship*. Lévi-Strauss had known Jakobson during their time together in New York during WWII and was influenced by both Jakobson's structuralism as well as the American anthropological tradition. In *Elementary Structures* he examined kinship systems from a structural point of view and demonstrated how apparently different social organizations were in fact different permutations of a few basic kinship structures. In the late 1950s he published *Structural Anthropology*, a collection of essays outlining his programme for structuralism.

By the early 1960s structuralism as a movement was coming into its own and some believed that it offered a single unified approach to human life that would embrace all disciplines. Roland Barthes and Jacques Derrida focused on how structuralism could be applied to literature. Blending Freud and De Saussure, the French (post)structuralist Jacques Lacan applied structuralism to psychoanalysis and, in a different way, Jean Piaget applied structuralism to the study of psychology. But Jean Piaget, who would better define himself as constructivist, considers structuralism as "a method and not a doctrine" because for him "there exists no structure without a construction, abstract or genetic"

Michel Foucault's book *The Order of Things* examined the history of science to study how structures of epistemology, or episteme, shaped the way in which people imagined knowledge and knowing (though Foucault would later explicitly deny affiliation with the structuralist movement). In much the same way, American historian of science Thomas Kuhn addressed the structural formations of science in his seminal work *The Structure of Scientific Revolutions* - its title alone evincing a stringent structuralist approach. Though less concerned with "episteme," Kuhn nonetheless remarked at how coteries of scientists operated under and applied a standard praxis of 'normal science,' deviating from a standard 'paradigm' only in instances of irreconcilable anomalies that question a significant body of their work.

Blending Marx and structuralism another French theorist Louis Althusser introduced his own brand of structural social analysis, giving rise to "structural Marxism". Other authors in France and abroad have since extended structural analysis to practically every discipline. The definition of 'structuralism' also shifted as a result of its popularity. As its popularity as a movement waxed and waned, some authors considered themselves 'structuralists' only to later eschew the label. The term has slightly different meanings in French and English. In the US, for instance, Derrida is considered the paradigm of post-structuralism while in France he is labeled a structuralist. Finally, some authors wrote in several different styles. Barthes, for instance, wrote some books which are clearly structuralist and others which clearly are not.

REACTIONS TO STRUCTURALISM

Today structuralism is less popular than approaches such as post-structuralism and deconstruction. There are many reasons for this. Structuralism has often been criticized for being ahistorical and for favoring deterministic structural forces over the ability of individual people to act. As the political turbulence of the 1960s and 1970s (and particularly the student uprisings of May 1968) began affecting academia, issues of power and political struggle moved to the centre of people's attention.

The ethnologist Robert Jaulin defined another ethnological method which clearly pitted itself against structuralism. In the 1980s, deconstruction and its emphasis on the fundamental ambiguity of language—rather than its crystalline logical structure—became popular. By the end of the century structuralism was seen as a historically important school of thought, but it was the movements it spawned, rather than structuralism itself, which commanded attention.

FUNCTIONALISM, BEHAVIOURISM

FUNCTIONAL PSYCHOLOGY

Functional psychology or functionalism refers to a general psychological approach that views mental life and behaviour in terms of active adaptation to the person's environment. As such, it provides the general basis for developing psychological theories not readily testable in controlled experiments and for applied psychology. Functionalism was a position taken opposing the prevailing structuralism of the end of the 19th century in psychology. Edward Titchener, the leading structuralist, gave psychology its first definition as a science as the study of mental experience, of consciousness, to be studied by trained introspection.

William James, John Dewey, George Herbert Mead, Harvey A. Carr, and especially James Rowland Angell were the leading proponents of the functionalist point of view at the University of Chicago. Another group at Columbia, led by James McKeen Cattell, Edward L. Thorndike, and Robert S. Woodworth, were also called functionalist and shared some of the views of the Chicago school. Egon Brunswik represents a more recent, but Continental, version. The functionalists retained an emphasis on conscious experience.

Behaviorists also rejected the methodology of

introspection but criticized functionalism because it was not grounded in controlled experiments and its theories provided little predictive power. B. F. Skinner was a pioneer of behaviorism. He did not think that aspects of the mind had any impact on behaviour, for he viewed behaviour simply as a learned response to an external stimulus.

Contemporary Descendants

Evolutionary psychology is founded on the view that the function of all psychological phenomena in human evolution is a necessary perspective to their understanding. Even the project of studying the evolutionary functions of consciousness is now an active field of study.

BEHAVIOURISM

Behaviorism or Behaviourism, also called the learning perspective (where any physical action is a behaviour) is a philosophy of psychology based on the proposition that all things which organisms do — including acting, thinking and feeling—can and should be regarded as behaviors.

The school of psychology maintains that behaviors as such can be described scientifically without recourse either to internal physiological events or to hypothetical constructs such as the mind.

Behaviorism comprises the position that all theories should have observational correlates but that there are no philosophical differences between publicly observable processes (such as actions) and privately observable processes (such as thinking and feeling).

From early psychology in the 19th century, the behaviorist school of thought ran concurrently and shared commonalities with the psychoanalytic and Gestalt movements in psychology into the 20th century; but also differed from the mental philosophy of the Gestalt psychologists in critical ways. Its main influences were Ivan Pavlov, who investigated classical conditioning, Edward Lee Thorndike, John B. Watson who rejected introspective methods and sought to restrict psychology to experimental methods, and B.F. Skinner who conducted research on operant conditioning. In the second half of the twentieth century, behaviorism was largely eclipsed as a result of the cognitive revolution.

VERSIONS

There is no classification generally agreed upon, but some titles given to the various branches of behaviorism include:

- Methodological: The behaviorism of Watson; the objective study of behaviour; no mental life, no internal states; thought is covert speech.
- Radical: Skinner's behaviorism; is considered radical since it expands behavioral principles to processes within the organism; in contrast to methodological behaviorism; not mechanistic or reductionist; hypothetical (mentalistic) internal states are not considered causes of behaviour, phenomena must be observable at least to the individual experiencing them. Willard Van Orman Quine used many of radical behaviorism's ideas in his study of knowing and language.
- Teleological: Post-Skinnerian, purposive, close to microeconomics.
- Theoretical: Post-Skinnerian, accepts observable internal states ("within the skin" once meant "unobservable", but with modern technology we are not so constrained); dynamic, but eclectic in choice of theoretical structures, emphasizes parsimony.
- Biological: Post-Skinnerian, centered on perceptual and motor modules of behaviour, theory of behaviour systems.
- Interbehaviorism: Founded by J.R. Kantor; regarded by many as the most naturalistic psychology since the Greeks; eschews all notions of dualism, mentalism, and causality including the simple substitution of "spiritual" with "mental" and "neural"

Two popular subtypes are Neo: Hullian and post-Hullian, theoretical, group data, not dynamic, physiological, and

Purposive: Tolman's behavioristic anticipation of cognitive psychology.

B.F. Skinner and Radical Behaviorism

Skinner, who carried out experimental work mainly in comparative psychology from the 1930s to the 1950s, but remained behaviorism's best known theorist and exponent virtually until his death in 1990, developed a distinct kind of behaviorist philosophy, which came to be called radical behaviorism. He is credited with having founded a new version of psychological science, which has come to be called behaviour analysis or the experimental analysis of behaviour after variations on the subtitle to his 1938 work *The Behaviour of Organisms: An Experimental Analysis Of Behaviour.*

B.F. Skinner was influential in defining radical behaviorism, a philosophy codifying the basis of his school of research (named the Experimental Analysis of Behaviour, or EAB.) While EAB differs from other approaches to behavioral research on numerous methodological and theoretical points, radical behaviorism departs from methodological behaviorism most notably in accepting treatment of feelings, states of mind and introspection as existent and scientifically treatable.

This is done by identifying them as something non-dualistic, and here Skinner takes a divide-and-conquer approach, with some instances being identified with bodily conditions or behaviour, and others getting a more extended 'analysis' in terms of behaviour. However, radical behaviorism stops short of identifying feelings as causes of behaviour. Among other points of difference were a rejection of the reflex as a model of all behaviour and a defence of a science of behaviour complementary to but independent of physiology. Radical behaviorism has considerable overlap with other western philosophical positions such as American pragmatism.

Experimental and Conceptual Innovations

This essentially philosophical position gained strength from the success of Skinner's early experimental work with rats and pigeons, summarized in his books *The Behaviour of*

Organisms and *Schedules of Reinforcement*. Of particular importance was his concept of the operant response, of which the canonical example was the rat's lever-press. In contrast with the idea of a physiological or reflex response, an operant is a class of structurally distinct but functionally equivalent responses.

For example, while a rat might press a lever with its left paw or its right paw or its·tail, all of these responses operate on the world in the same way and have a common consequence. Operants are often thought of as species of responses, where the individuals differ but the class coheres in its function—shared consequences with operants and reproductive success with species. This is a clear distinction between Skinner's theory and S-R theory.

Skinner's empirical work expanded on earlier research on trial-and-error learning by researchers such as Thorndike and Guthrie with both conceptual reformulations – Thorndike's notion of a stimulus-response 'association' or 'connection' was abandoned – and methodological ones – the use of the 'free operant', so called because the animal was now permitted to respond at its own rate rather than in a series of trials determined by the experimenter procedures.

With this method, Skinner carried out substantial experimental work on the effects of different schedules and rates of reinforcement on the rates of operant responses made by rats and pigeons.

He achieved remarkable success in training animals to perform unexpected responses, and to emit large numbers of responses, and to demonstrate much empirical regularity at the purely behavioral level. This lent some credibility to his conceptual analysis. It is largely his conceptual analysis that made his work much more rigorous than his peers, a point which can be seen clearly in his seminal work *Are Theories of Learning Necessary?* in which he criticizes what he viewed to be theoretical weaknesses then common in the study of psychology. An important descendant of the experimental analysis of behaviour is the Society for Quantitative Analysis of Behaviour.

Relation to Language

As Skinner turned from experimental work to concentrate on the philosophical underpinnings of a science of behaviour, his attention turned to human language with *Verbal Behaviour* and other language-related publications; *Verbal Behaviour* laid out a vocabulary and theory for functional analysis of verbal behaviour, and was strongly criticized in a review by Noam Chomsky.

Skinner did not respond in detail but claimed that Chomsky failed to understand his ideas, and the disagreements between the two and the theories involved have been further discussed. What was important for a behaviorist's analysis of human behaviour was not language acquisition so much as the interaction between language and overt behaviour.

In an essay republished in his 1969 book *Contingencies of Reinforcement*, Skinner took the view that humans could construct linguistic stimuli that would then acquire control over their behaviour in the same way that external stimuli could. The possibility of such "instructional control" over behaviour meant that contingencies of reinforcement would not always produce the same effects on human behaviour as they reliably do in other animals. The focus of a radical behaviorist analysis of human behaviour therefore shifted to an attempt to understand the interaction between instructional control and contingency control, and also to understand the behavioral processes that determine what instructions are constructed and what control they acquire over behaviour.

Molar versus Molecular Behaviorism

Skinner's view of behaviour is most often characterized as a "molecular" view of behaviour; that is, each behaviour can be decomposed into atomistic parts or molecules. This view is inaccurate when one considers his complete description of behaviour as delineated in the 1981 article, *Selection by Consequences* and many other works. Skinner claims that a complete account of behaviour has involved an understanding of selection history at three levels: biology (the natural selection or phylogeny of the animal); behaviour (the reinforcement history or ontogeny of the behavioral repertoire of the animal); and for some species, culture (the cultural practices of the social group to which the animal belongs). This whole organism, with all those histories, then interacts with its environment. He often described even his own behaviour as a product of his phylogenetic history, his reinforcement history (which includes the learning of cultural practices) interacting with the environment at the moment.

Molar behaviorists, such as Howard Rachlin argue that behaviour can not be understood by focusing on events in the moment. That is, they argue that a behaviour can be understood best in terms of the ultimate cause of history and that molecular behaviorist are committing a fallacy by inventing a fictitious proximal cause for behaviour. Molar behaviorists argue that standard molecular constructs such as "associative strength" are such fictitious proximal causes that simply take the place of molar variables such as rate of reinforcement. Thus, a molar behaviorist would define a behaviour such as loving someone as exhibiting a pattern of loving behaviour over time, there is no known proximal cause of loving behaviour, only a history of behaviors (of which the current behaviour might be an example of) that can be summarized as love. Molectular behaviorists use notions from Melioration theory, Negative power function discounting or additive versions of negative power function discounting.

Behaviorism in Philosophy

Behaviorism is a psychological movement that can be contrasted with philosophy of mind. The basic premise of *radical behaviorism* is that the study of behaviour should be a natural science, such as chemistry or physics, without any reference to hypothetical inner states of organisms as causes for their behaviour. A modern example of such analysis would be Fantino and colleagues' work on behavioral approaches to reasoning. Other varieties, such as *theoretical behaviorism*, permit internal states, but do not require them to be mental or have any relation to subjective experience. Behaviorism takes a functional view of behaviour. There are points of view within analytic philosophy that have called themselves, or have been called by others, behaviorist.

In *logical behaviorism* (as held, e.g., by Rudolf Carnap and Carl Hempel), the meaning of psychological statements are their verification conditions, which consist of performed overt behaviour. W. V. Quine made use of a type of behaviorism, influenced by some of Skinner's ideas, in his own work on language. Gilbert Ryle defended a distinct strain of philosophical behaviorism, sketched in his book *The Concept of Mind.*

Ryle's central claim was that instances of dualism frequently represented 'category mistakes,' and hence that they were really misunderstandings of the use of ordinary language. Daniel Dennett likewise acknowledges himself to be a type of behaviorist. It is sometimes argued that Ludwig Wittgenstein defended a behaviorist position, but while there are important relations between his thought and behaviorism, the claim that he was a behaviorist is quite controversial (e.g., the *Beetle in a box* argument). Mathematician Alan Turing is also sometimes considered a behaviorist, but he himself did not make this identification.

21st Century Behaviour Analysis

As of 2007, modern day behaviorism, known as "behaviour analysis," is a thriving field. The Association for Behaviour Analysis: International currently has 32 state and regional chapters within the United States. Approximately 30 additional chapters have also developed throughout Europe, Asia, South America, and Australia. In addition to 34 annual conferences held by ABAI in the United States and Canada, ABAI will hold the 5th annual International conference in Norway in 2009.

The interests among behaviour analysts today are wide ranging, as a review of the 30 Special Interest Groups (SIGs) within ABAI indicates. Such interests include everything from developmental disabilities and autism, to cultural psychology, clinical psychology, and Organizational Behaviour

Management (OBM; behaviour analytic I/O psychology). OBM has developed a particularly strong following within behaviour analysis, as evidenced by the formation of the OBM Network and the influential Journal of Organizational Behaviour Management (JOBM; recently ratest the 3rd highest impact journal in applied psychology by ISI JOBM rating.

Modern behaviour analysis has also witnessed a massive resurgence in research and applications related to language and cognition, with the development of Relational Frame Theory (RFT; described as a "Post-Skinnerian account of language and cognition." RFT also forms the empirical basis for the highly successful and data-driven Acceptance and Commitment Therapy (ACT).

In fact, researchers and practitioners in RFT/ACT have become sufficiently prominent that they have formed their own specialized organization, known as the Association for Contextual Behavioral Science (ACBS).

Some of the current prominent behaviour analytic journals include the Journal of Applied Behaviour Analysis (JABA), the Journal of the Experimental Analysis of Behaviour (JEAB) JEAB website, the Journal of Organizational Behaviour Management (JOBM), Behaviour and Social Issues (BSI), as well as the Psychological Record. Currently, the U.S. has 14 ABAI accredited MA and PhD programs for comprehensive study in behaviour analysis.

RESEARCH METHODS IN PSYCHOLOGY: OBSERVATION

As with most research, the study of developmental psychology begins with a hypothesis. A hypothesis is a testable statement that reflects what the researcher expects to find in a study. For example, a study on gender and learning disabilities might begin with a hypothesis that one gender will be more impacted by learning disorders. The goal of research is to analyze the area of interest, collect information and data about topic, draw conclusions based upon this research and data, and then adds or expand upon previously existing theories of development.

TYPES OF RESEARCH

There are a number of different ways to conduct psychological research. The two major types of research are:

- Cross-sectional Research

Cross-sectional research involves looking at different groups of people of different ages. For example, a research might measure or observe a group of young adults and compare this data with information gathered about a group of elderly participants. The benefit of this type of research is that it can be done relatively quickly; the research data is all gathered at the same point in time. However, because data is gathered from generations of people who share the same cultural experiences, these shared events may play a role in development. This makes it difficult to determine if something is caused by experience or the aging process.

- Longitudinal Research

Longitudinal research involves studying the same group of individuals over an extended period of time. Data is first collected at the outset of the study, and may then be gathered repeatedly throughout the length of the study. In some cases, longitudinal studies can last several decades. The benefit of this type of research is that it allows researchers to look at changes over time. However, longitudinal studies require enormous amounts of time and are often quite expensive. Because of this, these studies often have only a small group of subjects, which makes it difficult to apply the results to a larger population. Another problem is that participants sometimes drop out of the study, shrinking the sample size and decreasing the amount of data collected.

DATA COLLECTION

Once it has been decided which type of research to use, the next step is to determine how the information will be gathered. There are a number of different research methods that are used in the study of developmental psychology, each with its own strengths and weaknesses. Some common approaches include observation, case studies, questionnaires, and experimentation.

OBSERVATION

There are two different types of observation. The first involves viewing the subject of interest in a laboratory setting. The benefit of this is that the situation can be controlled by the experimental.

The drawbacks of lab observation are that the setting can be unnatural and the subject is aware that they are being studied. Both of these factors can have an impact on results of the study. Naturalistic observation allows researchers to observe participants in real-world settings. The strength of this method is that it allows researchers to view behaviour as it really happens in a natural setting. The drawback is that the researcher cannot control outside variables that might impact behaviour.

CASE STUDIES

A case study is an in-depth analysis of a particular individual. While this research method provides a great deal of information about a specific person, the results are often difficult to generalize to larger populations. For this reason, case studies are most often used in clinical research or other cases where certain aspects of the subject's life cannot be reproduced or duplicated.

QUESTIONNAIRES

Questionnaires offer researchers a quick, easy way to collect a great deal of information. One weakness of this method is that it reduces variety, creativity, and individuality of responses. In cases where the subject is unable to fill out a questionnaire, with very young children for example, questions are often posed through a structured interview.

EXPERIMENTATION

Experiments involve the manipulation and measurement of variables. This research method is the most scientific, but it can be difficult to use if the variables of interest are abstract or internal concepts. Another problem is that some variables of interest cannot be studied through experimentation for ethical reasons. Examples of this would be research on the effects of child abuse on development.

CORRELATION AND THE EXPERIMENTAL METHOD

In the early days, psychology was primarily investigated using a method known as rationalism. This approach simply involved thinking about something, and then coming up with an explanation as to why it may be that way. However whilst rationalism may be a useful approach for subjects such as philosophy, in psychology, rationalism can often lead to contradictory ideas.

One such example can be found with John Locke, who believed that at birth the mind was a blank slate. Yet later using same approach, Immanuel Kant concluded that there are some inborn ideas at birth. This is one of the problems of using rationalism in psychology, as it can lead to two different people coming up with two different ideas. To produce more concrete ideas, another approach was called for and it came in the form of empiricism.

EMPIRICISM

Empiricism involves gathering information by using the senses, (*e.g. hearing, touch, sight, taste and smell*) and marks the beginnings of the modern day research methods we use in psychology today. No longer were psychologists confined to the ideas created by the rationalistic approach, but they could now prove or disprove those ideas with real evidence. This is how William James believed psychology should be, as he argued that psychology should be treated like a science and therefore investigated in a scientific manner.

THE SCIENTIFIC METHOD

The scientific method represents the way psychological data is researched and collected today, and is something which evolved from the early methods of rationalism and empiricism that were previously described. The scientific method aims to gather information in a scientific way, so that it is both accurate and reliable. There are three main steps that must be followed when using this method.

Form A Hypothesis

The first step is to make an educated guess as to why something is the way it is, or in other words, form a hypothesis. For example, a teacher reads an article about how omega 3 supplements can increase concentration, so they form a hypothesis that omega 3 supplements will have an effect on student test scores.

Gather Data

After forming a hypothesis, the next step is to gather data so that we can test it. For example, the teacher may split the class into two, giving one half omega 3 supplements and the other half nothing.

Accept or Reject The Hypothesis

From the data we have collected, we can then determine whether our hypothesis was correct or incorrect. So if the teacher found that the children who received the omega 3 supplements had higher test scores than those who received no supplements, they can accept their hypothesis that omega 3 affects test scores. Should however no difference be found between the two groups, the teacher would then reject their hypothesis as the supplements produced no significant difference between the two test scores.

Inaccurate Information

Whilst the scientific method attempts to obtain accurate and reliable information, sometimes it is possible that the information collected was wrong. This is known as a decision error, of which there are two types.

TYPE I ERROR

A type I error occurs when a hypothesis has been accepted when it should have been rejected. A famous example of a type I error occurred when the astronomer Percival Lowell concluded that there were canals on Mars, when later research showed this was not the case. He made a type I error, because what his evidence told him was correct was actually incorrect.

TYPE II ERROR

A type II error occurs when a hypothesis is rejected when it should have been accepted. For example, before the research done by Louis Pasteur, many doctors rejected the idea that invisible germs cause disease and so saw no point in washing their hands when operating on patients. They made a type II error, because they rejected something which was correct. Now that we have looked at how modern day psychologists gather their information, lets look at some of the research methods they can use.

NATURALISTIC OBSERVATION

Naturalistic observation involves studying behaviour in its natural setting, without any influence from the researcher. This method can be used to study both animals and humans, and works best when the research subjects do not know they are being observed. This is because people and animals tend to act differently when they know someone is watching them. If it is not possible for the researcher to hide their presence, they may spend some time with the people or animals they are studying before they begin to record their behaviour. This allows the researcher to become accepted by the individual or group, so that they will act more naturally and better data can be collected.

THE CLINICAL METHOD

The clinical method involves treating people with various disorders, and then using that information for research. For example, a therapist may have been treating their patient for a number of years, and later decides that because this was an interesting or unique case, they will write about it and maybe even publish it in a scientific journal. A good example of the clinical method can be found with Sigmund Freud, who from his time spent with patients, came up with many new ideas as to how and why people get sick or have emotional problems in their life.

THE CASE STUDY METHOD

A case study studies one person over a prolonged period of time. Sometimes this might be for a few months, whilst other times it might be a whole lifetime.

Although case studies take a long time to complete, the information they provide is extremely valuable because they allow us to see the long term effects something may have. One such example can be found with adults were followed up 40 years after an experiment they had done when they were children.

In brief, what the case study found was that the children who were able to delay gratification became much more successful as adults than the children who were unable to delay gratification. Case studies are also common in medical research, where people are monitored over a period of time so that side effects to drugs can be identified.

THE SURVEY METHOD

In order understand the behaviour of a large group of people, it is necessary to take a sample of that group which is considered to be representative of the whole. This sample should be taken at random, so that it incorporates as many different types of people whilst also allowing for chance to operate. The people within this sample can then be surveyed using methods such as questionnaires or interviews to obtain the relevant data.

One famous example of such a survey was performed by the researcher Alfred Kinsey, who surveyed both males and females about their sexual behaviour. A film about this was released a few years ago called "Kinsey", which starred Liam Neeson as Alfred Kinsey.

One drawback however of using the survey method is that because you are only sampling a small subset of a population, you may get biased results if your sample group is not truly representative of the whole.

THE TESTING METHOD

As the name suggests, the testing methods uses various tests such as intelligence or personality tests to investigate behaviour. An example everyone should be able to relate to is the IQ test, which is designed to measure your average level of intelligence. Some researchers believe that the higher your IQ score is, the more likely you are to have good health and a high income. However in order for a test to be considered accurate, it needs to be both valid and reliable.

VALID TEST

A valid test will test what it is suppose to test. For example, an intelligence test should test your intelligence and not your personality. If a test tests something it is not suppose to, it is then considered to be invalid.

RELIABLE TEST

A reliable test is one that produces the same (*or very similar*) results when it is repeated. For example, if I get 80% on a test, and tomorrow when I repeat that test I get 82%, that test could be considered as reliable.

THE CORRELATION METHOD

Correlation simply means a relationship between two things (*variables*), and the correlation method is used to determine this by seeing how different things affect each other. The results of which, are usually being displayed on a graph as X and Y.

If one variable can be used to predict the scores of the second variable, they are said to be "covary", or exhibit "covariance", which means they vary together. For example, if X is the size of my left hand and Y is the size of my right hand, I can predict the size of Y by looking at the size of X and vice versa.

However it is important to realise that just because both variables seem to predict each other, it doesn't necessarily mean that they cause those effects to occur (*causation*). Using the same example given above, this would mean the size of my left hand does not cause the size of my right hand. The reason they covary (*vary together*) is due to something else, genetics.

TYPES OF CORRELATIONS

There are two main types of correlations:

Positive Correlation: This occurs when increasing one variable causes another variable to increase.

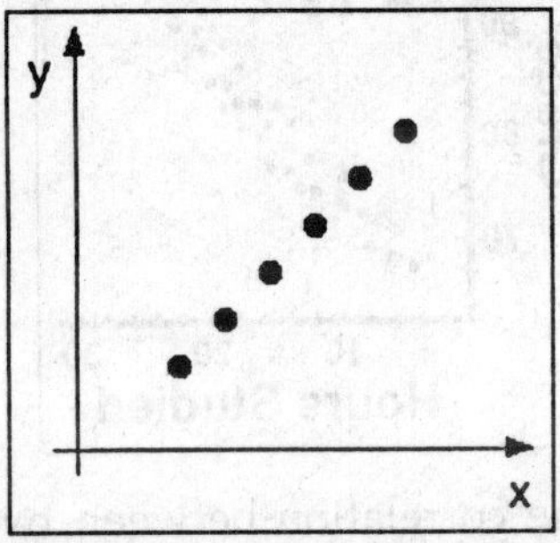

e.g. the more time I spend practicing tennis the better a player I become.

or, Increase in X = Increase in Y

Negative Correlation: This occurs when increasing one variable causes the other to decrease.

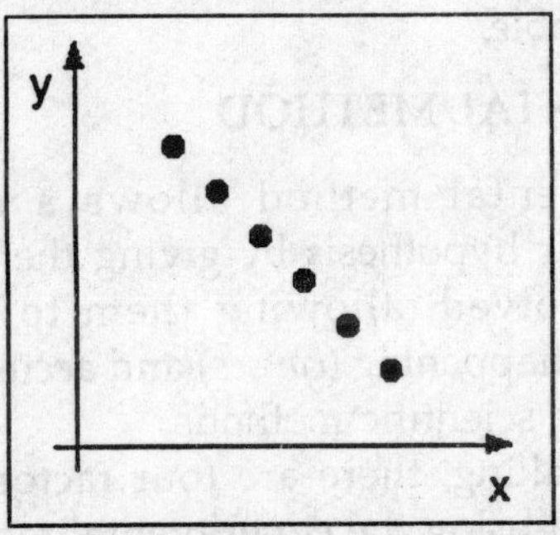

e.g. the more time I spend watching TV, the worse a tennis player I become.

Or, Increase in X = Decrease in Y

CORRELATION COEFFICIENT

In order to determine how closely two things are

correlated, we use a correlation coefficient which ranges from -1.00 (*perfect negative correlation*) to +1.00 (*perfect positive correlation*).

+.77 would be a strong positive correlation, -.33 would be a strong negative correlation.

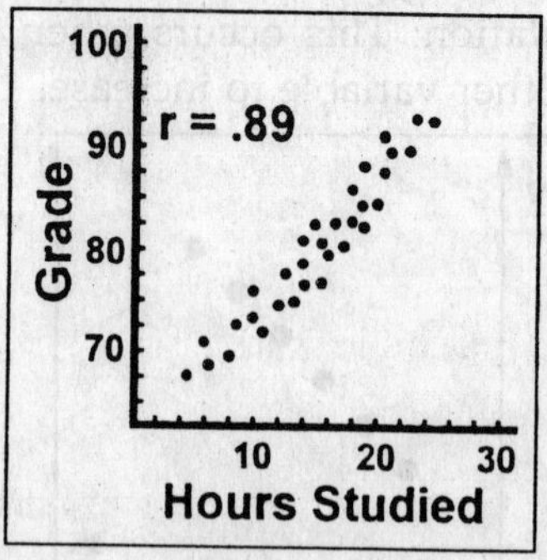

Determining the correlation between two variables can also be used to determine how valid and reliable a test is.

For example, if an intelligence test has a high positive correlation with grades, then we can say that the test is valid. If a test is repeated on two separate days and there is a strong positive correlation between the test results, then we can say that the test is reliable.

THE EXPERIMENTAL METHOD

The experimental method allows a researcher to accurately test their hypothesis by giving them control over the variables involved, allowing them to identify why something may be happening (*causes*) and accurately measure behaviour by using scientific methods.

Generally speaking, there are four factors to take into consideration when using the experimental method.

The Control Group

The control group is used to represent a group that has not been interfered with in any way. This group shall then be compared to other groups, to see the effects an intervention may have had.

The Experimental Group

This group is who you experiment on, and see how what you do changes their behaviour.

Independent Variable

An independent variable is something which you think will affect another variable. For example, putting a puppy in a room full of people will cause them to feel happy (*change their mood*).

Dependent Variable

A dependent variable measures the resulting effect of another variable. For example, happiness (*dependent variable*) was a result of bringing the puppy (*independent variable*) into the room. The independent variable causes the effect, and the dependent variable measures that effect.

Putting it All Together

If we put all this information together using the example I gave previously about omega 3 and test scores, you may be able to gain a better understanding of the experimental method in action.

Hypothesis - Omega 3 supplements will have an effect on test results.

The first thing we need to do is create two groups, a control (*students who will receive no omega 3 supplements*) and an experimental group (*students who will receive omega 3*). In order for these groups to be fair, we need to divide them by random. This could involve each student writing their name down on paper and being randomly drawn. This randomisation process will help to cancel out individual differences between the students, which may have given inaccurate or biased results. The independent variable we are testing is omega 3, because we predict that it will have an effect on test scores. This will be given to the experimental group at a predetermined dose.

The dependent variable is the test score, because we are seeing how students are affected by the omega 3. If we find that after the experiment omega 3 supplementation results in higher test scores in the experimental group (*a positive correlation*) we can perform a statistical analysis to see if the result are due to chance. If they are not, we can then conclude with some degree of certainty that omega 3 supplementation results in better grades.

ETHICAL ISSUES IN PSYCHOLOGICAL RESEARCH

Most psychological research is conducted with human participants. Working with humans requires that we consider their welfare as part of our research planning process. Ethical guidelines such as those developed by the American Psychological Association (APA) and the federal policy outlined in the Federal Register (1991) emphasize sensitive and humane treatment that minimizes risks to research participants. When we begin our ethical decision-making process, we should consider each of the following issues.

- Benefits of the Research
- Responsibility
- Physical and Psychological Risks
- Deception
- Reducing Risk and/or Minimizing Harm
- Informed Consent
- Privacy
- Summary of Results

We do research because we want to make contributions to our profession and to society. Those who agree to be a part of our studies join with us to meet these larger goals. They become partners in research and, as such, deserve to be treated well. Our ethical guidelines help us to think through how we can do high-quality research at the same time that we treat our research participants with respect. When we conduct research, we make an implicit contract with our participants that our study has the potential to yield some larger benefit beyond our own personal interests. We ask questions that are grounded in theory and previous psychological research. We also make sure that our studies are sufficiently well designed to provide meaningful information. Anything other than our most careful work would be a waste of participants' time and effort.

What are some of the ways students can insure that their research has some larger benefit? As researchers, we must take full responsibility for our studies. Even if we are in a class or working on a thesis where others are helping us with our research, we must take full responsibility for how we conduct the study. This responsibility extends to research assistants. If we have students helping us to collect or compile data, we also must make sure that they know about and follow ethical principles.

Psychological research can cause physical and/or psychological discomfort. For example, imaging studies are increasingly popular in research on cognitive processing. Participants may feel physical discomfort from the heat generated by the imaging machines or anxious and claustrophobic from the noise and enclosed space. As researchers, we are obligated to accurately estimate the degree of risk in our research. We typically do this by reading the literature and consulting with colleagues.

Institutional Review Boards (IRBs) also will help researchers estimate the degree of risk involved in their studies. An IRB is a group of professionals and members of the community at large who review research proposals to make sure that they follow ethical standards. Every institution that receives federal funding is required to submit all proposals for research with human participants to the IRB. The IRB is an important safeguard but the ethical responsibility for the research ultimately rests with the investigator. Student research, especially research conducted as part of a class, typically involves little or no risk.

Let's try a risk assessment. A group of students wants to study how college undergraduates cope with stress. They plan to survey their peers about circumstances that cause stress and the strategies used to reduce stress. They want to administer a questionnaire that asks undergraduates to identify on a list of 51 events those that occurred in the past year and to rate the stressfulness (1 - not at all stressful; 7 - extremely stressful) of each event experienced. Events ranged from very low stress (e.g., falling asleep in class) to very high stress (e.g., being raped, death of a close friend). Following this scale, they want to ask the research participants to complete a questionnaire about different coping strategies for reducing stress.

What is the level of risk in this study (none, minimal/low, moderate, high, very high)? How did you arrive at your decision? Many experiments require that participants have no knowledge about the study hypothesis; this translates into deceiving research participants about the true purpose of the research. For example, the famous Asch study asked participants to judge the length of lines drawn on a series of cards in the presence of "confederates" who either gave a correct or incorrect answer. Knowing that the study was examining conformity to group pressure may alter the response to the task, so participants were told that they were participating in a visual perception experiment. This type of deception is not "outlawed" in psychological research.

Ethical standards, however, acknowledge that not revealing the true nature of the research at the outset incurs special ethical obligations. The APA ethics code requires that we use deception only when study risks are mild and there are no feasible alternatives to the deception. In addition, we must provide an explanation of the deception immediately following the conclusion of the experiment and give the research participants the choice to withdraw from the study at that time. Finally, we may not deceive participants about aspects of the research that might influence their willingness to participate, such as physical or emotional discomforts or time commitment involved. Deceptions in psychological research can range from setting up false expectations about the purpose of the study to giving incorrect feedback about study performance. The use of deception in psychological research is a controversial topic. Some believe it should never be used, others believe that to outlaw deception would rule out our ability to study important questions about human behaviour.

What is your opinion? What are some of the costs and

benefits of using deception in psychological research? Any time that our research involves some level of risk, it is our ethical obligation to try to reduce the risk or address any harm experienced by participants in the study. Wherever possible, we try to prevent discomfort for our research participants. When that is not possible because of the nature of what we are studying, we must try to alleviate any distress after it has occurred. For example, in our survey study of stress and coping, we might prevent emotional discomfort by choosing an instrument that addresses daily hassles and mild stressors rather than more extreme events. This would change the question, though, from coping with all types of stressors to coping with everyday problems. You might also tell the participant before the study begins that you will ask questions about a wide range of stressors, including major life events.

Participants who might become distressed by the study can then choose not to participate, thereby preventing emotional discomfort. There might be no way to prevent discomfort with the original question as a small segment of the population will experience major stressors. Perhaps the most important principle built into ethics codes is the right of the participant to refuse to be in the study or discontinue participation at any time.

Ethical researchers, therefore, cannot coerce participants to agree to be in the study or prevent participants from discontinuing the study. When participants are children who cannot legally give consent, are incapacitated by a mental or emotional disorder, or have difficulty understanding information or giving consent, there is an even greater obligation on the part of the researcher to make sure that participants' rights are protected.

We still need to ask those who may not legally be able to give consent if they wish to participate in the study; we call this obtaining assent. If they say no, their wishes should be respected even if others have given permission for them to participate in the study. Incentives to participate in a study cannot be so great that a reasonable person would feel that he or she could not refuse to participate. This is particularly important when substantial sums of money are offered to participants or in an institutional setting in which even small rewards have great value. When obtaining informed consent, the researcher must provide participants with enough information to make a sound decision.

What are some of the elements of the study you think are essential to include when obtaining informed consent? Psychological research often involves matters that may be personally sensitive. Thus, it is important that the researcher maintain strict confidentiality of information gathered about participants. When possible, information should be gathered anonymously. If this is not possible, researchers should use code numbers rather than participants' names on all research records. Information should be stored in a locked and safe location. Data files should also be maintained in a manner that maintains participant privacy.

The right to privacy also extends to the publication or presentation of information. Information should be analyzed and reported in a manner that maintains the privacy of all research participants. Psychologists are expected to give participants an opportunity to obtain the results of the study. Some researchers will mail a study summary once the data are analyzed and conclusions drawn. Other researchers will post the results on a Web site. The summary does not need to include all analyses and conclusions but it should provide a good overview of the study findings and implications for the field. Providing a research summary not only allows the participants to see the end result of their efforts, it also provides the researcher an opportunity to thank the participants for their contribution to science.

Now that we have learned some ethical issues that must be considered when designing a study, let's put it all together into preparing a consent form. Presented below is a sample consent form. Look it over and identify all of the necessary elements of consent.

PERSONAL RELATIONSHIPS IN ADULTHOOD

Information is being gathered as part of an introductory

class in statistics at Local University. We are asking all students in the class who complete this questionnaire to discuss their beliefs and feelings about themselves and their relationships with others. While there may be no direct benefit to you from participating in this project, we hope to provide students in the class with a learning experience in which the data that they analyze is interesting to them and reflects an established area of study in the field of psychology. We will enter the information gathered anonymously into a database that students will use in the class and a computer laboratory. We are asking you to answer questions about how you see yourself and your relationships with others. We are also gathering social background data. It should take about 20-25 minutes to answer all of the questions on the survey form. When you are finished, please return the questionnaire to the designated envelope in your computer lab.

There are no known problems or risks with these types of surveys. Some people, though, find it difficult, at times, to think about personal matters. You can decide not to answer specific questions. You also can stop filling out the questions at any time. You can choose not to participate in the project without any consequences for your class grade.

Information is being gathered as part of an introductory class in statistics at Local University. [(1) Who is doing the study] We are asking all students in the class who complete this questionnaire to discuss their beliefs and feelings about themselves and their relationships with others. [(2) Brief description of study and why the participant is being recruited] While there may be no direct benefit to you from participating in this project, we hope to provide students in the class with a learning experience in which the data that they analyze is interesting to them and reflects an established area of study in the field of psychology. We will enter the information gathered anonymously into a database that students will use in the class and a computer laboratory. We are asking you to answer questions about how you see yourself and your relationships with others. We are also gathering social background data. It should take about 20-25 minutes to answer all of the questions on the survey form. When you are finished, please return the questionnaire to the designated envelope in your computer lab. [(3) What is required of the research participants]

There are no known problems or risks with these types of surveys. Some people, though, find it difficult, at times, to think about personal matters. [(4) Risks associated with the study] You can decide not to answer specific questions. You also can stop filling out the questions at any time. You can choose not to participate in the project without any consequences for your class grade. [(5) Participant's rights] If you find that the questions are stressful or you wish to discuss any part of the project, you may telephone Dr. Nice Teacher, the course instructor, on campus, at 555-6753. [(6) Contact information] Your answers to questions will be strictly confidential. Your name will not appear anywhere on the questionnaire. Your answers will be used only for teaching purposes and will be presented to the class as part of group statistics. [(7) & (8) What will be done with the data and how to obtain the results] If you have any questions about the project, feel free to contact Dr. Teacher. Because the questionnaire will be completely anonymous, filling out the questionnaire will be considered consent to participate in the project. Please keep this form for your personal records.

Unit II

Human Development

PHYSICAL GROWTH AND DEVELOPMENT

Human development is the scientific study of systematic psychological changes that occur in human beings over the course of the life span. Originally concerned with infants and children, the field has expanded to include adolescence and adult development, aging, and the entire life span.

This field examines change across a broad range of topics including motor skills and other psycho-physiological processes; cognitive development involving areas such as problem solving, moral understanding, and conceptual understanding; language acquisition; social, personality, and emotional development; and self-concept and identity formation.

Developmental psychology includes issues such as the extent to which development occurs through the gradual accumulation of knowledge versus stage-like development, or the extent to which children are born with innate mental structures versus learning through experience. Many researchers are interested in the interaction between personal characteristics, the individual's behaviour, and environmental factors including social context, and their impact on development; others take a more narrowly focused approach.

Developmental psychology informs several applied fields, including: educational psychology, child psychopathology, and forensic developmental psychology. Developmental psychology complements several other basic research fields in psychology including social psychology, cognitive psychology, ecological psychology, and comparative psychology.

APPROACHES

Many theoretical perspectives attempt to explain development; among the most prominent are: Jean Piaget's Stage Theory, Lev Vygotsky's Social Contextualism (and its heirs, the Cultural Theory of Development of Michael Cole, and the Ecological Systems Theory of Urie Bronfenbrenner), Albert Bandura's Social learning theory, and the information processing framework employed by cognitive psychology. To a lesser extent, historical theories continue to provide a basis for additional research. Among them are Erik Erikson's eight stages of psychosocial development and John B. Watson's and B. F. Skinner's behaviorism. Many other theories are prominent for their contributions to particular aspects of development. For example, attachment theory describes kinds of interpersonal relationships and Lawrence Kohlberg describes stages in moral reasoning. Folklore also describes a good method to the growth of child psychology.

THEORISTS AND THEORIES

Piagetian Stages of Cognitive Development

Piaget was a French speaking Swiss theorist who posited that children learn through actively constructing knowledge through hands-on experience. He suggested that the adult's role in helping the child learn was to provide appropriate materials for the child to interact and construct. He would use Socratic questioning to get the children to reflect on what they were doing. He would try to get them to see contradictions in their explanations. He also developed stages of development. His approach can be seen in how the curriculum is sequenced in schools, and in the pedagogy of preschool centers across the United States.

Vygotsky's Cultural-historical Theory

Vygotsky was a theorist from the Soviet era, who posited

that children learn through hands-on experience, as Piaget suggested. However, unlike Piaget, he claimed that timely and sensitive intervention by adults when a child is on the edge of learning a new task (called the "zone of proximal development") could help children learn new tasks. This technique is called "scaffolding," because it builds upon knowledge children already have with new knowledge that adults can help the child learn.

Vygotsky was strongly focused on the role of culture in determining the child's pattern of development, arguing that development moves from the social level to the individual level.

ECOLOGICAL SYSTEMS THEORY

Also called "Development in Context" or "Human Ecology" theory, Ecological Systems Theory, originally formulated by Urie Bronfenbrenner specifies four types of nested environmental systems, with bi-directional influences within and between the systems. The four systems are Microsystem, Mesosystem, Exosystem, and Macrosystem.

Each system contains roles, norms and rules that can powerfully shape development.

Since its publication in 1979, Bronfenbrenner's major statement of this theory, *The Ecology of Human Development* has had widespread influence on the way psychologists and others approach the study of human beings and their environments.

As a result of this conceptualization of development, these environments — from the family to economic and political structures — have come to be viewed as part of the life course from childhood through adulthood.

ATTACHMENT THEORY

Attachment theory, originally developed by John Bowlby, focuses on close, intimate, emotionally meaningful relationships. Attachment is described as a biological system that evolved to ensure the survival of the infant. A child who is threatened or stressed will move toward caregivers who create a sense of physical, emotional and psychological safety for the individual. Later Mary Ainsworth developed the Strange Situation Protocol and the concept of the secure base.

NATURE/NURTURE

A significant question in developmental psychology is the relationship between innateness and environmental influence in regard to any particular aspect of development. This is often referred to as "nature versus nurture" or nativism versus empiricism. A nativist account of development would argue that the processes in question are innate, that is, they are specified by the organism's genes. An empiricist perspective would argue that those processes are acquired in interaction with the environment. Today developmental psychologists rarely take such extreme positions with regard to most aspects of development; rather they investigate, among many other things, the relationship between innate and environmental influences. One of the ways in which this relationship has been explored in recent years is through the emerging field of evolutionary developmental psychology.

One area where this innateness debate has been prominently portrayed is in research on language acquisition. A major question in this area is whether or not certain properties of human language are specified genetically or can be acquired through learning. The empiricist position on the issue of language acquisition suggests that the language input provides the necessary information required for learning the structure of language and that infants acquire language through a process of statistical learning.

From this perspective, language can be acquired via general learning methods that also apply to other aspects of development, such as perceptual learning. The nativist position argues that the input from language is too impoverished for infants and children to acquire the structure of language. Linguist Noam Chomsky asserts that, evidenced by the lack of sufficient information in the language input, there is a universal grammar that applies to all human languages and is pre-specified. This has led to the idea that there is a special cognitive module suited for learning language, often called the language acquisition device. Chomsky's critique of the behaviorist model of language acquisition is regarded by many as a key turning point in the decline in the prominence of the theory of behaviorism generally. But Skinner's conception of "Verbal Behaviour" has not died, perhaps in part because it has generated successful practical applications.

MECHANISMS OF DEVELOPMENT

Developmental psychology is concerned not only with describing the characteristics of psychological change over time, but also seeks to explain the principles and internal workings underlying these changes. Psychologists have attempted to better understand these factors by using models. Developmental models are sometimes computational, but they do not need to be. A model must simply account for the means by which a process takes place. This is sometimes done in reference to changes in the brain that may correspond to changes in behaviour over the course of the development. Computational accounts of development often use either symbolic, connectionist (neural network), or dynamical systems models to explain the mechanisms of development.

RESEARCH AREAS

Cognitive Development

Cognitive development is primarily concerned with the ways in which infants and children acquire, develop, and use internal mental capabilities such as problem solving, memory, and language. Major topics in cognitive development are the study of language acquisition and the development of perceptual and motor skills. Piaget was one of the influential early psychologists to study the development of cognitive abilities. His theory suggests that development proceeds through a set of stages from infancy to adulthood and that there is an end point or goal.

Other accounts, such as that of Lev Vygotsky, have suggested that development does not progress through stages, but rather that the developmental process that begins at birth and continues until death is too complex for such structure and finality. Rather, from this viewpoint, developmental processes proceed more continuously, thus development should be analyzed, instead of treated as a product to be obtained. Modern cognitive development has largely moved away from Piagetian stage theories, and is influenced by accounts of domain-specific information processing, which posit that development is guided by innate evolutionarily specified and content-specific information processing mechanisms.

SOCIAL AND EMOTIONAL DEVELOPMENT

Developmental psychologists who are interested in social development examine how individuals develop social and emotional competencies. For example, they study how children form friendships, how they understand and deal with emotions, and how identity develops. Research in this area may involve study of the relationship between cognition or cognitive development and social behaviour.

RESEARCH METHODS

Developmental psychology employs many of the research methods used in other areas of psychology. However, infants and children cannot always be tested in the same ways as adults, so different methods are often used to study their development.

METHODS AND TECHNIQUES

When studying older children, especially adolescents, adult measurements of behaviour can often be used, but they may need to be simplified to allow children to perform certain tasks.

Adults

Developmental psychologists have a number of methods to study changes in individuals over time. In a longitudinal study, a researcher observes many individuals born at or around the same time (a cohort) and carries out new observations as members of the cohort age. This method can be used to draw conclusions about which types of development are universal (or normative) and occur in most members of a cohort. Researchers may also observe ways in which development varies between individuals and hypothesize about the causes of variation observed in their data. Longitudinal studies often require large amounts of time and funding, making them unfeasible in some situations. Also, because members of a cohort all experience historical events unique to their generation, apparently normative developmental trends may in fact be universal only to their cohort.

In a cross-sectional study, a researcher observes differences between individuals of different ages at the same time. This generally requires fewer resources than the longitudinal method, and because the individuals come from different cohorts, shared historical events are not so much of a confounding factor. By the same token, however, cross-sectional research may not be the most effective way to study differences between participants, as these differences may result not from their different ages but from their exposure to *different* historical events.

An accelerated longitudinal design or cross-sequential study or cohort-sequential design combines both methodologies. Here, a researcher observes members of different birth cohorts at the same time, and then tracks all participants over time, charting changes in the groups. By comparing differences and similarities in development, one can more easily determine what changes can be attributed to individual or historical environment, and which are truly universal. Clearly such a study can be even more resource-consuming than a longitudinal study. Additionally, these are all correlational, not experimental, designs, and so one cannot readily infer causation from the data they yield. Nonetheless, correlational research methods are common in the study of development, in part due to ethical concerns. In a study of the effects of poverty on development, for instance, one cannot easily randomly assign certain families to a poverty condition and others to an affluent one, and so observation alone has to suffice.

STAGES OF DEVELOPMENT

The prenatal development of human beings is viewed in three separate stages, which are not the same as the trimesters of a woman's pregnancy:

- Germinal (conception through week 2)
- Embryonic (weeks 3 through 8)
- Fetal (week 9 through birth)

The germinal stage begins when a sperm penetrates an egg in the act of conception (normally the result of sexual intercourse between a man and a woman). At this point a zygote is formed. Through the process of mitosis, the cells divide and double. The embryonic stage occurs once the zygote has firmly implanted itself in the uterine wall. It is in this stage that the vital organs are formed, and while the external body is still extremely dissimilar from an adult human, some features such as eyes and arms, and eventually ears and feet, become recognizable.

The fetal period is the pre-natal period when the brain has its greatest development, becoming more and more complex over the last few months. During pregnancy there is a risk to the developing child from drugs and other teratogens, spousal abuse and other stress on the mother, nutrition and the age of the mother. Genetic testing prior to pregnancy is also increasingly available. Three methods of determining fetal defects and health include the ultrasound, amniocentesis, and chorionic villus sampling. Although difficult, some methods of treating fetal disorders have been developed, both surgical and drug based.

Infancy

From birth until the onset of speech, the child is referred to as an infant. Developmental psychologists vary widely in their assessment of infant psychology, and the influence the outside world has upon it, but certain aspects are relatively clear. While no agreement has yet been reached regarding the level of stimulation an infant requires, a normal level of stimulation is very important, and a lack of stimulation and affection can result in learning difficulties and a host of other developmental and social disorders Some feel that classical music, particularly Mozart is good for an infant's mind. While some tentative research has shown it to be helpful to older children, no conclusive evidence is available involving infants. The majority of a newborn infant's time is spent in sleep. At first this sleep is evenly spread throughout the day and night, but after a couple of months, infants generally become diurnal.

Infants can be seen to have 6 states, grouped into pairs:

- Quiet sleep and active sleep (dreaming, when REM occurs)
- Quiet waking, and active waking
- Fussing and crying

Infants respond to stimuli differently in these different states. Habituation is frequently used in testing psychological phenomenon. Both infants and adults attend less as a result of consistent exposure to a particular stimulus. The amount of time spent attending to an alternate stimulus (after habituation to the initial stimulus) is indicative of the strength of the remembered percept of the previous stimulus, or dishabituation. Habituation is used to discover the resolution of perceptual systems, for example, by habituating a subject to one stimulus, and then observing responses to similar ones, one can detect the smallest degree of difference that is detectable by the subject.

Infants have a wide variety of reflexes, some of which are permanent (blinking, gagging), and others transient in nature. Some have obvious purposes, some are clearly vestigial, and some do not have obvious purposes. Primitive reflexes reappear in adults under certain conditions, such as neurological conditions like dementia or traumatic lesions. A partial list of infantile reflexes includes:

- Moro reflex or startle reflex:
  - Startle
  - Spreading out the arms (adduction)

  - Unspreading the arms (abduction)
  - Crying (usually)
- Tonic neck reflex or fencer's reflex
- Rooting reflex, sucking reflex, suckling reflex: can be initiated by scratching the infant's cheek; the reaction is pursing of the lips for sucking.
- Stepping reflex, step-up reflex: can be initiated if you support the infant upright from its armpits below a given surface so the baby lifts its foot and steps up on the surface (like climbing a stair).
- Grasp reflex: can be initiated by scratching the infant's palm.
- Parachute reflex: the infant is suspended by the trunk and suddenly lowered as if falling for an instant. The child spontaneously throws out the arms as a protective mechanism. The parachute reflex appears before the onset of walking.
- Plantar reflex or Babinski reflex: a finger is stroked firmly down the outer edge of the baby's sole; the toes spread and extend out.

Infants have significantly worse vision than older children. Infant sight, blurry in early stages, improves over time. Infants less than 2 months old are thought to be colour blind. Hearing is well-developed prior to birth, however, and a preference for the mother's heartbeat is well established. Infants are fairly good at detecting the direction from which a sound comes, and by 18 months their hearing ability is approximately equal to that of adults. Smell and taste are present, with infants having been shown to prefer the smell and taste of a banana, while rejecting the taste of shrimp. There is good evidence for infants preferring the smell of their mother to that of others. Infants have a fully developed sense of touch at birth, and the myth believed by some doctors even today that infants feel no pain is inaccurate. Doctors are slowly becoming aware of the need for pain prevention for newborns.

Piaget asserted that there were several sensorimotor stages within his broader Theory of cognitive development.

- The first sub-stage occurs from birth to six weeks and

is associated primarily with the development of reflexes. Three primary reflexes are described by Piaget: sucking of objects in the mouth, following moving or interesting objects with the eyes, and closing of the hand when an object makes contact with the palm (palmar grasp). Over these first six weeks of life, these reflexes begin to become voluntary actions; for example, the palmar reflex becomes intentional grasping.

- The second sub-stage occurs from six weeks to four months and is associated primarily with the development of habits. Primary circular reactions or repeating of an action involving only ones own body begin. An example of this type of reaction would involve something like an infant repeating the motion of passing their hand before their face. Also at this phase, passive reactions, caused by classical or operant conditioning, can begin.
- The third sub-stage occurs from four to nine months and is associated primarily with the development of coordination between vision and prehension. Three new abilities occur at this stage: intentional grasping for a desired object, secondary circular reactions, and differentiations between ends and means. At this stage, infants will intentionally grasp the air in the direction of a desired object, often to the amusement of friends and family. Secondary circular reactions, or the repetition of an action involving an external object occur begin; for example, moving a switch to turn on a light repeatedly. The differentiation between means also occurs. This is perhaps one of the most important stages of a child's growth as it signifies the dawn of logic. Towards the late part of this sub-stage infants begin to have a sense of object permanence, passing the A-not-B error test.
- The fourth sub-stage occurs from nine to twelve months and is associated primarily with the development of logic and the coordination between

means and ends. This is an extremely important stage of development, holding what Piaget calls the "first proper intelligence." Also, this stage marks the beginning of goal orientation, the deliberate planning of steps to meet an objective.

- The fifth sub-stage occurs from twelve to eighteen months and is associated primarily with the discovery of new means to meet goals. Piaget describes the child at this juncture as the "young scientist," conducting pseudo-experiments to discover new methods of meeting challenges.
- The sixth sub-stage is associated primarily with the beginnings of insight, or true creativity. This marks the passage into the preoperational stage.

When studying infants, the habituation methodology is an example of a method often used to assess their performance. This method allows researchers to obtain information about what types of stimuli an infant is able to discriminate. In this paradigm, infants are habituated to a particular stimulus and are then tested using different stimuli to evaluate discrimination. The critical measure in habituation is the infants' level of interest. Typically, infants prefer stimuli that are novel relative to those they have encountered previously. Several methods are used to measure infants' preference. These include the high-amplitude sucking procedure, in which infants suck on a pacifier more or less depending on their level of interest, the conditioned foot-kick procedure, in which infants move their legs to indicate preference, and the head-turn preference procedure, in which the infant's level of interest is measured by the amount of time spent looking in a particular direction.

A key feature of all these methods is that, in each situation, the infant controls the stimuli being presented. This gives researchers a means of measuring discrimination. If an infant is able to discriminate between the habituated stimulus and a novel stimulus, they will show a preference for the novel stimulus. If, however, the infant cannot discriminate between the two stimuli, they will not show a preference for one over the other. Object permanence is an important stage of cognitive development for infants. Numerous tests regarding it have been done, usually involving a toy, and a crude barrier which is placed in front of the toy, and then removed, repeatedly. In sensorimotor stages 1 and 2, the infant is completely unable to comprehend object permanence. Jean Piaget conducted experiments with infants which led him to conclude that this awareness was typically achieved at eight to nine months of age. Infants before this age are too young to understand object permanence, which explains why infants at this age do not cry when their mothers are gone. "Out of sight, out of mind." A lack of Object Permanence can lead to A-not-B errors, where children reach for a thing at a place where it should not be.

Toddler

Intelligence is demonstrated through the use of symbols, language use matures, and memory and imagination are developed. Thinking is done in a nonlogical, nonreversible manner. Egocentric thinking predominates. Socially, toddlers are little people attempting to become independent at this stage, which they are commonly called the "terrible twos". They walk, talk, use the toilet, and get food for themselves. Self-control begins to develop. If taking the initiative to explore, experiment, risk mistakes in trying new things, and test their limits is encouraged by the caretaker(s) the child will become autonomous, self-reliant, and confident. If the caretaker is overprotective or disapproving of independent actions, the toddler may begin to doubt their abilities and feel ashamed for the desire for independence. The child's autonomic development will be inhibited, and be less prepared to successfully deal with the world in the future.

Early Childhood

When children attend preschool, they broaden their social horizons and become more engaged with those around them. Impulses are channeled into fantasies, which leaves the task of the caretaker to balance eagerness for pursuing adventure, creativity and self expression with the development of responsibility. If caretakers are properly encouraging and consistently disciplinary, children are more likely to develop positive self-esteem while becoming more responsible, and will follow through on assigned activities. If not allowed to decide which activities to perform, children may begin to feel guilt upon contemplating taking initiative. This negative association with independence will lead them to let others make decisions in place of them.

Childhood

In middle childhood, intelligence is demonstrated through logical and systematic manipulation of symbols related to concrete objects. Operational thinking develops, which means actions are reversible, and egocentric thought diminishes. Children go through the transition from the world at home to that of school and peers. Children learn to make things, use tools, and acquire the skills to be a worker and a potential provider. Children can now receive feedback from outsiders about their accomplishments. If children can discover pleasure in intellectual stimulation, being productive, seeking success, they will develop a sense of competence. If they are not successful or cannot discover pleasure in the process, they may develop a sense of inferiority and feelings of inadequacy that may haunt them throughout life. This is when children think of them selves as industrious or as inferior.

Adolescence

Adolescence is the period of life between the onset of puberty and the full commitment to an adult social role, such as worker, parent, and/or citizen. It is the period known for the formation of personal and social identity and the discovery of moral purpose. Intelligence is demonstrated through the logical use of symbols related to abstract concepts and formal reasoning. A return to egocentric thought often occurs early in the period. Only 35% develop the capacity to reason formally during adolescence or adulthood. The adolescent asks "Who am I? Who do I want to be?" Like toddlers, adolescents must explore, test limits, become autonomous, and commit to an identity, or sense of self. Different roles, behaviors and ideologies must be tried out to select an identity. Role confusion and inability to choose vocation can result from a failure to achieve a sense of identity.

The person must learn how to form intimate relationships, both in friendship and love. The development of this skill relies on the resolution of other stages. It may be hard to establish intimacy if one has not developed trust or a sense of identity. If this skill is not learned the alternative is alienation, isolation, a fear of commitment, and the inability to depend on others. However, an Inuit proverb claims that 'privation and suffering are the basis of all great things', so ultimately this isolation may be to an individual's long-term best interest. A related framework for studying this part of the life span is that of Emerging adulthood, introduced in 2000 by Jeffrey Arnett. Scholars of emerging adulthood are interested not only in relationship development (focusing on the role of dating in helping individuals settle on a long-term spouse/partner), but also the development of sociopolitical views and occupational choice.

Middle Age

Middle adulthood generally refers to the period between ages 40 to 65. During this period, the middle-aged experience a conflict between generativity and stagnation. They may either feel a sense of contributing to the next generation and their community or a sense of purposelessness. Physically, the middle-aged experience a decline in muscular strength, reaction time, sensory keenness, and cardiac output. Also, women experience menopause and a sharp drop in the hormone estrogen. Men do not have an equivalent to menopause, but they do experience a decline in sperm count and speed of ejaculation and erection. Most men and women remain capable of sexual satisfaction after middle age.

Old Age

This stage generally refers to those over 75 years. During old age, people experience a conflict between integrity vs.

despair. When reflecting on their life, they either feel a sense of accomplishment or failure. Physically, older people experience a decline in muscular strength, reaction time, stamina, hearing, distance perception, and the sense of smell. They also are more susceptible to severe diseases such as cancer and pneumonia due to a weakened immune system. Mental disintegration may also occur, leading to Dementia or Alzheimer's Disease.

However, partially due to a lifetime's accumulation of antibodies, the elderly are less likely to suffer from common diseases such as the cold. Whether or not intellectual powers increase or decrease with age remains controversial. Longitudinal studies have suggested that intellect declines, while cross-sectional studies suggest that intellect is stable. It is generally believed that crystallized intelligence increases up to old age, while fluid intelligence decreases with age.

OTHER FINDINGS

Parenting

In Western developed societies, mothers (and women generally) were emphasized to the exclusion of other caregivers, particularly as the traditional role of the father was more the breadwinner, and less the direct caregiver of an infant, he has been traditionally viewed as impacting an infant indirectly through interactions with the mother of the child. The emphasis of study has shifted to the primary caregiver (regardless of gender or biological relation), as well as all persons directly or indirectly influencing the child (the family system). The roles of the mother and father are more significant than first thought as we moved into the concept of primary caregiver.

Affirming a role for fathers, studies have shown that children as young as 15 months benefit significantly from substantial engagement with their father. In particular, a study in the U.S.A. and New Zealand found the presence of the natural father was the most significant factor in reducing rates of early sexual activity and rates of teenage pregnancy in girls.

Covariate factors used included early conduct problems, maternal age at first childbirth, race, maternal education, father's occupational status, family living standards, family life stress, early mother-child interaction, measures of psychosocial adjustment and educational achievement, school qualifications, mood disorder, anxiety disorder, suicide attempts, violent offending, and conduct disorder.

Further research has found fathers have an impact on child academic performance, including involved nonresident fathers. However, father absence is associated with a range of negative outcomes for children, including child and later criminal behaviour.

The modern form of developmental psychology has its roots in the rich psychological tradition represented by Aristotle, Tabari, Rhazes, Alhazen, and Descartes. William Shakespeare had his melancholy character *Jacques* (in As You Like It) articulate the seven ages of man: these included three stages of childhood and four of adulthood.

In the mid-eighteenth century Jean Jacques Rousseau described three stages of childhood: *infans* (infancy), *puer* (childhood) and *adolescence* in *Emile: Or, On Education*. Rousseau's ideas were taken up strongly by educators at the time.

In the late nineteenth century, psychologists familiar with the evolutionary theory of Darwin began seeking an evolutionary description of psychological development; prominent here was G. Stanley Hall, who attempted to correlate ages of childhood with previous ages of mankind.

A more scientific approach was initiated by James Mark Baldwin, who wrote essays on topics that included *Imitation: A Chapter in the Natural History of Consciousness* and *Mental Development in the Child and the Race: Methods and Processes*. In 1905, Sigmund Freud articulated five psychosexual stages. Later, Rudolf Steiner articulated stages of psychological development throughout human life. By the early to mid-twentieth century, the work of Vygotsky and Piaget, mentioned above, had established a strong empirical tradition in the field.

PERCEPTUAL DEVELOPMENT – COGNITIVE DEVELOPMENT: PIAGET'S THEORY

Cognitive development is a field of study in neuroscience and psychology focusing on a child's development in terms of information processing, conceptual resources, perceptual skill, and other topics in cognitive psychology.

A large portion of research has gone into understanding how a child conceptualizes the world. Jean Piaget was a major force in the founding of this field, forming his "theory of cognitive development". Many of his claims have since fallen out of favour. A major topic in cognitive development is nativism versus empiricism. Another is the question of convergance or homology with animals when humans have similar cognition. These two debates are present in nearly every smaller part of the field.

CORE SYSTEMS OF COGNITION

Nativists theorize that children are born with many innate cognitive systems designed to tackle problems that the human species have faced over a very long evolutionary time. Empiricists study how these skills may be learned in such a short time. The debate is over whether these systems are learned by general-purpose learning devices, or domain-specific cognition.

Number

Infants appear to have two systems for dealing with numbers. One deals with small numbers, often called subitizing. Another deal with larger numbers in an approximate fashion.

Navigation

Very young children appear to have some skill in dead reckoning. This basic "sense of direction" does not change very much through development. Later in life, adults can use natural language to store additional navigational information. Making them use their language skills for something else makes them perform like children or rats.

Visual Perception

One of the original nativist versus empiricist debates was over depth perception. There is some evidence that children less than 72 hours old can perceive such complex things as biological motion.

Essentialism

Young children seem to be predisposed to think of things in an essentialistic way.

Language Acquisition

A major, well-studied feat of cognitive development is language acquisition. The modern consensus is that this draws on many innate systems.

Creation of New Representational Resources

Of course, the human mind expands far beyond these simple forms of cognition. For example, children are not born knowing what force is, but they are capable of eventually learning.

Whorf's Hypothesis

Whorf believed that a person cannot think what they cannot say in language.

Quine's Bootstrapping Hypothesis

Quine suggests that words are commonly used to help create new thoughts.

PIAGET'S THEORY

Jean Piaget believed that people move through stages of development that allow them to think in new, more complex ways. Many of his claims have fallen out of favour. For example, he claimed that young children cannot conserve number.

However, further experiments show that children did not really understand what was being asked of them. When the experiment is done with candies, and the children are asked which set they *want* rather than tell an adult which is more, they show no confusion about which group has more items.

Neuroscience

During development, especially the first few years of life, children show interesting patterns of neural development and a high degree of neuroplasticity. The Theory of Cognitive Development, one of the most historically influential theories was developed by Jean Piaget, a Swiss psychologist (1896–1980).

His theory provided many central concepts in the field of developmental psychology and concerned the growth of intelligence, which for Piaget, meant the ability to more accurately represent the world and perform logical operations on representations of concepts grounded in the world.

The theory concerns the emergence and acquisition of schemata—schemes of how one perceives the world—in "developmental stages", times when children are acquiring new ways of mentally representing information. The theory is considered "constructivist", meaning that, unlike nativist theories (which describe cognitive development as the unfolding of innate knowledge and abilities) or empiricist theories (which describe cognitive development as the gradual acquisition of knowledge through experience), it asserts that we construct our cognitive abilities through self-motivated action in the world. For his development of the theory, Piaget was awarded the Erasmus Prize. Piaget divided schemes that children use to understand the world through four main periods, roughly correlated with and becoming increasingly sophisticated with age:

- Sensorimotor period (years 0–2)
- Preoperational period (years 2–7)
- Concrete operational period (years 7–12)
- Formal operational period (years 12–adulthood)

SENSORIMOTOR PERIOD

Infants are born with a set of congenital reflexes, according to Piaget, in addition to a drive to explore their world. Their initial schemas are formed through differentiation of the congenital reflexes

The *sensorimotor period* is the first of the four periods. According to Piaget, this stage marks the development of essential spatial abilities and understanding of the world in six sub-stages:

- The first sub-stage, known as *the reflex schema* stage, occurs from birth to six weeks and is associated primarily with the development of reflexes.
- The second sub-stage, *primary circular reaction phase,* occurs from six weeks to four months and is associated primarily with the development of habits.
- The third sub-stage, the *secondary circular reactions phase,* occurs from four to nine months and is associated primarily with the development of coordination between vision and prehension.
- The fourth sub-stage, called *the co-ordination of secondary circular reactions stage,* which occurs from nine to twelve months, is when Piaget (1954) thought that object permanence developed.
- The fifth sub-stage, *the tertiary circular reactions phase,* occurs from twelve to eighteen months and is associated primarily with the discovery of new means to meet goals.
- The sixth sub-stage, considered "beginnings of symbolic representation", is associated primarily with the beginnings of insight, or true creativity.

PREOPERATIONAL STAGE

The Preoperational stage is the second of four stages of cognitive development. By observing sequences of play, Piaget was able to demonstrate that towards the end of the second year a qualitatively new kind of psychological functioning occurs. (Pre)Operatory Thought in Piagetian theory is any procedure for mentally acting on objects. The hallmark of the preoperational stage is sparse and logically inadequate mental operations. During this stage the child learns to use and to represent objects by images and words, in other words they learn to use symbolic thinking. Thinking is still egocentric: The child has difficulty taking the viewpoint of others.

The child can classify objects by a single feature: e.g. groups together all the red blocks regardless of shape or all the square blocks regardless of colour. According to Piaget, the Pre-Operational stage of development follows the Sensorimotor stage and occurs between 2–7 years of age. In this stage, children develop their language skills. They begin representing things with words and images. However, they still use intuitive rather than logical reasoning. At the beginning of this stage, they tend to be egocentric, that is, they are not aware that other people do not think, know and perceive the same as them. Children have highly imaginative minds at this time and actually assign emotions to inanimate objects. The theory of mind is also critical to this stage.

The Preconceptual stage (2-4 years) is marked by egocentric thinking and animistic thought. A child who displays animistic thought tends to assign living attributes to inanimate objects, for example that a glass would feel pain if it were broken. The Intuitive (4-7 years) stage is when children start employing mental activities to solve problems and obtain goals but they are unaware of how they came to their conclusions. For example a child is shown 7 dogs and 3 cats and asked if there are more dogs then cats. The child would respond positively. However when asked if there are more dogs then animals the child would once again respond positively. Such fundamental errors in logic show the transition between intuitiveness in solving problems and true logical reasoning acquired in later years.

CONCRETE OPERATIONAL STAGE

The Concrete operational stage is the third of four stages of cognitive development in Piaget's theory. This stage, which follows the Preoperational stage, occurs between the ages of 6 and 12 years and is characterized by the appropriate use of logic. Important processes during this stage are:

- Seriation—the ability to sort objects in an order according to size, shape, or any other characteristic.

For example, if given different-shaded objects they may make a colour gradient.

- Classification—the ability to name and identify sets of objects according to appearance, size or other characteristic, including the idea that one set of objects can include another. A child is no longer subject to the illogical limitations of animism (the belief that all objects are alive and therefore have feelings).
- Decentering—where the child takes into account multiple aspects of a problem to solve it. For example, the child will no longer perceive an exceptionally wide but short cup to contain less than a normally-wide, taller cup.
- Reversibility—where the child understands that numbers or objects can be changed, then returned to their original state. For this reason, a child will be able to rapidly determine that if 4+4 equals 8, 8"4 will equal 4, the original quantity.
- Conservation—understanding that quantity, length or number of items is unrelated to the arrangement or appearance of the object or items. For instance, when a child is presented with two equally-sized, full cups they will be able to discern that if water is transferred to a pitcher it will conserve the quantity and be equal to the other filled cup.
- Elimination of Egocentrism—the ability to view things from another's perspective (even if they think incorrectly). For instance, show a child a comic in which Jane puts a doll under a box, leaves the room, and then Melissa moves the doll to a drawer, and Jane comes back. A child in the concrete operations stage will say that Jane will still think it's under the box even though the child knows it is in the drawer.

FORMAL OPERATIONAL STAGE

The formal operational period is the fourth and final of the periods of cognitive development in Piaget's theory. This stage, which follows the Concrete Operational stage, commences at around 11 years of age (puberty) and continues into adulthood. It is characterized by acquisition of the ability to think abstractly, reason logically and draw conclusions from the information available.

During this stage the young adult is able to understand such things as love, "shades of gray", logical proofs, and values. Lucidly, biological factors may be traced to this stage as it occurs during puberty (the time at which another period of neural pruning occurs), marking the entry to adulthood in Physiology, cognition, moral judgment (Kohlberg), Psychosexual development (Freud), and social development (Erikson). Some two-thirds of people do not develop this form of reasoning fully enough that it becomes their normal mode for cognition, and so they remain, even as adults, concrete operational thinkers.

GENERAL INFORMATION REGARDING THE STAGES

These four stages have been found to have the following characteristics:

- Although the timing may vary, the sequence of the stages does not.
- Universal (not culturally specific)
- Generalizable: the representational and logical operations available to the child should extend to all kinds of concepts and content knowledge
- Stages are logically organized wholes
- Hierarchical nature of stage sequences (each successive stage incorporates elements of previous stages, but is more differentiated and integrated)
- Stages represent qualitative differences in modes of thinking, not merely quantitative differences

CHALLENGES TO PIAGETIAN STAGE THEORY

Piagetians accounts of development have been challenged on several grounds. First, as Piaget himself noted, development does not always progress in the smooth manner his theory seems to predict. 'Decalage', or unpredicted gaps in the developmental progression, suggest that the stage model is at best a useful approximation. More broadly, Piaget's theory is 'domain general', predicting that cognitive maturation occurs concurrently across different domains of knowledge (such as mathematics, logic, understanding of physics, of language, etc).

However, more recent cognitive developmentalists have been much influenced by trends in cognitive science away from domain generality and towards domain specificity or modularity of mind, under which different cognitive faculties may be largely independent of one another and thus develop according to quite different time-tables.

In this vein, many current cognitive developmentalists argue that rather than being domain general learners, children come equipped with domain specific theories, sometimes referred to as 'core knowledge', which allows them to break into learning within that domain.

For example, even young infants appear to understand some basic principles of physics (e.g. that one object cannot pass through another) and human intention (e.g. that a hand repeatedly reaching for an object has that object, not just a particular path of motion, as its goal). These basic assumptions may be the building block out of which more elaborate knowledge is constructed.

POST PIAGETIAN AND NEO-PIAGETIAN STAGES

There are three major changes to the number of stages and their definitions. First and foremost, the half stages are now shown to be stages. Pascual Leone discovered this. Almost all Post Piagetians accept this. Second, postformal stages have been shown to exist. Kurt Fischer suggested two, Michael Commons presents evidence for four postformal stages: the systematic, metasystematic, paradigmatic and cross paradigmatic. Fischer has considered a stage suggested by Biggs and Biggs. It is a stage before the early preoperational. Commons and Richards call this stage the sentential because organisms can sequence representations of concepts.

Piagetian and post-Piagetian stage theories/heuristics:

- Michael Barnes' stages of religious and scientific thinking
- Michael Lamport Commons' Model of Hierarchical Complexity
- Kieran Egan's stages of understanding
- Suzy Gablik's stages of art history
- Christopher Hallpike's stages of moral understanding
- Lawrence Kohlberg's stages of moral development
- Don Lepan's theory of the origins of modern thought and drama
- Charles Raddings theory of the medieval intellectual development
- R.J. Robinson's stages of history and theory of the origins of intelligence

MORAL DEVELOPMENT: KOHLBERG'S STAGES OF MORAL UNDERSTANDING

IMPLICATIONS FOR THEOLOGY

Lawrence Kohlberg is a moral philosopher and student of child development. He is director of Harvard's Centre for Moral Education. His special area of interest is the moral development of children - how they develop a sense of right, wrong, and justice. Kohlberg observed that growing children advance through definite stages of moral development in a manner similar to their progression through Piaget's well-known stages of cognitive development. His observations and testing of children and adults, led him to theorize that human beings progress consecutively from one stage to the next in an invariant sequence, not skipping any stage or going back to any previous stage. These are stages of thought processing, implying qualitatively different modes of thinking and of problem solving at each stage.

These conclusions have been verified in cross-cultural studies done in Turkey, Taiwan, Yucatan, Honduras, India, United States, Canada, Britain, and Israel.

An outline of these developmental stages follows:

Kohlberg's concept of consecutive stages of moral

development is rich with theological implications. An application of his theory to the story of God's dealing with ancient Israel, offers a rational explanation of actions on God's part which may seem harsh or unduly severe from our perspective. An application of Kohlberg's stage theory is especially relevant to current discussions of the gospel, the atonement, the Law, and the true character of God.

KOHLBERG'S STAGES OF MORAL DEVELOPMENT

- PREMORAL OR PRECONVENTIONAL STAGES: Behaviour motivated by anticipation of pleasure or pain.

Stage 1: Punishment and Obedience:

Avoidance of physical punishment and deference to power. Punishment is an automatic response of physical retaliation. The immediate physical consequences of an action determine its goodness or badness. The atrocities carried out by soldiers during the holocaust who were simply "carrying out orders" under threat of punishment, illustrate that adults as well as children may function at stage one level.

Stage 2: instrumental exchange:

Marketplace exchange of favors or blows. "You scratch my back, I'll scratch yours." Justice is: "Do unto others as they do unto you." Individual does what is necessary, makes concessions only as necessary to satisfy his own needs. Right action consists of what instrumentally satisfies one's own needs. Vengeance is considered a moral duty. People are valued in terms of their utility.

- Conventional Morality: Acceptance of the rules and standards of one's group.

Stage 3: Interpersonal Conformity: Right is conformity to the behavioral expectations of one's society or peers. Individual acts to gain approval of others. Good behaviour is that which pleases or helps others within the group. "Everybody is doing it." One earns approval by being conventionally "respectable" and "nice." Sin is a breach of the expectations of the social order. Retribution, however, at this stage is collective. Individual vengeance is not allowed. Forgiveness is preferable to revenge. Punishment is mainly for deterrence. Failure to punish is "unfair." "If he can get away with it, why can't I?"

Stage 4: Law And Order: Respect for rules, laws and properly constituted authority. Defence of the given social and institutional order for it's own sake. Responsibility toward the welfare of others in the society. "Justice" normally refers to criminal or forensic justice.

Justice demands that the wrongdoer be punished, that he "pay his debt to society," and that law abiders be rewarded. "A good day's pay for a good day's work." Injustice is failing to reward work or punish demerit. Right behaviour consists of maintaining the social order for its own sake. Authority figures are seldom questioned. "He must be right. He's the Pope (or the President, or the Judge, or God)." Consistency and precedent must be maintained.

Stage 4 ½: Between the conventional stages and the post-conventional Levels 5 and 6, there is a transitional stage. College-age students that have come to see conventional morality as relative and arbitrary, but have not yet discovered universal ethical principles, may drop into a hedonistic ethic of "do your own thing." This was well noted in the hippie culture of the 1960's. Disrespect for conventional morality was especially infuriating to the Stage 4 mentality, and indeed was calculated to be so.

- Postconventional or Principled Morality: Ethical Principles

Stage 5: Prior Rights and Social Contract: Moral action in a specific situation is not defined by reference to a checklist of rules, but from logical application of universal, abstract, moral principles. Individuals have natural or inalienable rights and liberties that are prior to society and must be protected by society. Retributive justice repudiated. Justice distributed proportionate to circumstances and need. "Situation ethics." The statement, "Justice demands punishment," which is a self-evident truism to the Stage 4 mind, is just as self-evidently nonsense at Stage 5. Retributive punishment is neither rational nor just, because it does not promote the rights and welfare of the individual. Only legal sanctions that fulfill that purpose are imposed— protection of future victims, deterrence, and rehabilitation. Individual acts out of mutual obligation and a sense of public good. Right action tends to be defined in terms of general individual rights, and in terms of standards that have been critically examined and agreed upon by the whole society—e.g. the Constitution. The freedom of the individual should be limited by society only when it infringes upon someone else's freedom.

Stage 6: Universal Ethical Principles: An individual who reaches this stage acts out of universal principles based upon the equality and worth of all human beings. Persons are never means to an end, but are ends in themselves. Having rights means more than individual liberties. It means that every individual is due consideration of his interests in every situation, those interests being of equal importance with ones own. This is the "Golden Rule" model. A list of rules inscribed in stone is no longer necessary. At this level, God is understood to say what is right because it is right; His sayings are not right, just because it is God who said them. Persons at this level have accepted God's invitation to "come and let us reason together".

THE FOLLOWING ARE OBSERVATIONS THAT WERE MADE BY KOHLBERG

- Stage Development Is Invariant.

One must progress through the stages in order, and one cannot get to a higher stage without passing through the stage immediately preceding it. A belief that such a leap into moral maturity is possible is in sharp contrast to the facts of developmental research. Moral development is growth, and like all growth, takes place according to a pre-determined sequence. To expect someone to grow into high moral maturity overnight would be like expecting someone to walk before he crawls.

- In Stage Development, Subjects Cannot Comprehend Moral Reasoning At A Stage More Than One Stage Beyond Their Own.

If Johnny is oriented to see good almost exclusively as that which brings him satisfaction, how will he understand a concept of good in which the "good" may bring him no tangible pleasure at all.

The moral maxim "It is better to give than to receive" reflects a high level of development. The child who honestly asks you why it is better to give than to receive, does so because he does not and cannot understand such thinking. To him, "better" means better for him. And how can it be better for him to give, than to get.

- In Stage Development Individuals Are Cognitively Attracted To Reasoning One Level Above Their Own Present Predominant Level.

The person has questions and problems the solutions for which are less satisfying at his present level. Since reasoning at one stage higher is intelligible and since it makes more sense and resolves more difficulties, it is more attractive. For example, two brothers both want the last piece of pie. The bigger, stronger brother will probably get it. The little brother suggests they share it. He is thinking at level two, rather than at level one. The solution for him is more attractive: getting some rather than none. An adult who functions at level one consistently will end up in prison or dead.

- In Stage Development, Movement Through The Stages Is Effected When Cognitive Disequilibrium Is Created, That Is, When A Person's Cognitive Outlook Is Not Adequate To Cope With A Given Moral Dilemma.

The person who is growing, will look for more and more adequate ways of solving problems. If he has no problems, no dilemmas, he is not likely to look for solutions. He will not grow morally. In the apple pie example. The big brother, who can just take the pie and get away with it, is less likely to look for a better solution than the younger brother who will get none and probably a beating in the struggle.

- It Is Quite Possible For A Human Being To Be Physically Mature But Not Morally Mature.

If a child is spoiled, never having to accommodate for others needs, if he is raised in an environment where level two thinking by others gets the job done, he may never generate enough questions to propel him to a higher level of moral reasoning.

- Kohlberg Believed That Only About 25% Of Persons Ever Grow To Level Six, The Majority Remaining At Level Four.

The Bible enjoins principles of modesty, humility, and wise stewardship of the money. Application of these principles might preclude the purchase of expensive jewelry, furs, flashy cars, or other items primarily for show. A person functioning at level six would have no problem applying these principles. Persons functioning at a level four on the other hand, might make rules about "jewelry" (in a church for instance) or red dresses, or cosmetics. But they might not even notice a flashy car or the lady who wears a new dress every single week. Those things aren't on the list. If Kohlberg's observation is true, then level 6 thinkers would be in the minority. They might even be misunderstood and persecuted by a level 4 majority (Christ being the primary example).

THEOLOGICAL APPLICATIONS

How was God to deal with human beings functioning just barely at level two. One million slaves, not yet freed from the lash. To them "good" was more to eat and not being punished. How is He to convince them to follow Him out into a desert wilderness, to face the most hostile tribes of people then on earth, to believe that He will lead them to a "land flowing with milk and honey." More importantly, how is God to teach moral principles to such a group of people.

It is apparent to some students of scripture that God stooped to reach those people where they were. He began by using reasoning they could accept: level one reasoning.

These slaves, functioning at level one, could be stimulated to think at level three if it presented a better solution to their problem, (and there were many "problems" in the Sinai desert.) At stage one a ruler establishes his right to rule by displays of power and vengeance upon his enemies. He rules by threat of punishment and hope of reward. Mercy, or failure to punish, is seen as evidence of weakness, not morality by stage one standards. God first established His credentials to rule Israel by acts of vengeance upon the Egyptians, and by mighty, spectacular miracles. "I did this so that you might know that I am the Lord your God." (*Deut. 29:6* NIV) Each of the plagues of Egypt was directed at an object to worship to the Egyptians - the River Nile, the frog (a fertility symbol), the cattle, the sun, the "first born" (They were considered dedicated to the gods.).

In many instances this situation of God vs the other "gods" (Dagon for example, the god of the Philistines), was involved when God acted in seemingly destructive ways. When we realise that these civilizations were for the most part functioning at level two, or at best level three, the picture becomes clear. If God had done nothing when directly challenged to prove Himself, He would have lost hope of any further influence over those peoples. To initiate a connection with Himself, a point of contact, from which to begin a reeducation He had to use forceful means. It is evident that sometimes these means involved the death of many people (the 185,000 Assyrians for example). If God had done nothing. Or worse If God had tried to use level 5-6 reasoning, the people would have judged Him weak and unworthy of worship. His word would fall upon no receptive ear. The story of Israel is the story of a Father guiding, not one child, but a whole nation of moral children (a whole world of moral children) from childhood to maturity.

Instances of this type of direct confrontation between God and the pagan gods, or between God and individuals who wished to challenge His right to be their God and to rule them, include:

The plagues of Egypt (*Exodus 4-13*)

The death penalty laws given by God to young Israel (*Leviticus 20*)

The rebellion of Nadab and Abihu (*Leviticus 10*)

The Tribe of Levi blessed by God for killing idolaters at Sinai. (*Exodus 32-34*)

The rebellion of Korah, Dathan, and Abiram (*Numbers l6*)

The 50,000 slain who looked into the Ark after it was

returned by the Philistines. (*I Sam. 6:19*) The plague upon the Philistines who took the Ark (*I Sam. 3-7*)

Sampson verses the Philistines in the temple of Dagon. (*Judges 16*)

The Soldiers of the King of Samaria vs Elijah the prophet (*II Kings 1:1-17*)

The mocking juveniles versus the prophet Elisha (*II Kings 2:24*)

The Valley of Jehoshaphat when the enemy was confused into fighting against each other. (*II Chron. 20*)

The command to kill in war with assurance of victory. (*Joshua 6:17*)

Fifty days after Israel was rescued from Egypt God appeared to them on Mt. Sinai. The people were terrified of the thunder and the glory. Moses, who apparently was functioning at a higher level, tried to explain that there was no need to be afraid. The people preferred a mediator. They said, "Moses, you go talk with God, and come tell us what He said." (*Exodus 20:18*). God gave them His law in the form of ten simple, concrete rules, punctuated with threats of punishment. He deliberately portrayed Himself as a angry, jealous ruler, threatening not only to punish the disobedient, but the children for the parents' sins, (a concept which leaves us aghast but would seem perfectly normal to the pre-conventional mind). (*Exodus 20:5*). Today we almost automatically reinterpret these words to refer to the working to cause and effect, but this does violence to the context in which it was given and would have been a meaningless concept to a pre-scientific culture.

Belief that God punishes children for their parent's sins was chronic in Israel, persisting to the time of Christ. When the disciples saw a blind man they asked, "Who sinned, this man or his parents?" When Christ pronounced a blessing upon the poor, the persecuted, the meek, this seemed incredible, because these were the very ones whom the Israelites thought God was punishing. If you were prosperous, it was a sure sign that you were right with God, because He was blessing you. (The three friends of Job held this belief.) Perhaps the wording of the 2nd commandment - "visting the iniquity of the doctrine. So also, Noah's curse upon Canaan for the sin of Ham (*Exodus 20:5)*," strengthened belief in this statement of the Lord, "The fathers shall not be put to death for their children, nor shall the children be put to death for their fathers; a person shall be put to death for his own sin". Apparently God had decided it was time to deal with Israel at a higher level.

Today, we understand the words of the second commandment to mean that the wicked habi8ts and unbelief of the Fathers were passed down by teaching and example, to their children who then suffered the consequences. In the time of Moses, the "law" of cause and effect might not have been so understood by a nation of slaves. After the conquest of Canaan the spectacular displays of power ceased, perhaps because God no longer wished to deal with men at this level. He was seeking to draw them into a higher level of functioning. They however, returned to their idols, in true stage one fashion, as soon as their fear abated. God demonstrated in this way, for all who care to observe, the futility of punishment as a learning tool. Punishment only buys time, until other positive reinforcement techniques can effect permanent changes in behaviour.

What was God to do with such a people, when they adopted the pagan gods, even sacrificing their own children on the red hot arms of Dagon. He did the only thing that could be done under the circumstances: He punished them severely, "in furious anger and great wrath," as they perceived it. (*Deut. 19:28*) At stage 1 they expected Him to do this, or He would have appeared weak in their eyes, hardly worthy of notice, let alone obedience and worship. To be taken seriously at all, God had to punish. By this time in Canaan however, God did not punish them directly, He simply withdrew His protection, and allowed them to be beaten by their many enemies (*II Chron. 29:8-9*). When they returned to God and burned their idols, God rescued them again and again. Israel was a tiny nation, which could not have survived without God's special protection.

Ezekiel states the stage 1 and 2 reasons: "So I will spend

my wrath upon them, and they will know that I am the Lord, when their people lie slain..." (*Ezekiel 6:12,13*) God clearly runs the risk of appearing to gain some sort of satisfaction or catharsis from avenging Himself on His enemies, as would a heathen deity. Look at *Micah 5:15* : "In anger and in wrath I will execute vengeance." Or *Ezekiel 5:13*: "Then my anger will cease and my wrath against them will subside, and I will be avenged." In the Old Testament, we see God saying, in effect: "Because you aren't sufficiently afraid of sin, I will have to make you afraid of Me, lest you destroy yourselves and the hope of all future generations."

God had problems over and over with men interpreting His mercy as weakness and a license to do as they pleased without consequences. "I will be safe, even though I persist in going my own way." (*Deut. 29:19*) At stage 2, and in a more sophisticated way at stages 3 and 4, God's mercy is challenged as unjust. "Where is the God of justice?" "It is vain to serve God...evildoers not only prosper, but when they put God to the test, they escape" (*Malachi 2:17, 3:14,15*) Even the prophet Jeremiah remonstrated with God. "I would speak with you about your justice: Why does the way of the wicked prosper?" (*Jer. 12:1*). God's tantalizing answer in verse 5 says, in effect, "Jeremiah, this is too advanced for you to understand." (*Jer. 12:5*). "For My thoughts are not your thoughts, nor are your ways My ways, says the Lord." (*Isa. 55:8*)

The problem of God's mercy to the wicked is not resolvable at lower stage thinking. It doesn't even arise as a question at stages 5 or 6. Isaiah even says that God shows mercy "because He is just" (*Isa. 30:18*), a totally incomprehensible statement to early stage moral reasoning. Stage one is partly characterized by an inability to generalize from principles to their application. Rules are understood very concretely, so they have to be spelled out in complete detail. An example of such detailed instruction is found in the 2nd, 4th, and especially the 10th Commandments. After God has told the Israelites not to covet their neighbor's house, lest they assume that they are left free to covet his other possessions, the Lord adds, "your neighbor's wife or his manservant." But if God had stopped there, Israel would have concluded that it would be permissible to covet the "maidservant", so God spells that out too, and "his ox, nor his ass." Redundantly He adds "nor anything that belongs to your neighbour."

This detailed instruction is what makes the first four books of the Bible so lengthy. At stage 6, the Law may be summed up in two statements: "Thou shalt love the Lord thy God with all thy heart and with all thy soul and with all thy mind, and thou shalt love thy neighbour as thyself." (*Luke 10:27*) and (*Deut 6:5, Lev 19:18*). These are not New Testament concepts. They are as old as the Law. It's just that they could not be understood when they were first spoken. The people were morally immature. After the golden calf debacle at Sinai, God begins to relate to Israel more at the stage 2 level of marketplace bargaining and mutual exchange. He makes an agreement or "covenant" with them: If they obeyed God, He would cause them to prosper, and if they disobeyed then they would not prosper, and might be cut down by their enemies. (*Deut. 7:6-26*)

Many of the civil and criminal laws were based on the preconventional concept of justice. "Show no pity: life for life, tooth for tooth, hand for hand, foot for foot" (*Deut. 19:21*) God made provision to soften the brutality of stage 1 "blood vengeance" by providing "cities of refuge" where a man could flee who had unintentionally killed someone. (*Deut. 19:6*) Intention counts at stage 2, so the "avenger of blood" (a classic preconventional phrase!) would have to be functioning at stage 1, where intention did not count. Of course the premeditated murderer was not safe even in the city of refuge. He would be safe only until a proper trial was held. Then he would be executed. What a far cry from "Love your enemies. Do good to them that hate you", spoken by Christ. But that was level 6.

The cities of refuge gradually fell out of use, as such, as the people matured. By the time of Christ, we see the people comfortable in their conventional morality, but cheating the poor and abusing the powerless because everybody does it. (Stage 3) We see them carrying out a multitude of ceremonial observances, some not even given by God, just to make sure that they are being obedient to the Law. (Stage 4) God says through the prophet Amos: "I hate, I despise your religious feasts; I cannot stand your assemblies...but let justice roll on like a river, and righteousness like a never-failing stream!" (*Amos 5:21,24*) God is trying to lead them to the heart of the Law, and not just the letter. He would rather have them "act justly and love mercy" than to bring Him "thousands of rams with ten thousand rivers of oil." (*Micah 6:6-8*)

Justice at the conventional levels (3-4) is understood in the sense of what we commonly mean when we talk about "criminal justice." Justice demands that a lawbreaker be punished, that the penalty must be paid. In Ezekiel's time the people protested that God was unjust if He did not punish a wicked man who had repented (*Ezekiel 18:25*). God's answer was, "But if a wicked man turns away from the wickedness he has committed...he will surely live, he will not die. Yet the house of Israel says, 'The way of the Lord is not just.' Is my ways unjust, O house of Israel? Is it not your ways that are unjust?" (*Ezekiel 18:27-29*)

Listed in *Lev. 20,* is the penalty for adultery - death by stoning. But Christ Himself forgave the woman caught in the act of adultery, and she began a process of rehabilitation. Here again is contrasted stage two level thinking with stage 6. In fact all of Christ's teaching was level 6 or level 7. At stage 4, the saying "a good day's work for a good day's pay" is a truism. In the parable of the workers (*Matt. 20:1-16*), those who worked only one hour were paid the same as those who had worked all day (unjust?). Christ confronted the Pharisees with the contrast between conventional justice and God's justice. Those who come to Christ at the last hour will receive the same reward, the same eternal life, as those who have walked with Christ all of their lives.

In the parable of the Pharisee and the publican, the conventional respectability of the Jewish ruling class came under fire. The publican had a true heart repentance and love of God, and so was acceptable and savable. The Pharisee had only outward form and ceremony (level 4 morality). He felt no need of God, and so could not grow morally. He was self-satisfied. No question or problem called for a higher level solution. In the time of Christ the fear of a punishing God had generated a compulsion for rule making, and a backbreaking mass of regulations covering every detail of living. Much of the teaching of Christ seems to have been directed at weaning the people away from mechanical rule keeping. The Pharisees were threatened because they felt He didn't have enough respect for the rules (or for themselves). What they did not perceive was the higher stage thinking (level 5-6) that He was trying to lead them towards.

The Sermon on the Mount, (*Matt. 5*) is an excellent example of level 5-6 morality. It is heavy with principle not prescription, yet some would use this, in true stage 4 fashion, as a more rigorous rule book, providing more detailed regulations on such things as divorce and remarriage. To do this is to miss the overall intent of the sermon. Christ's teaching and example of Sabbath keeping provides another example of the superiority of principles over rule keeping.

The statement "the Sabbath was made for man and not man for the Sabbath" revealed a level 5-6 understanding of the nature of rules. Rules are valid only insofar as they promote the freedom and value of persons. God knew that human beings needed time with Him, time to consider who they are, time to turn attention to their relationship with their Heavenly Father. Level 6 people have no problem enjoying the Sabbath Day. It is at level 1-4 that the Sabbath seems a duty to be performed.

At stage 5-6, commands become promises. "Thou shalt not kill", becomes "I can stop hurting myself or others through the power of God in my life." What wonderful good news! This is righteousness by faith. At level 6 God's commands just make good sense. For instance God' commanded Israel not to eat fat or blood under any circumstances. (*Lev. 7:22-27*) Just think what health benefits would have come from adherence to this prescription. Level 6 individuals see God as the one who tells you to do, what you would want to do anyway, if you knew what was really good for you. And He doesn't just tell you to do it, He helps you do it. Jesus' healing of the paralytic illustrates wonderfully the concept of forgiveness at level 6.

The young man was paralyzed, a consequence of his own foolish choices. His friends let his bed down through the roof, right at the feet of Jesus in the middle of a great crowd. Jesus said to him simply "Your sins are forgiven." The Pharisees questioned this statement, because to them forgiveness is a legal maneuver and unjustly releases the guilty party from punishment. So Jesus then said "Which is easier to say, your sins are forgiven', or get up and walk.'" You see, healing the damage done by sin is what forgiveness is all about. It is not just juggling the heavenly books so Uncle Harry can get in. Forgiveness means giving Uncle Harry a "new heart (or mind)," healed now from the damage done by sin.

Kohlberg suggests that there may be (I believe there is) a level 7. Whether it stands totally outside of the other moral stages, I do not know. Stage 6 implies a perfect equivalence of duties and rights. "Love your neighbour as yourself." "Do unto others as you would have them do unto you." The stage 6 person believes he may expect of others the same things that he is willing to give to them. But the love of the saints goes beyond expecting anything of others. Agape acts are of grace, without regard for merit or return. They go a giant step beyond. This is a self-sacrificing love. Agape love creates value in its object. This is why the command to "Love one another as I have loved you," was a "new commandment." This is why Christ said, "You must be born again."

Stage development exhibits a phenomenon called lateral decollage. That is, it may take a person just reaching Stage 5, for example, a long time for the implications of his new way of thinking to filter out into all areas of his thinking. Since religious thought is often tightly compartmentalized, with its own jargon and thought forms, insulated from the rest of our thinking, theological concepts may take on a life of their own and be relatively impervious to advancements in the rest of our thinking. In other words, a person's theology may lag at least one stage behind the rest of his thinking processes. This may explain why highly educated persons may have very primitive theological notions, or why successful business men or even educators may not be able to relate to their own children at home.

A great many of the problems within the church may be explained by these differences in stage thinking. Level 4 people are anxious that the rules be kept, while level 6 persons who want to discuss general principles, are called "liberal." Level 6 persons may become very bored with legalistic sermons aimed at level 4, or with level 2 -the fiery hell and damnation threats, while level 4 members feel threatened by questions which seem to undermine the authority of God and His Law or His church. Those Christians who are functioning at higher levels of maturity must realise that stage development is normal and necessary. They must not be prejudiced towards those who are functioning at lower levels, who cannot understand many of those things which the more mature take for granted. They must be patient, seeking to draw others towards a higher level of understanding without belittling them or diminishing their current experience in faith. To do this is to work with God.

The story of Israel, miraculously written down and preserved for 3,500 years, is the story of God and man, in miniature. God's efforts to save men from themselves, to lead them to greater understanding, to pull them into a relationship with Himself, are a revelation of His character. Reading this story, we may consider the evidence, and decide for ourselves if God truly loves us.

STAGE THEORY AND THE ATONEMENT

The sacrifice of Christ, His substitutionary death, "the Atonement," takes on greater and deeper meaning at each level of moral development. God chose the perfect way to win mankind back to Himself. He chose an act which could be understood and accepted at each level of development, an act which while comprehensible to the person at level 2, takes on greater and greater significance at each level.

Level 1:Man sinned and offended God. God responded with angry vengeance taking the life of Jesus.

Level 2:God somehow struck a bargain with the Devil, a market place exchange of Christ's life, paid as a ransom to the Devil, in trade for the devil's releasing his hostages. In the popular version, Satan found out too late that God had conned him, when Christ rose from the dead.

Level 3-4 :The Law must be kept. Man broke the Law. Someone had to pay the penalty. "The wages of sin is death." Jesus paid that penalty. The integrity of the Law was maintained.

Level 5-6: He demonstrated that separation from God is death. ("Why have you forsaken me?") Since we separate ourselves from Him, not He from us, He is not our executioner. He allowed Satan to play out his hand, exposing his selfish character for all both man and angels to see, and thus erasing all sympathy for the accusations of the fallen foe. God's character was vindicated.

Level 7: Atonement becomes at-one-ment. God did what it took to win our love and trust. His love for us is greater than any man can comprehend, that the eternal God of the universe should so value a human being, that He would die to win his love. Neither God, nor His law, defined as the eternal principles upon which He bases His government, change, but our understanding of His law changes, and God speaks to us at each level of our understanding. It is a mistake to cling to expressions appropriate to an earlier age of understanding, regardless of how valid and useful they were in their own context, when more appropriate expressions exist. But we must be patient with our brethren who perhaps are just beginning their maturing process, and allow the pastor to preach for them sometimes. For even as God was laying down detailed concrete rules for the Israelites, He was already looking forward to the day when He would "write His laws on our hearts."

SOCIAL AND EMOTIONAL DEVELOPMENT - KEY FACTORS IN SOCIAL DEVELOPMENT

The test to raise a child who is literate, non-violent, drug-free, caring and responsible has been around for hundreds of years. This was a task for parents and other family members.

But in recent years the task has spread to the school system. This is considered the missing pieces of education. When teachers are involved in these aspects they are educating the whole child. These things are all parts of social emotional development. According to Erik Erickson, Abraham Maslow, Maurice Elias and many other social development theorist, children all have common needs. These needs are necessary to develop a young healthy adult, who can properly function in society.

SKILLS

One skill that is becoming more and more important each day is for children to have good commutation skills. Children also need to have good work ethics. Children also need to learn to take responsibility for their actions and health. Children need to develop social relationships, so that they can work in groups. Children need to learn to be caring. They also need to develop good problem solving skills. Finally they need to develop a good character and sound morals. All of these things are essential needs of all children, in order to properly develop socially.

Communication is the act of communicating verbally and non-verbally. Communication skills are important skills for children to learn because communication is a tool that is used everyday by everyone. It's important for children to develop this skill because not being able to communicate properly can and has led to major problems. So much depends on effective communication. Entire countries have gone to war as a result of its absence. Work ethics is another important skill for children to develop. Work ethics can be described as a set of values based on the moral merits of hard work and assiduousness. Work ethics are needed because a child who lacks them, may end up steeling or participating in some sort of malpractice.

Children also need to learn to take responsibility for their actions and health. It is essential for children to learn to take care of their health. It's also very important that children learn to take risibility for their actions. When I say health I am referring to cleanliness and nutrition. Taking responsibility for ones actions is saying yes I did that and excepting the consequences, whether they be bad or good. These are very important life and social skills especially when seeking employment. Being caring is a very important skill that many people are lacking today. Children need to learn to be caring. Children need to be able to care about others feelings. Meaning they take into consideration others feelings.

Caring can be described as feeling and exhibiting concern and empathy for others. At a young age children usually develop this skill. In a preschool setting Tommy may start crying after his mother dropped him off. When all of a sudden another child (Jack) walks up to him and says what's wrong? It's okay I miss my mommy too. But she always comes back after work. Jack wants to know, what's wrong with Tommy and reinsure him that his mom will be back. Jack is trying to use his skill of caring to let Tommy know that sometimes he feels the same way. Problem solving is an important skill for children to develop. Problem solving is the application of knowledge. A good problem solver can take the skills that they have learned and apply them to problems, to find an answer.

It's common for parents and families to wish and hope that their child will turn out right. Developing morals and a good character are two important social skills that can lead to this. Morals are personal principles, standards. This is important for children, because it aides in determining what is right and what is wrong. A persons character can be described as a description of a person's attributes, traits, or personality None of the above skills can be adequately developed if the environment doesn't support them.

FAMILY ENVIRONMENT

Families play a very important role in the development of social emotional skills in children. Families are the first influences or first teachers that children have. Children learn how to groom themselves and how to communicate with others from watching their families. It's a good idea for families to build strong relationships with their child at a young age, and continue it through out adolescents. There are many things that families can do to contribute to the development social development.

Parents need to keep close relationships with their child. It has been proven that teens who have a close relationship with their parents are less likely to engage is risky behaviour. When parent child relationships are close this makes way for open commutation.

Children and teens who have a close relationship with their parents are more likely to come to them when they have a problem. Parents also need to know where their child is at all times. This is called parental monitoring.

Parents who are positive role models help to support healthy life styles and development in their children. Children and teens need support from their parents. This helps them to feel that they are cared for. A very simple way for parents to help support social development is by simply setting down and eating with their child or teen.

It has been shown that teens who regularly eat meals with their families are more likely to eat fruits and vegetables it has also been shown that these teens are less likely to skip breakfast. All of these things can contribute to a healthy life style. However, parents and families must be careful not to overstep.

By overstepping parents can leave children feeling helpless and inhibit social development. Parents who don't allow their children to explore are inhibiting social development. Abuse of any kind is damaging to anyone no matter their age, especially children and teens. If children feel let down or that know one cares for them, they may never learn how to care for others. If children are not taught healthy eating habits and how to care for themselves they may never be able to do so.

When parents are not practicing parental mentoring their child may be anywhere. Parental mentoring is not spying on children but simply making sure that they are safe and not doing any thing they shouldn't be doing. A lack of this can lead to children being injured or arrested. Without parental mentoring children are at a great risk to become violent, use drugs and be involved in criminal activity. "Children love and want to be loved and they very much prefer the joy of accomplishment to the triumph of hateful failure. Do not mistake a child for his symptom". Out side of the home parents also have an major influences on their child's social development skills. I have observed this many times while shopping at the local dollar store. On a few occasion I have noticed children screaming for a toy or candy bar. Sometimes the parents buy whatever the child wants, while other times they don't. Buy giving in while the child is screaming parents are teaching their child that this is an effective way to communicate. But on the other hand parents who simple ignore their child and never talk about what happened are inhibiting many self help skills. Such as communication skills, problem solving skills and conflict resolution.

GENDER DEVELOPMENT

Gender refers to an individual's anatomical sex, or sexual assignment, and the cultural and social aspects of being male or female. An individual's personal sense of maleness or femaleness is his or her gender identity. Outward expression of gender identity, according to cultural and social expectations, is a gender role. Either gender may live out a gender role (a man or a woman, for instance, can be a homemaker) but not a sex role, which is anatomically limited to one gender (only a woman can gestate and give birth).

GENDER IDENTITY

Gender identity appears to form very early in life and is most likely irreversible by age 4. Although the exact cause of gender identity remains unknown, biological, psychological, and social variables clearly influence the process. Genetics, prenatal and postnatal hormones, differences in the brain and the reproductive organs, and socialization all interact to mold a toddler's gender identity. The differences brought about by physiological processes ultimately interact with social-learning influences to establish clear gender identity.

PSYCHOLOGICAL AND SOCIAL INFLUENCES ON GENDER IDENTITY

Gender identity is ultimately derived from chromosomal makeup and physical appearance, but this derivation of gender identity does not mean that psychosocial influences are missing. Gender socialization, or the process whereby a child learns the norms and roles that society has created for his or her gender, plays a significant role in the establishment of her or his sense of femaleness or maleness. If a child learns she is a female and is raised as a female, the child believes she is a female; if a child is told he is a male and is raised as a male, the child believes he is male.

Beginning at birth, most parents treat their children according to the appearance of their genitals. Parents even handle their baby girls less aggressively than their baby boys. Children quickly develop a clear understanding that they are either female or male, as well as a strong desire to adopt gender-appropriate mannerisms and behaviors. This understanding normally occurs within 2 years of age, according to many authorities. In short, biology sets the stage, but children's interactions with social environments actually determine the nature of gender identity.

GENDER ROLES

Gender roles are both cultural and personal. These roles determine how males and females think, speak, dress, and interact within the context of society. Learning plays a role in this process of shaping gender roles. These gender schemas are deeply embedded cognitive frameworks regarding what defines masculine and feminine.

While various socializing agents—educators, peers, movies, television, music, books, and religion—teach and reinforce gender roles throughout a child's life span, parents probably exert the greatest influence, especially when their children are very young.

Developmentalists indicate that adults perceive and treat female and male infants differently. Parents probably do this in response to having been recipients of gender expectations as young children themselves. Traditionally, fathers teach boys how to fix and build things; mothers teach girls how to cook, sew, and keep house. Children then receive parental approval when they conform to gender expectations and adopt culturally accepted and conventional roles. All of these lessons are reinforced by additional socializing agents, such as the media. In other words, learning gender roles always occurs within a social context, with the values of the parents and society being passed along to the children of successive generations.

EDUCATIONAL IMPLICATIONS

The notion that individuals differ in various abilities, capacities and personality characteristics necessitates the adoption of individual tendencies in education. It compels the teachers to realise following facts:

- In any group there are individuals, who deviate from the norms of the group. Along with the average, the presence of very superior and extremely dull is equally possible in his class.
- Every teacher should try to have the desired knowledge of the abilities, capacities, interests, attitudes, aptitudes and other personality traits of his pupils and in the light of this knowledge should render individual guidance to children for maximum utilization of their potentialities.
- It is wrong to expect uniformity in gaining proficiency or success in a particular field from a group of students. On account of their subnormal intelligence, previous background, lack of proper interest, aptitude and attitude some students have to lag behind in some or other area of achievement.
- All students can not be benefited by one particular method of instruction and a uniform and rigid curriculum.

Provisions for 'individual differences' in Schools:

Realization of the above facts or some more of their nature makes us think that we must have some provision for the wide individual differences among our pupils in our schools. Emphasizing this need Crow and Crow (1973) write –

"Since we supposedly are teaching individuals, not groups of individuals, it is the function of the school within its budgetary personnel and curricular limitations to provide adequate schooling for every learner no matter how much he differs from every other learner."

How can we accomplish this task is a pertinent question to be asked at this stage. In fact, to provide adequate schooling or learning experience for every learner according to his individuality is not a simple task. However, the following suggestions can be helpful for any teacher –

- Proper knowledge of individual personalities: The first step in making provisions for individual differences are not how abilities, capacities, interests, aptitudes and other personality traits of individual pupils. For this purpose, frequent assessment in the form of intelligence tests, cumulative record card, interest inventories, attitude scales, aptitude tests and measures for assessing personality traits shall be carried out.
- Ability grouping: In the light of results derived from various tests of knowing individual differences in terms of individual potentialities in various dimensions, the students in a class or area of activity can be divided into homogeneous groups. Such divisions can prove beneficial in adjusting the method of instruction to varying individual differences.
- Adjusting the curriculum: To meet the requirement of varying individual differences among the pupils, the curriculum should be as flexible and differentiated as possible. It should have the provision for a number of diversified courses and curriculum experiences so that the pupils may get opportunity to study and work in the areas of their own interests and abilities. It should provide adjustment to suit the local requirements and

potentialities of students of different groups.

- Adjusting the methods of teaching: Considering the varying individual differences, adjustment with regard to the adoption of methods of teaching is very effective. Every teacher should be somewhat free to formulate his own plan and strategy and adopt different instructional procedures which he finds most suited to different pupils. He should follow different procedures or methods of instruction to suit the requirements of varying ability groups of his pupils.
- Adopting social programs or methods for individualizing instruction: Schools may also adopt some social programs or methods of teaching like the Dalton plan, the Winnekta plan, project method or use programmed learning material for enabling students to learn at their own individual pace.
- Other causes of individualizing instruction: For the purpose of individualizing instruction a few practical measures can also prove beneficial :-
- The student strength of the class or section should be made as small as possible.
- The teacher should try to pay individual attention to the group under instruction.
- The teacher should keep in view the individual difference of his students while engaging them in drill or practice work in the class-room or assigning home-task.
- In case where ability grouping is not possible and more specifically under the prevalent system of class teaching, special coaching and guidance programme for both the dull and the gifted children are most helpful.

Thus, the problem of individual differences can be tackled with multi dimensional tasks. The teacher, school authorities, the parents and the government as well as voluntary agencies – all should join hands to meet the individual requirements of children who possess tremendous individual differences.

Unit III

Theories of Learning

HULLS SYSTEMATIC BEHAVIOUR THEORY

Biological motives are those that are "wired into the nervous system." They include hunger, thirst, the pursuit of pleasure, and the avoidance of pain. Most living creatures do what they must to obtain food and water. That is why these are termed primary reinforcers.

Hull's theory was one of the first systematic attempts to explain motivation. Hull thought he would explain *all* behaviour of *all* organisms. It was a very ambitious undertaking. Few theories in the history of psychology have soared so high or fallen so low. Hull's theory once dominated American psychology; now it has all but disappeared. What stereotype is due partly to Hull's theory?

Research on Hull's theory is largely responsible for an old stereotype of experimental psychologists as lab-coated figures watching rats run through mazes for cheese reinforcement. Hull and other researchers performed many thousands of experiments with rats in mazes, trying to discover basic laws of motivation.

For beginning students, Hull's theory remains relevant in several ways. First, the story of its rise and fall is a case study in scientific research. Second, Hull's emphasis on homeostasis is echoed in present day studies of biological motives as regulatory systems. Third, understanding a little about Hull's theory helps one understand the motivational theories that came later, many of which arose in response to deficiencies in Hull's theory. In this respect, Hull's theory is like Freud's: one must know about it in order to make sense of what came after it. It was a very *influential* theory.

THE HULLIAN APPROACH

In the 1930s, Clark Hull undertook to construct a grand theory that he thought would unite all psychology. He based his theory on the concept of *homeostasis,* which he borrowed from biology. Homeostasis is a word that refers to the active regulation of critical biological variables. For example, your kidney regulates the salt and water balance in your body, and your pancreas regulates blood sugar. To Hull, behaviour was another way the organism regulated itself or kept itself alive and healthy, so to him it made sense that a theory of motivation would borrow from scientific knowledge about homeostatic processes.

Scientists knew about biological regulation as early as the mid-1800s, but the concept of homeostasis was not widely discussed until Walter B. Cannon's 1932 book *The Wisdom of the Body*. Cannon pointed out that organisms work to keep biological variables within a healthy or normal range. There are many homeostatic systems in the body. Levels of blood pressure, salt, glucose, water, and carbon dioxide (among other things) must be maintained within normal ranges, for the health of the organism. Hull reasoned that homeostatic mechanisms might provide a scientific explanation of motivation.

Behaviour could be regarded as an outward expression of the organism's pursuit of biological health. For example, you shiver to get warm. That is a homeostatic mechanism built into the body. If that fails, you are motivated to carry out a behaviour such as putting on a sweater or finding a heater. Many behaviors are extensions of homeostatic mechanisms. Think how many human behaviors are related to eating, which is itself aimed at maintaining glucose and fat levels in our bodies. Hull conceived of all motivation as coming originally from biological imbalances or *needs*. The organism was thrown into movement (was *motivated*) when it needed something that was not present at its current location. A *need,* in Hull's system, was a *biological requirement of the organism*. Hunger was the need for more energy. Thirst was the need for more water. Motivation, to Hull, was aimed at making up or erasing a *deficiency* or *lack* of something in the organism.

Hull used the word *drive* to describe the state of behavioral arousal resulting from a biological need. In Hull's system, drive was the energy that powered behaviour. But drive was not pleasant. Drive was an uncomfortable state resulting from a biological need, so drive was something the animal tried to eliminate. The animal searched for food in order to *reduce* the hunger drive. Hull believed *the animal would repeat any behaviour that reduced a drive*, if the same need occurred again. Therefore Hull's theory was called a *drive-reduction* theory of motivation.

Hull's theory inspired an enormous amount of research. No other psychological theory was so daringly precise. Hull used specific formulas to predict the likelihood of specific behaviors. He specified that the probability that a particular stimulus would lead to a particular response (the "excitation potential") using a formula. You do not have to memorize this; it is offered as an example of the precision to which Hull aspired:

Excitation potential = S H R [D x K x J x V]...where....

S H R was the number of reinforced training trials

D was the amount of biological deprivation or drive

K was the size or magnitude of the goal

J was the delay before the animal was allowed to pursue the goal

V was the intensity of the stimulus that set off the behaviour

Each variable was given a precise operational definition, to aid research and replication. Hull hoped to make psychology as scientific and precise in its predictions as physics or chemistry. However, things did not work out that way. Many predictions based on Hull's equations did not come true. Researchers responded by altering the system, adding variables or subtracting others, adjusting parameters, trying to make it all work. Finally researchers began to realise it was never going to work. There could not be such a simple system for predicting animal behaviour.

The abandonment of Hull's theory occurred about 30 years after he proposed it. An entire generation of researchers had followed a false lead! By the early 1970s journal articles contained bitter references to "30 years of fruitless Hullian research." The study of learning veered off into different directions. Bolles (1990) commented, "Hull would have been unable to read a present-day research paper; none of it would have made any sense!" Hull's theory may have disappeared from present day motivational research, but not before it had a big impact on the field. Many motivational theories of the 1950s and 1960s were reactions to then-dominant Hullian theories. These included the proposals for cognitive motives as well as Maslow's motivational psychology, both discussed later in this chapter. All were conceived as alternatives to Hull's drive-reduction approach.

FAT REGULATION

One idea from Hull's theory remains very current. That is the idea that biological motives resemble control systems or regulatory systems in the body. Research has shown that biological motives like hunger and thirst do indeed operate as homeostatic systems, regulating basic biological variables. Weight control, for example, is related to energy regulation in the body. Which idea from Hull's theory remains current? Keeley and colleagues coined the term *set-point* to refer to the level of fat in the body that is kept at a certain level. Fat cells are elastic. If animals are given access to adequate supplies of food and left alone, the fat cells stay constant in size. This indicates some sort of regulatory process.

Why is fat regulated so closely? Fat is the most energy-dense substance in the body. By regulating levels of fat, the body regulates storage of reserve energy. The natural or ideal level of fat in your body is the set-point. The concept of a set-point is particularly reminiscent of Hull's assumption that motivation is homeostatic—aimed at maintaining a crucial variable within an ideal range. The set-point determines what level of fat the body will return to, other things being equal. A dieter does not lose fat cells; rather, each fat cell shrinks. When the fat cells get small enough, the organism takes action to restore fat levels to the set-point. That is what it means to say the organism *defends* the set-point.

The following compensations occur when fat levels fall below the set-point, as part of the organism's active defence of the set-point:

- The basal metabolic rate or BMR, the background level of energy consumption in the body, is reduced. Body heat is lowered.
- More calories are extracted from food as it is digested; fewer calories are excreted in waste products.
- Activity level, except for that directed at food, decreases to conserve energy.

These changes make it harder to lose weight when one is below the set-point...and easier to regain weight after a diet. The body acts as though it wants to restore the level of fat to the set-point. That is why many people regain the weight they have lost during a successful diet.

Some people generate low numbers of fat cells. They are naturally thin. They find it difficult to gain weight no matter how much they eat. The more calories they consume, the more efficiently their bodies burn off the excess calories. Thus they "defend" their low weight. This energy burn-off takes the form of metabolic adjustments that are the opposite of those listed above. After a big meal, the naturally thin person will experience the following compensations:

- Basal metabolic rate and body heat rise as the body's cellular engines are turned up a notch and extra calories are burned off.
- Less energy will be absorbed from food, as the body cuts back on insulin, which converts food to energy.
- Activity levels and fidgeting increase after a brief rest.

Most people do not consider natural thinness to be a problem. Fatness is more of a worry. A person with a high set-point can lose weight but usually will put it right back on, if he or she resumes previous eating patterns. To make matters worse, each rebound from dieting tends to raise the set-point a little bit.

So is dieting hopeless? Not entirely. The existence of a storage system for fat does not mean fat levels are permanently fixed and cannot change. The opposite is true. To be useful, the fat must be accessible. Fat is like money in a bank account. It is only helpful if you can get it out when you need it; otherwise there is no point in storing it. How does one withdraw fat from the fat bank? Create conditions in which the body must draw upon its energy supplies. There are three options: take in fewer calories, increase energy consumption by exercising, or do both. To maintain a low weight without the rebound to a higher weight, the change in dietary patterns must be permanent. This is why sophisticated diets emphasize a change of lifestyle rather than a temporary change of diet. Some weight-loss programs refuse to use the word "diet" at all, because it implies a temporary change. They work with a philosophy more like alcoholism treatment programs. One is encouraged to give up old ways and adopt a new way of living.

For some people trying to lose weight, overeating is like an addiction. Like some drug addicts, some overweight people succeed in changing their lives and altering their behaviour patterns without a dramatic intervention like surgery. However, eating is different from other addictions in one crucial respect: nobody can abstain from eating completely. So temptation is constant, and recidivism (backsliding) is common. Statistics show 90% of diets are failures, if success is defined as permanent weight loss.

CONSEQUENCES OF SEVERE DIETING

What about people who succeed in taking off enormous amounts of weight, going from 300 or 400 pounds down to normal weight? Although they may look more normal to the outside world, such people are often quite abnormal in their body physiology. Rockefeller University researchers followed a group of successful dieters from Overeaters Anonymous, all of whom lost more than 200 pounds. After such a severe diet, these individuals had a normal weight according to "ideal weight" tables. But the researchers found they were biologically abnormal. Their fat cells were tiny and the dieters' hormonal output was like that of a starving person. Fat tissue itself acts like an endocrine gland: it puts out hormones (over 20 different hormones, according to recent research). Therefore fat is not an inert glob; it is tissue that actively changes the rest of the body. The changes caused by obesity can lead to the so-called metabolic syndrome, a group of problems that often occur together in overweight people. The metabolic syndrome includes heart disease, high blood pressure, and diabetes.

Inflammation-normally the result of an infection-can be stimulated by excess fat. Chronic inflammation may itself may itself invite heart disease and strokes, because inflammation of artery walls is now thought to trigger formation of plaque deposits on the walls of blood vessels, and plaque deposits can ultimately burst, causing heart attacks and strokes. In light of all these complications, the lack of hormones produced by a severe diet may be preferable to the abundance of hormones produced by too much fat. A person with *anorexia nervosa*—the starvation disease—has tiny fat cells. Such a person is likely to experience disturbances such as irregular heartbeat, insomnia, intolerance of cold, and mood fluctuation. They have low white blood-cell counts and abnormally low heart rate and blood pressure. Anorectic women (women with anorexia nervosa) do not menstruate. They are intolerant of cold. They tend to be obsessed with food.

The Rockefeller University researchers found the same exact characteristics in people who were formerly obese and now at so-called normal weight. To maintain their weight loss, they had to eat 25% less than people without a history of obesity. To keep their fat cells almost empty of fat, they had to tolerate being cold much of the time. Virtually all the women stopped menstruating. They tended to be obsessed with food. In summary, it is *possible* to go from extremely obese to normal in weight, but the price is great. One remains in a perpetual state of starvation, physiologically.

LEWIN'S FIELD THEORY

Kurt Lewin (1890-1947) was a famous, charismatic psychologist who is now viewed as the father of social psychology. Born in Germany, Lewin emigrated to the USA as a result of World War II. Lewin viewed the social environment as a dynamic field which impacted in an interactive way with human consciousness. Adjust elements of the social environment and particular types of psychological experience predictably ensue. In turn, the person's psychological state influences the social field or milieu. Lewin was well known for his terms "life space" and "field theory". He was perhaps even better known for practical use of his theories in studying group dynamics, solving social problems related to prejudice, and group therapy (t-groups). Lewin sought to not only describe group life, but to investigate the conditions and forces which bring about change or resist change in groups.

In the field (or 'matrix') approach, Lewin believed that for change to take place, the total situation has to be taken into account. If only part of the situation is considered, a misrepresented picture is likely to develop. Later on, yoda in Star Wars brought field theory back into vogue, with his kind wish for Luke Skywalker, "may the force [field] be with you." But likewise, Luke had to influence the force. The following two passages offer a more detailed summary of Lewin's field theory.

From Smith (2001):

For Kurt Lewin behaviour was determined by totality of an individual's situation. In his field theory, a 'field' is defined as 'the totality of coexisting facts which are conceived of as mutually interdependent'. Individuals were seen to behave differently according to the way in which tensions between perceptions of the self and of the environment were worked through. The whole psychological field, or 'lifespace', within which people acted had to be viewed, in order to understand behaviour. Within this individuals and groups could be seen in topological terms (using map-like representations). Individuals participate in a series of life spaces (such as the family, work, school and church), and these were constructed under the influence of various force vectors.

Hall and Lindzey (1978: 386) summarize the central features of Kurt Lewin's field theory as follows:

Behaviour is a function of the field that exists at the time the behaviour occurs,

Analysis begins with the situation as a whole from which are differentiated the component parts, and

The concrete person in a concrete situation can represented mathematically.

Kurt Lewin also looked to the power of underlying forces (needs) to determine behaviour and, hence, expressed 'a preference for psychological as opposed to physical or physiological descriptions of the field' (*op. cit.*). In this we can see how Kurt Lewin drew together insights from topology (e.g. lifespace), psychology (need, aspiration etc.), and sociology (e.g. force fields – motives clearly being dependent on group pressures). As Allport in his foreword to *Resolving Social Conflict* (Lewin 1948: ix) put it, these three aspects of his thought were not separable. 'All of his concepts, whatever root-metaphor they employ, comprise a single well-integrated system'. It was this, in significant part, which gave his work its peculiar power.

From Jones (n.d.):

Lewin is most renown for his development of the field theory. The field theory is the "proposition that human behaviour is the function of both the person and the environment: expressed in symbolic terms, B = f (P, E)." (Deaux 9) This means that one's behaviour is related both to one's personal characteristics and to the social situation in which one finds oneself. The field theory may seem obvious to us now, but most early psychologist did not believe in behaviorism. Many psychologists at the time believed in the psychoanalytic theory that held human motives to be blind pushes from within. Lewin thought of motives as goal-directed forces. He believed "that our behaviour is purposeful; we live in a psychological reality or life space that includes not only those parts of our physical and social environment that are important to us but also imagined states that do not currently exist".

Lewin's field theory lead to the development of actual field research on human behaviour. With boldness, Lewin manipulated complex situational variables in natural settings. His approach has guided experiments in the field of social cognition, social motivation, and group processes. Most importantly Lewin helped develop action research. Action research uses empirical social research, social action, and controlled evaluation.

GUTHRIE'S THEORY

Edwin Guthrie's contiguity theory was similar to John Watson's perspective in that it placed S-R connections at the centre of the learning process. Guthrie's basic principle of learning was as follows: A stimulus that is followed by a particular response will, upon its recurrence, tend to be followed by the same response again. This S-R connection gains its full strength on one trial. In other words, if an organism responds to a particular stimulus in a particular way on one occasion, the organism will make the same response the next time it encounters the same stimulus; in this manner, a habit is formed. Guthrie contended that the critical factor in learning is the contiguity—the more or less simultaneous occurrence—of a stimulus and a response.

Guthrie also shared Watson's belief that recency is critical in learning: An organism will respond to a stimulus in the way that it has most recently responded to that stimulus. Guthrie's notion of one-trial learning—that an S-R connection is fully formed on one pairing— was a radical one in its time. Most other early behaviorists believed that S-R connections were acquired only gradually, primarily through practice. Guthrie explained the seemingly gradual learning of complex behaviors by proposing that such behaviors are actually composed of many tiny S-R connections; with each practice trial, more and more appropriate S-R connections are formed, thus leading to slow, incremental changes observed in overall performance.

The parsimony of Guthrie's theory—his proposal that the contiguity of stimuli and responses is the basis of all learning—is certainly appealing. Guthrie conducted little research to support his views, however, and later research has cast doubt on the notion that learning is as simple as Guthrie described it. Nevertheless, three techniques for breaking S-R habits that Guthrie derived from his theory continue to be used in educational and therapeutic practice.

OBSERVATIONAL LEARNING: BASIC PRINCIPLES AND PRACTICAL APPLICATIONS

Social learning theory is the theory that people learn new behaviour through overt reinforcement or punishment, or via observational learning of the social actors in their environment. If people observe positive, desired outcomes in the observed behaviour, they are more likely to model, imitate, and adopt the behaviour themselves.

THEORY

Social learning theory is derived from the work of Gabriel Tarde (1843-1904) which proposed that social learning occurred through four main stages of limitation:

- Close contact,
- Imitation of superiors,
- Understanding of concepts,
- Role model behaviour

It consists of 3 parts observing, imitating, and reinforcements.

Julian Rotter moved away from theories based on psychosis and behaviourism, and developed a learning theory. In *Social Learning and Clinical Psychology* (1954), Rotter suggests that the effect of behaviour has an impact on the motivation of people to engage in that specific behaviour. People wish to avoid negative consequences, while desiring positive results or effects. If one expects a positive outcome from a behaviour, or thinks there is a high probability of a positive outcome, then they will be more likely to engage in that behaviour. The behaviour is reinforced, with positive outcomes, leading a person to repeat the behaviour. This social learning theory suggests that behaviour is influenced by these environmental factors or stimulus, and not psychological factors alone.

Albert Bandura (1977) expanded on the Rotter's idea, as well as earlier work by Miller & Dollard (1941), and is related to social learning theories of Vygotsky and Lave. This theory incorporates aspects of behavioural and cognitive learning. Behavioural learning assumes that people's environment (surroundings) cause people to behave in certain ways.

Cognitive learning presumes that psychological factors are important for influencing how one behaves. Social learning suggests a combination of environmental (social) and psychological factors influence behaviour. Social learning theory outlines three requirements for people to learn and model behaviour include attention: retention (remembering what one observed), reproduction (ability to reproduce the behaviour), and motivation (good reason) to want to adopt the behaviour.

CRIMINOLOGY

In criminology, Ronald Akers and Robert Burgess (1966) developed social learning theory to explain deviancy by combining variables which encouraged delinquency (e.g. the social pressure from delinquent peers) with variables that discouraged delinquency (e.g. the parental response to discovering delinquency in their children). The first two stages were used by Edwin Sutherland in his Differential Association Theory. Sutherland's model for learning in a social environment depends on the cultural conflict between different factions in a society over who has the power to determine what is deviant. But his ideas were difficult to put into operation and measure quantitatively. Burgess, a behavioral sociologist, and Akers revised Sutherland's theory and included the idea of reinforcement, which increases or decreases the strength of a behaviour, and applied the principles of Operant Psychology, which holds that behaviour is a function of its consequences.

Functionalism had been the dominant paradigm but, in the 1960s, there was a shift towards Social Control Theories,

Conflict Criminology, and Labeling Theories that tried to explain the emerging and more radical social environment.

Moreover, people believed that they could observe behaviour and see the process of social learning, e.g., parents watched their own children and saw the influence of other children on their own; they could also see what kind of affect they had on their own children, i.e. the processes of differential association and reinforcement.

The conservative political parties were advocating an increase in punishment to deter crime. Unlike Labeling Theory, Social Learning Theory actually supports the use of punishment which translates into longer sentences for those convicted, and helps to explain the increase in the prison population that began in the early 1970s.

Unlike situational crime prevention, the theory ignores the opportunistic nature of crime. To learn one must first observe criminal behaviour, but the morals from his mother's purse; where was this behaviour learned?

The theory does explain how criminal behaviour is 'transmitted' from one person to an animal, which can explain increases in types of crimes, but it does not consider how criminal acting can be prevented although it may be fairly assumed that the processes of learning behaviors can be changed.

There is also a definite problem. What may be reinforcement for one person may not be for another.

Also, reinforcements can be both social involving attention and behaviour between more than one person, and non-social reinforcement would not involve this interaction Social Learning Theory has been used in mentoring programs that should, in theory, prevent some future criminal behaviour. The idea behind mentoring programs is that an adult is paired with a child, who supposedly learns from the behaviour of the adult and is positively reinforced for good behaviour. In the classroom, a teacher may use the theory by changing the seating arrangements to pair a behaving child and a misbehaving child, but the outcome may be that the behaving child begins to be very bad.

HUMAN MEMORY: THE ATKINSON AND SHIFFRIN MODEL

In 1968 Atkinson and Shiffrin proposed a model of human memory which posited two distinct memory stores: short-term memory, and long-term memory.

Later a third memory store (actually the first in sequence) was added: sensory memory. In this chapter I describe this augmented three-store model and indicate some of the characteristics of each memory system.

SENSORY MEMORY

Information enters the human information processing system via a variety of channels associated with the different senses. Perceptual systems operate on this information to create perceptions. But because of a limited processing ability at the higher levels, most incoming information cannot be immediately dealt with.

Instead, we *attend* only to certain information. However, information not immediately attended to is held briefly in a very temporary "buffer" memory, making it possible to attend to some of it a bit later — as when you can still hear someone asking you a question even though you weren't really listening when they asked it. This buffer memory is called sensory memory.

Sensory memory is really many sensory memory systems, one associated with each sense. For example, there is a sensory memory for vision, called *iconic memory,* and one for audition (hearing), called *echoic memory*. Here are some characteristics of these two sensory memory systems:

- Iconic Memory (vision)
  - Capacity: Essentially that of the visual system (Sperling)
  - Duration: About 0.5 to 1.0 seconds (Sperling)
  - Processing: None additional beyond raw perceptual processing
- Echoic Memory (hearing}
  - Capacity
  - Duration: About 4 to 5 seconds

- Processing: None additional beyond raw perceptual processing

SHORT-TERM MEMORY (STM) OR "WORKING MEMORY"

Information that is attended to arrives in another temporary store called short-term or working memory. The more recent term "working memory" is intended to convey the idea that information here is available for further processing. In general information in working memory is information you are conscious of and can work with. Here are some properties of STM:

- Capacity: About 7 plus or minus 2 "chunks" of information
- Duration: About 18 to 20 seconds
- Processing: To hold information in STM, it is often encoded verbally, although other strategies may also be used such as visualization. These strategies make it possible to "rehearse" the information.

The low capacity of STM was first noted by George Miller in a famous paper intitled *The Magical Number Seven, Plus or Minus Two*. Miller concluded that about seven (plus or minus two) "chunks" of information could reside in STM simultaneously. Miller defined a "chunk" as an independent item of information — one whose recall did not aid in the further recall of the other items. Random letters such as "GJK" would each be considered a chunk, but letters that form a recognizable larger whole, such as "CAR" would not. (In this case the word "car" is a single chunk.)

Information that enters STM fades away, or *decays* as soon as it is no longer attended to. (The duration of 18-20 seconds assumes that the information is not being actively rehearsed.) Information that is being actively attended to is represented by a pattern of neural activity in the brain may become represented more permanently by guiding changes in neural connectivity in the brain, a process referred to as *storage*. But information that is not more permanently stored is simply lost shortly after attention is directed elsewhere. Because STM presents severe limits on the amount of information that can be held in mind simultaneously and on the duration for which it lasts once attention is withdrawn from it, STM has been described as the *bottleneck* of the human information processing system.

LONG-TERM MEMORY (LTM)

Long-term memory is the relatively permanent memory store in which you hold information even when you are no longer attending to it. Information held in LTM is not represented as patterns of neural activity (as in STM), but rather as changes in brain wiring — in the "conductivity" of existing synapses, and in the formation new synapses and destruction of old ones. Storing information in LTM is equivalent to a computer writing information out to its hard drive, or to a tape recorder writing patterns of magnetization onto tape to record music. The recording process is called storage and the "playback" process, retrieval.

Here are some properties of LTM:

- Capacity: Virtually unlimited
- Duration: Up to a lifetime
- Processing: Information is organized according to *meaning* and is associatively linked

Capacity is unlimited in the sense that nobody seems to run out of the capacity to store new information, even if they live beyond 100 years. If they did, then either they would stop learning entirely or new learning could only take place by first erasing something already stored in LTM. This does not appear to happen — when storage/retrieval capability is lost it is due to deterioration of brain systems rather than to systems exceeding their holding capacity. It is difficult to determine how long memories can exist in LTM. If you cannot remember something you once knew, is it because it has been lost from the system, or because you have developed a problem locating it for retrieval?

Permanent losses do occur as a result of brain damage, and it is possible that some memories simply decay away if they are not accessed for a very long time. We do know with certainty, however, that some failures of retrieval are due to temporary blockages and not to the loss of the information in memory.

You may be unable to remember someone's name at present, for example, but later it comes to you. Obviously, it was there in memory all the while. A common idea is that everything we have ever experienced has created a long-term memory, but this is unlikely to be so. Much of what we experience is never attended to, or not attended to beyond a few brief moments, and probably does not result in activation of the storage process.

EVIDENCE THAT STM AND LTM ARE PHYSICALLY DISTINCT SYSTEMS

The latter changes supposedly make it possible for certain inputs to regenerate something like the original patterns of neural firing that were present when the long-term memories were being laid down.

One especially convincing piece of evidence for this distinction is found in the case of "H. M.," a victim of severe epilepsy who received experimental surgery in an attempt to control the symptoms.

The surgery involved destruction of the hippocampus in both cerebral hemispheres. Following the surgery, H. M. could no longer store new information in LTM (with certain exceptions to be discussed elsewhere), although he could still retrieve information that had been stored there in the years before the surgery.

His STM was unaffected. He had become like a tape recorder that could still play back old tapes but could no longer record new ones. The fact that his LTM was severely affected without damaging his STM shows that these are two functionally distinct systems. There is also evidence that LTM involves a rather slow process requiring many hours to complete, called consolidation. If an individual is rendered unconscious (as in an accident), memories just beginning to consolidate at that time may not form. Of course, STM involves no such consolidation process.

NEURAL NETWORKS MODELS

Traditionally, the term neural network had been used to refer to a network or circuit of biological neurons. The modern usage of the term often refers to artificial neural networks, which are composed of artificial neurons or nodes. Thus the term has two distinct usages:

- Biological neural networks are made up of real biological neurons that are connected or functionally related in the peripheral nervous system or the central nervous system. In the field of neuroscience, they are often identified as groups of neurons that perform a specific physiological function in laboratory analysis.
- Artificial neural networks are made up of interconnecting artificial neurons (programming constructs that mimic the properties of biological neurons). Artificial neural networks may either be used to gain an understanding of biological neural networks, or for solving artificial intelligence problems without necessarily creating a model of a real biological system. The real, biological nervous system is highly complex and includes some features that may seem superfluous based on an understanding of artificial networks.

This chapter focuses on the relationship between the two concepts; for detailed coverage of the two different concepts refer to the separate articles: Biological neural network and Artificial neural network. In general a biological neural network is composed of a group or groups of chemically connected or functionally associated neurons. A single neuron may be connected to many other neurons and the total number of neurons and connections in a network may be extensive. Connections, called synapses, are usually formed from axons to dendrites, though dendrodendritic microcircuits and other connections are possible. Apart from the electrical signaling, there are other forms of signaling that arise from neurotransmitter diffusion, which have an effect on electrical signaling. As such, neural networks are extremely complex.

Artificial intelligence and cognitive modeling try to simulate some properties of neural networks. While similar in their techniques, the former has the aim of solving particular tasks, while the latter aims to build mathematical models of biological neural systems.

In the artificial intelligence field, artificial neural networks have been applied successfully to speech recognition, image analysis and adaptive control, in order to construct software agents (in computer and video games) or autonomous robots. Most of the currently employed artificial neural networks for artificial intelligence are based on statistical estimation, optimization and control theory.

The cognitive modelling field involves the physical or mathematical modeling of the behaviour of neural systems; ranging from the individual neural level (e.g. modelling the spike response curves of neurons to a stimulus), through the neural cluster level (e.g. modelling the release and effects of dopamine in the basal ganglia) to the complete organism (e.g. behavioural modelling of the organism's response to stimuli).

The concept of neural networks started in the late-1800s as an effort to describe how the human mind performed. These ideas started being applied to computational models with Turing's B-type machines and the perceptron. In early 1950s Friedrich Hayek was one of the first to posit the idea of spontaneous order in the brain arising out of decentralized networks of simple units (neurons). In the late 1940s, Donald Hebb made one of the first hypotheses for a mechanism of neural plasticity (i.e. learning), Hebbian learning. Hebbian learning is considered to be a 'typical' unsupervised learning rule and it (and variants of it) was an early model for long term potentiation.

The Perceptron is essentially a linear classifier for classifying data $x \in R^n$ specified by parameters $\omega \in R^n, b \in R$ and an output function $f = w'x + b$. Its parameters are adapted with an ad-hoc rule similar to stochastic steepest gradient descent. Because the inner product is a linear operator in the input space, the Perceptron can only perfectly classify a set of data for which different classes are linearly separable in the input space, while it often fails completely for non-separable data. While the development of the algorithm initially generated some enthusiasm, partly because of its apparent relation to biological mechanisms, the later discovery of this inadequacy caused such models to be abandoned until the introduction of non-linear models into the field.

The Cognitron (1975) was an early multilayered neural network with a training algorithm. The actual structure of the network and the methods used to set the interconnection weights change from one neural strategy to another, each with its advantages and disadvantages. Networks can propagate information in one direction only, or they can bounce back and forth until self-activation at a node occurs and the network settles on a final state. The ability for bi-directional flow of inputs between neurons/nodes was produced with the Hopfield's network (1982), and specialization of these node layers for specific purposes was introduced through the first hybrid network.

The parallel distributed processing of the mid-1980s became popular under the name connectionism. The rediscovery of the backpropagation algorithm was probably the main reason behind the repopularisation of neural networks after the publication of "Learning Internal Representations by Error Propagation" in 1986 (Though backpropagation itself dates from 1974). The original network utilised multiple layers of weight-sum units of the type $f = g(w'x + b)$, where g was a sigmoid function or logistic function such as used in logistic regression. Training was done by a form of stochastic steepest gradient descent. The employment of the chain rule of differentiation in deriving the appropriate parameter updates results in an algorithm that seems to 'backpropagate errors', hence the nomenclature. However it is essentially a form of gradient descent.

Determining the optimal parameters in a model of this type is not trivial, and steepest gradient descent methods cannot be relied upon to give the solution without a good starting point. In recent times, networks with the same architecture as the back propagation network are referred to as Multi-Layer Perceptrons. This name does not impose any limitations on the type of algorithm used for learning. The back propagation network generated much enthusiasm at the time and there was much controversy about whether such learning could be implemented in the brain or not, partly because a mechanism for reverse signalling was not obvious at the time, but most importantly because there was no plausible source for the 'teaching' or 'target' signal.

THE BRAIN, NEURAL NETWORKS AND COMPUTERS

Neural networks, as used in artificial intelligence, have traditionally been viewed as simplified models of neural processing in the brain, even though the relation between this model and brain biological architecture is debated. A subject of current research in theoretical neuroscience is the question surrounding the degree of complexity and the properties that individual neural elements should have to reproduce something resembling animal intelligence.

Historically, computers evolved from the von Neumann architecture, which is based on sequential processing and execution of explicit instructions. On the other hand, the origins of neural networks are based on efforts to model information processing in biological systems, which may rely largely on parallel processing as well as implicit instructions based on recognition of patterns of 'sensory' input from external sources. In other words, at its very heart a neural network is a complex statistical processor (as opposed to being tasked to sequentially process and execute).

NEURAL NETWORKS AND ARTIFICIAL INTELLIGENCE

An *artificial neural network* (ANN), also called a *simulated neural network* (SNN) or commonly just *neural network* (NN) is an interconnected group of artificial neurons that uses a mathematical or computational model for information processing based on a connectionistic approach to computation. In most cases an ANN is an adaptive system that changes its structure based on external or internal information that flows through the network. In more practical terms neural networks are non-linear statistical data modeling or decision making tools. They can be used to model complex relationships between inputs and outputs or to find patterns in data.

An artificial neural network involves a network of simple processing elements (artificial neurons) which can exhibit complex global behaviour, determined by the connections between the processing elements and element parameters. Artificial neurons were first proposed in 1943 by Warren McCulloch, a neurophysiologist, and Walter Pitts, an MIT logician.

One classical type of artificial neural network is the Hopfield net. In a neural network model simple nodes, which can be called variously "neurons", "neurodes", "Processing Elements" (PE) or "units", are connected together to form a network of nodes — hence the term "neural network". While a neural network does not have to be adaptive *per se,* its practical use comes with algorithms designed to alter the strength (weights) of the connections in the network to produce a desired signal flow.

In modern software implementations of artificial neural networks the approach inspired by biology has more or less been abandoned for a more practical approach based on statistics and signal processing. In some of these systems neural networks, or parts of neural networks (such as artificial neurons) are used as components in larger systems that combine both adaptive and non-adaptive elements. The concept of a neural network appears to have first been proposed by Alan Turing in his 1948 paper "Intelligent Machinery".

APPLICATIONS

The utility of artificial neural network models lies in the fact that they can be used to infer a function from observations and also to use it. This is particularly useful in applications where the complexity of the data or task makes the design of such a function by hand impractical.

REAL LIFE APPLICATIONS

The tasks to which artificial neural networks are applied tend to fall within the following broad categories:

- Function approximation, or regression analysis, including time series prediction and modelling.
- Classification, including pattern and sequence recognition, novelty detection and sequential decision making.
- Data processing, including filtering, clustering, blind signal separation and compression.

Application areas include system identification and control (vehicle control, process control), game-playing and decision making (backgammon, chess, racing), pattern recognition (radar systems, face identification, object recognition, etc.), sequence recognition (gesture, speech, handwritten text recognition), medical diagnosis, financial applications, data mining (or knowledge discovery in databases, "KDD"), visualization and e-mail spam filtering.

NEURAL NETWORK SOFTWARE

Neural network software is used to simulate, research, develop and apply artificial neural networks, biological neural networks and in some cases a wider array of adaptive systems.

LEARNING PARADIGMS

There are three major learning paradigms, each corresponding to a particular abstract learning task. These are supervised learning, unsupervised learning and reinforcement learning. Usually any given type of network architecture can be employed in any of those tasks.

SUPERVISED LEARNING

In supervised learning, we are given a set of example pairs $(x, y) x \in X, y \in Y$ and the aim is to find a function f in the allowed class of functions that matches the examples. In other words, we wish to *infer* how the mapping implied by the data and the cost function is related to the mismatch between our mapping and the data.

UNSUPERVISED LEARNING

In unsupervised learning we are given some data x, and a cost function which is to be minimized which can be any function of x and the network's output, f. The cost function is determined by the task formulation. Most applications fall within the domain of estimation problems such as statistical modeling, compression, filtering, blind source separation and clustering.

REINFORCEMENT LEARNING

In reinforcement learning, data x is usually not given, but generated by an agent's interactions with the environment. At each point in time t, the agent performs an action y_t and the environment generates an observation x_t and an instantaneous cost c_t, according to some (usually unknown) dynamics. The aim is to discover a *policy* for selecting actions that minimizes some measure of a long-term cost, i.e. the expected cumulative cost. The environment's dynamics and the long-term cost for each policy are usually unknown, but can be estimated. ANNs are frequently used in reinforcement learning as part of the overall algorithm. Tasks that fall within the paradigm of reinforcement learning are control problems, games and other sequential decision making tasks.

LEARNING ALGORITHMS

There are many algorithms for training neural networks; most of them can be viewed as a straightforward application of optimization theory and statistical estimation. They include: Back propagation by gradient descent, Rprop, BFGS, CG etc. Evolutionary computation methods, simulated annealing, expectation maximization and non-parametric methods are among other commonly used methods for training neural networks. Recent developments in this field also saw the use of particle swarm optimization and other swarm intelligence techniques used in the training of neural networks.

NEURAL NETWORKS AND NEUROSCIENCE

Theoretical and computational neuroscience is the field

concerned with the theoretical analysis and computational modeling of biological neural systems.

Since neural systems are intimately related to cognitive processes and behaviour, the field is closely related to cognitive and behavioural modeling. The aim of the field is to create models of biological neural systems in order to understand how biological systems work. To gain this understanding, neuroscientists strive to make a link between observed biological processes (data), biologically plausible mechanisms for neural processing and learning (biological neural network models) and theory (statistical learning theory and information theory).

TYPES OF MODELS

Many models are used in the field, each defined at a different level of abstraction and trying to model different aspects of neural systems. They range from models of the short-term behaviour of individual neurons, through models of how the dynamics of neural circuitry arise from interactions between individual neurons, to models of how behaviour can arise from abstract neural modules that represent complete subsystems. These include models of the long-term and short-term plasticity of neural systems and its relation to learning and memory, from the individual neuron to the system level.

CURRENT RESEARCH

While initially research had been concerned mostly with the electrical characteristics of neurons, a particularly important part of the investigation in recent years has been the exploration of the role of neuromodulators such as dopamine, acetylcholine, and serotonin on behaviour and learning. Biophysical models, such as BCM theory, have been important in understanding mechanisms for synaptic plasticity, and have had applications in both computer science and neuroscience. Research is ongoing in understanding the computational algorithms used in the brain, with some recent biological evidence for radial basis networks and neural backpropagation as mechanisms for processing data.

CRITICISM

A common criticism of neural networks, particularly in robotics, is that they require a large diversity of training for real-world operation. Dean Pomerleau, in his research presented in the paper "Knowledge-based Training of Artificial Neural Networks for Autonomous Robot Driving," uses a neural network to train a robotic vehicle to drive on multiple types of roads (single lane, multi-lane, dirt, etc.). A large amount of his research is devoted to (1) extrapolating multiple training scenarios from a single training experience, and (2) preserving past training diversity so that the system does not become overtrained (if, for example, it is presented with a series of right turns – it should not learn to always turn right). These issues are common in neural networks that must decide from amongst a wide variety of responses.

A. K. Dewdney, a former *Scientific American* columnist, wrote in 1997, "Although neural nets do solve a few toy problems, their powers of computation are so limited that I am surprised anyone takes them seriously as a general problem-solving tool." Arguments for Dewdney's position are that to implement large and effective software neural networks, much processing and storage resources need to be committed. While the brain has hardware tailored to the task of processing signals trough a graph of neurons, simulating even a most simplified form on Von Neuman technology may compel a NN designer to fill many millions of database rows for its connections - which can lead to abusive RAM and HD necessities.

Furthermore, the designer of NN systems will often need to simulate the transmission of signals through many of these connections and their associated neurons - which must often be matched with incredible amounts of CPU processing power and time. While neural networks often yield *effective* programs, they too often do so at the cost of time and money *efficiency*. Arguments against Dewdney's position are that neural nets have been successfully used to solve many complex and diverse tasks, ranging from autonomously flying aircraft to detecting credit card fraud.

Technology writer Roger Bridgman commented on Dewdney's statements about neural nets:

Neural networks, for instance, are in the dock not only because they have been hyped to high heaven, (what hasn't?) but also because you could create a successful net without understanding how it worked: the bunch of numbers that captures its behaviour would in all probability be "an opaque, unreadable table...valueless as a scientific resource". In spite of his emphatic declaration that science is not technology, Dewdney seems here to pillory neural nets as bad science when most of those devising them are just trying to be good engineers. An unreadable table that a useful machine could read would still be well worth having.

Some other criticisms came from believers of hybrid models (combining neural networks and symbolic approaches). They advocate the intermix of these two approaches and believe that hybrid models can better capture the mechanisms of the human mind.

WORKING MEMORY

Working memory (also referred to as short-term memory, depending on the specific theory) is a theoretical construct within cognitive psychology that refers to the structures and processes used for temporarily storing and manipulating information. There are numerous theories as to both the theoretical structure of working memory as well as to the specific parts of the brain responsible for working memory. However, most researchers agree that the frontal cortex, parietal cortex, anterior cingulate, and parts of the basal ganglia are crucial for functioning. Much of the understanding of the neural basis of working memory has come from lesion experiments in animals and imaging experiments in humans.

The term was first used in the 1960s in the context of theories that likened the mind to a computer. Atkinson and Shiffrin (1968) used this term, "working memory" (p.92) to describe their "short-term store." What we now call working memory was referred to as a "short-term store" or short-term memory, primary memory, immediate memory, operant memory, or provisional memory. Short-term memory is the ability to remember information over a brief period of time (in the order of seconds). Most theorists today use the concept of working memory to replace or include the older concept of short-term memory, thereby marking a stronger emphasis on the notion of manipulation of information instead of passive maintenance.

The earliest mention of experiments on the neural basis of working memory can be traced back to over 100 years ago, when Hitzig and Ferrier described ablation experiments of the prefrontal cortex (PFC). They concluded that the frontal cortex was important for cognitive processes rather than sensory ones. In 1935 and 1936, Jacobsen and colleagues were the first to conclude that the cognitive processes in the PFC were notable in delay-dependent tasks; in other words, they suffered from short-term memory loss.

THEORIES OF WORKING MEMORY

There have been numerous models proposed regarding how working memory functions, both anatomically and cognitively. Of those, three have received the distinct notice of wide acceptance.

THE BADDELEY AND HITCH MODEL

Baddeley and Hitch (1974) introduced and made popular the multicomponent model of working memory. This theory proposes that two "slave systems" are responsible for short-term maintenance of information, and a "central executive" is responsible for the supervision of information integration and for coordinating the slave systems. One slave system, the phonological loop, stores phonological information (i.e., the sound of language) and prevents its decay by continuously articulating its contents, thereby refreshing the information in a rehearsal loop. It can, for example, maintain a seven-digit telephone number for as long as one repeats the number to oneself again and again. The other slave system, the visuo-spatial sketch pad, stores visual and spatial information. It can be used, for example, for constructing and manipulating visual images, and for the representation of mental maps. The sketch pad can be further broken down into a visual subsystem (dealing with, for instance, shape, colour, and texture), and a spatial subsystem (dealing with location).

The central executive is, among other things, responsible for directing attention to relevant information, suppressing irrelevant information and inappropriate actions, and for coordinating cognitive processes when more than one task must be done at the same time. Baddeley (2000) extended the model by adding a fourth component, the episodic buffer, which holds representations that integrate phonological, visual, and spatial information, and possibly information not covered by the slave systems (e.g., semantic information, musical information). The component is episodic because it is assumed to bind information into a unitary episodic representation. The episodic buffer resembles Tulving's concept of episodic memory, but it differs in that the episodic buffer is a temporary store.

THE THEORY OF COWAN

Cowan regards working memory not as a separate system, but as a part of long-term memory. Representations in working memory are a subset of the representations in long-term memory. Working memory is organized in two embedded levels. The first level consists of long-term memory representations that are activated. There can be many of these, there is no limit to activation of representations in long-term memory. The second level is called the focus of attention. The focus is regarded as capacity limited and holds up to four of the activated representations. Oberauer has extended the Cowan model by adding a third component, a more narrow focus of attention that holds only one chunk at a time.

The one-element focus is embedded in the four-element focus and serves to select a single chunk for processing. For example, you can hold four digits in mind at the same time in Cowan's "focus of attention". Now imagine that you wish to perform some process on each of these digits, for example, adding the number two to each digit. Separate processing is required for each digit, as most individuals can not perform several mathematical processes in parallel. Oberauer's attentional component selects one of the digits for processing, and then shifts the attentional focus to the next digit, continuing until all of the digits have been processed.

THE THEORY OF ERICSSON AND KINTSCH

Whereas most adults can repeat about seven digits in correct order, some individuals have shown impressive enlargements of their digit span - up to 80 digits. This feat is possible by extensive training on an encoding strategy by which the digits in a list are grouped (usually in groups of three to five) and these groups are encoded as a single unit (a chunk). To do so one must be able to recognize the groups as some known string of digits. One person studied by K. Anders Ericsson and his colleagues, for example, used his extensive knowledge of racing times from the history of sports. Several such chunks can then be combined into a higher-order chunk, thereby forming a hierarchy of chunks. In this way, only a small number of chunks at the highest level of the hierarchy must be retained in working memory.

At retrieval, the chunks are unpacked again. That is, the chunks in working memory act as retrieval cues that point to the digits that they contain. It is important to note that practicing memory skills such as these do not expand working memory capacity proper. This can be shown by using different materials - the person who could recall 80 digits was not exceptional when it came to recalling words. Ericsson and Kintsch (1995) have argued that we use skilled memory in most everyday tasks. Tasks such as reading, for instance, require to maintain in memory much more than seven chunks - with a capacity of only seven chunks our working memory would be full after a few sentences, and we would never be able to understand the complex relations between thoughts expressed in a novel or a scientific text.

We accomplish this by storing most of what we read in long-term memory, linking them together through retrieval structures. We need to hold only a few concepts in working memory, which serve as cues to retrieve everything associated to them by the retrieval structures. Anders Ericsson and Walter Kintsch refer to this set of processes as "long-term working memory". Retrieval structures vary according to the domain of expertise, yet as suggested by Gobet they can be categorized in three typologies: generic retrieval structures, domain knowledge retrieval structures and the episodic text structures. The first corresponds to Ericsson and Kintsch's 'classic' retrieval structure and the second to the elaborated memory structure.

The first kind of structure is developed deliberately and is arbitrary (e.g. the method of loci), the second one is similar to patterns and schemas and the last one takes place exclusively during text comprehension. Concerning this last typology, Kintsch, Patel and Ericsson consider that every confirmed reader is able to form an episodic text structure during text comprehension, if the text is well written and if the content is familiar. Guida and colleagues using this last feature have proposed the 'personalisation method' as a way to operationalise the long-term working memory.

WORKING MEMORY CAPACITY

Working memory is generally considered to have limited capacity. The earliest quantification of the capacity limit associated with short-term memory was the "magical number seven" introduced by Miller (1956). He noticed that the memory span of young adults was around seven elements, called chunks, regardless whether the elements were digits, letters, words, or other units. Later research revealed that span does depend on the category of chunks used (e.g., span is around seven for digits, around six for letters, and around five for words), and even on features of the chunks within a category.

For instance, span is lower for long words than for short words. In general, memory span for verbal contents (digits, letters, words, etc.) strongly depends on the time it takes to speak the contents aloud, and on the lexical status of the contents (i.e., whether the contents are words known to the person or not). Several other factors also affect a person's measured span, and therefore it is difficult to pin down the capacity of short-term or working memory to a number of chunks. Nonetheless, Cowan (2001) has proposed that working memory has a capacity of about four chunks in young adults (and fewer in children and old adults).

MEASURES OF WORKING-MEMORY CAPACITY AND THEIR CORRELATES

Working memory capacity can be tested by a variety of tasks. A commonly used measure is a dual-task paradigm combining a memory span measure with a concurrent processing task, sometimes referred to as "complex span". Daneman and Carpenter invented the first version of this kind of task, the "reading span", in 1980. Subjects read a number of sentences (usually between 2 and 6) and try to remember the last word of each sentence. At the end of the list of sentences, they repeat back the words in their correct order. Other tasks that don't have this dual-task nature have also been shown to be good measures of working memory capacity. The question of what features a task must have to qualify as a good measure of working memory capacity is a topic of ongoing research.

Measures of working-memory capacity are strongly related to performance in other complex cognitive tasks such as reading comprehension, problem solving, and with any measures of the intelligence quotient. Some researchers have argued that working memory capacity reflects the efficiency of executive functions, most notably the ability to maintain a few task-relevant representations in the face of distracting irrelevant information. The tasks seem to reflect individual differences in ability to focus and maintain attention, particularly when other events are serving to capture attention. These effects seem to be a function of frontal brain areas.

Others have argued that the capacity of working memory is better characterized as the ability to mentally form relations between elements, or to grasp relations in given information. This idea has been advanced, among others, by Graeme

Halford, who illustrated it by our limited ability to understand statistical interactions between variables. These authors asked people to compare written statements about the relations between several variables to graphs illustrating the same or a different relation, for example "If the cake is from France then it has more sugar if it is made with chocolate than if it is made with cream but if the cake is from Italy then it has more sugar if it is made with cream than if it is made of chocolate". This statement describes a relation between three variables (country, ingredient, and amount of sugar), which is the maximum most of us can understand. The capacity limit apparent here is obviously not a memory limit - all relevant information can be seen continuously - but a limit on how many relationships we can discern simultaneously.

EXPERIMENTAL STUDIES OF WORKING MEMORY CAPACITY

Why is working memory capacity limited at all? If we knew the answer to this question, we would understand much better why our cognitive abilities are as limited as they are. There are several hypotheses about the nature of the capacity limit. One is that there is a limited pool of cognitive resources needed to keep representations active and thereby available for processing, and for carrying out processes. Another hypothesis is that memory traces in working memory decay within a few seconds, unless refreshed through rehearsal, and because the speed of rehearsal is limited, we can maintain only a limited amount of information. Yet another idea is that representations held in working memory capacity interfere with each other. There are several forms of interference discussed by theorists.

One of the oldest ideas is that new items simply replace older ones in working memory. Another form of interference is retrieval competition. For example, when the task is to remember a list of 7 words in their order, we need to start recall with the first word. While trying to retrieve the first word, the second word, which is represented in close proximity, is accidentally retrieved as well, and the two compete for being recalled. Errors in serial recall tasks are often confusions of neighboring items on a memory list (so-called transpositions), showing that retrieval competition plays a role in limiting our ability to recall lists in order, and probably also in other working memory tasks. A third form of interference assumed by some authors is feature overwriting. The idea is that each word, digit, or other item in working memory is represented as a bundle of features, and when two items share some features, one of them steals the features from the other. The more items are held in working memory, and the more their features overlap, the more each of them will be degraded by the loss of some features.

None of these hypotheses can explain the experimental data entirely. The resource hypothesis, for example, was meant to explain the trade-off between maintenance and processing: The more information must be maintained in working memory, the slower and more error prone concurrent processes become, and with a higher demand on concurrent processing memory suffers. This trade-off has been investigated by tasks like the reading-span task described above. It has been found that the amount of trade-off depends on the similarity of the information to be remembered and the information to be processed. For example, remembering numbers while processing spatial information, or remembering spatial information while processing numbers, impair each other much less than when material of the same kind must be remembered and processed. Also, remembering words and processing digits, or remembering digits and processing words, is easier than remembering and processing materials of the same category.

These findings are also difficult to explain for the decay hypothesis, because decay of memory representations should depend only on how long the processing task delays rehearsal or recall, not on the content of the processing task. A further problem for the decay hypothesis comes from experiments in which the recall of a list of letters was delayed, either by instructing participants to recall at a slower pace, or by instructing them to say an irrelevant word once or three times in between recall of each letter. Delaying recall had virtually no effect on recall accuracy.. The interference hypothesis seems to fare best with explaining why the similarity between memory contents and the contents of concurrent processing tasks affects how much they impair each other. More similar materials are more likely to be confused, leading to retrieval competition, and they have more overlapping features, leading to more feature overwriting.

One experiment directly manipulated the amount of overlap of phonological features between words to be remembered and other words to be processed. Those to-be-remembered words that had a high degree of overlap with the processed words were recalled worse, lending some support to the idea of interference through feature overwriting. The theory most successful so far in explaining experimental data on the interaction of maintenance and processing in working memory is the "time-based resource sharing model". This theory assumes that representations in working memory decay unless they are refreshed. Refreshing them requires an attentional mechanism that is also needed for any concurrent processing task. When there are small time intervals in which the processing task does not require attention, this time can be used to refresh memory traces. The theory therefore predicts that the amount of forgetting depends on the temporal density of attentional demands of the processing task - this density is called "cognitive load".

The cognitive load depends on two variables, the rate at which the processing task requires individual steps to be carried out, and the duration of each step. For example, if the processing task consists of adding digits, then having to add another digit every half second places a higher cognitive load on the system than having to add another digit every two seconds. Adding larger digits takes more time than adding smaller digits, and therefore cognitive load is higher when larger digits must be added. In a series of experiments, Barrouillet and colleagues have shown that memory for lists of letters depends on cognitive load, but not on the number of processing steps (a finding that is difficult to explain by an interference hypothesis) and not on the total time of processing (a finding difficult to explain by a simple decay hypothesis). One difficulty for the time-based resource-sharing model, however, is that the similarity between memory materials and materials processed also affects memory accuracy.

TRAINING OF WORKING MEMORY

One theory of attention-deficit hyperactivity disorder states that ADHD can lead to deficits in working memory. Recent studies suggest that working memory can be improved by training in ADHD patients through the Cogmed computerized programme developed by Torkel Klingberg and his colleagues at the Karolinska Institute in Sweden. This random controlled study has found that a period of working memory training increases a range of cognitive abilities and increases IQ test scores. Consequently, this study supports previous findings suggesting that working memory underlies general intelligence.

Another study of the same group has shown that, after training, measured brain activity related to working memory increased in the prefrontal cortex, an area that many researchers have associated with working memory functions. A further study has shown that training with a working memory task (the dual n-back task) improves performance on a certain fluid intelligence test in healthy young adults. Further research is required to verify whether improving or augmenting the brain's working memory ability increases fluid intelligence. In 2009, it was reported in Science that working memory training led to measurable density changes for cortical dopamine neuroreceptors in test persons.

WORKING MEMORY IN THE BRAIN

Localizing Working Memory Functions

The first insights into the neuronal basis of working memory came from animal research. Fuster recorded the electrical activity of neurons in the prefrontal cortex (PFC) of monkeys while they were doing a delayed matching task. In that task, the monkey sees how the experimenter places a bit of food under one of two identical looking cups. A shutter is then lowered for a variable delay period, screening off the cups from the monkey's view. After the delay, the shutter opens and the monkey is allowed to retrieve the food from under the cups. Successful retrieval in the first attempt – something the animal can achieve after some training on the task – requires holding the location of the food in memory over the delay period. Fuster found neurons in the PFC that fired mostly during the delay period, suggesting that they were involved in representing the food location while it was invisible. Later research has shown similar delay-active neurons also in the posterior parietal cortex, the thalamus, the caudate, and the globus pallidus.

Localization of brain functions in humans has become much easier with the advent of brain imaging methods (PET and fMRI). This research has confirmed that areas in the PFC are involved in working memory functions. During the 1990s much debate has centered on the different functions of the ventrolateral (i.e., lower areas) and the dorsolateral (higher) areas of the PFC. One view was that the dorsolateral areas are responsible for spatial working memory and the ventrolateral areas for non-spatial working memory. Another view proposed a functional distinction, arguing that ventrolateral areas are mostly involved in pure maintenance of information, whereas dorsolateral areas are more involved in tasks requiring some processing of the memorized material. The debate is not entirely resolved but most of the evidence supports the functional distinction.

Brain imaging has also revealed that working memory functions are by far not limited to the PFC. A review of numerous studies shows areas of activation during working memory tasks scattered over a large part of the cortex. There is a tendency for spatial tasks to recruit more right-hemisphere areas, and for verbal and object working memory to recruit more left-hemisphere areas. The activation during verbal working memory tasks can be broken down into one component reflecting maintenance, in the left posterior parietal cortex, and a component reflecting subvocal rehearsal, in the left frontal cortex.

There is an emerging consensus that most working memory tasks recruit a network of PFC and parietal areas. One study has shown that during a working memory task the connectivity between these areas increases. Other studies have demonstrated that these areas are necessary for working memory, and not just accidentally activated during working memory tasks, by temporarily blocking them through transcranial magnetic stimulation (TMS), thereby producing an impairment in task performance. A current debate concerns the function of these brain areas. The PFC has been found to be active in a variety of tasks that require executive functions.

This has led some researchers to argue that the role of PFC in working memory is in controlling attention, selecting strategies, and manipulating information in working memory, but not in maintenance of information. The maintenance function is attributed to more posterior areas of the brain, including the parietal cortex. Other authors interpret the activity in parietal cortex as reflecting executive functions, because the same area is also activated in other tasks requiring executive attention but no memory. Most brain imaging studies of working memory have used recognition tasks such as delayed recognition of one or several stimuli, or the n-back task, in which each new stimulus in a long series must be compared to the one presented n steps back in the series. The advantage of recognition tasks is that they require minimal movement (just pressing one of two keys), making fixation of the head in the scanner easier.

Experimental research and research on individual differences in working memory, however, has used largely recall tasks. It is not clear to what degree recognition and recall tasks reflect the same processes and the same capacity limitations. A few brain imaging studies have been conducted with the reading span task or related tasks. Increased activation during these tasks was found in the PFC and, in several studies, also in the anterior cingulate cortex (ACC). People performing better on the task showed larger increase of activation in these areas, and their activation was correlated more over time, suggesting that their neural activity in these two areas was better coordinated, possibly due to stronger connectivity.

How does the brain maintain memories over the short term? Much has been learned over the last two decades on where in the brain working memory functions are carried out. Much less is known on how the brain accomplishes short-term maintenance and goal-directed manipulation of information.

The persistent firing of certain neurons in the delay period of working memory tasks shows that the brain has a mechanism of keeping representations active without external input. Keeping representations active, however, is not enough if the task demands maintaining more than one chunk of information. In addition, the components and features of each chunk must be bound together to prevent them from being mixed up. For example, if a red triangle and a green square must be remembered at the same time, one must make sure that "red" is bound to "triangle" and "green" is bound to "square".

One way of establishing such bindings is by having the neurons that represent features of the same chunk fire in synchrony, and those that represent features belonging to different chunks fire out of sync. In the example, neurons representing redness would fire in synchrony with neurons representing the triangular shape, but out of sync with those representing the square shape.

So far, there is no direct evidence that working memory uses this binding mechanism, and other mechanisms have been proposed as well.

It has been speculated that synchronous firing of neurons involved in working memory oscillates with frequencies in the theta band (4 to 8 Hz). Indeed, the power of theta frequency in the EEG increases with working memory load, and oscillations in the theta band measured over different parts of the skull become more coordinated when the person tries to remember the binding between two components of information.

WORKING MEMORY AND LEARNING

There is now extensive evidence that working memory is linked to key learning outcomes in literacy and numeracy. In a recent large-scale screening study, one in ten children in mainstream classrooms were identified with working memory deficits. The majority of them performed very poorly in academic achievements, independent of their IQ. Without appropriate intervention, these children lag behind their peers. Recent research has also confirmed that working memory capacity, but not IQ, predicts learning outcomes two years later.

This suggests that working memory impairments are associated with low learning outcomes and constitute a high risk factor for educational under achievement for children. In children with learning disabilities such as dyslexia, ADHD, and developmental coordination disorder, a similar pattern is evident. In a classroom, common characteristics of working memory impairment include a failure to remember instructions and an inability to complete learning activities. Without early diagnosis, working memory impairment negatively impacts a child's performance throughout their scholastic career.

RESEARCH

Today there are hundreds of research laboratories around the world studying various aspects of working memory. There are numerous applications of working memory in the field, such as using working memory capacity to explain intelligence, success at emotion regulation, and other cognitive abilities, furthering the understanding of autism, ADHD, motor dyspraxia, and improving teaching methods,, and creating artificial intelligence based on the human brain.

HOW PSYCHOLOGISTS STUDY MEMORY: MEMORY FOR FACTUAL INFORMATION AND MEMORY FOR SKILLS

Human memory, like memory in a computer, allows us to store information for later use. In order to do this, however, both the computer and we need to master three processes involved in memory. The first is called encoding; the process we use to transform information so that it can be stores. For a computer this means transferring data into 1's and 0's. For us, it means transforming the data into a meaningful form such as an association with an existing memory, an image, or a sound.

Next is the actual storage, which simply means holding onto the information.

For this to take place, the computer must physically write the 1' and 0's onto the hard drive.

It is very similar for us because it means that a physiological change must occur for the memory to be stored. The final process is called retrieval, which is bringing the memory out of storage and reversing the process of encoding. In other words, return the information to a form similar to what we stored.

The major difference between humans and computers in terms of memory has to do with how the information is stored. For the most part, computers have only two types; permanent storage and permanent deletion. Humans, on the other hand are more complex in that we have three distinct memory storage capabilities (not including permanent deletion). The first is Sensory memory, referring to the information we receive through the senses. This memory is very brief lasting only as much as a few seconds.

Short Term Memory (STM) takes over when the information in our sensory memory is transferred to our consciousness or our awareness (Engle, Cantor, & Carullo, 1993; Laming, 1992).

This is the information that is currently active such as reading this page, talking to a friend, or writing a paper. Short term memory can definitely last longer than sensory memory (up to 30 seconds or so), but it still has a very limited capacity. According to research, we can remember approximately 5 to 9 (7 +/- 2) bits of information in our short term memory at any given time (Miller, 1956) If STM lasts only up to 30 seconds, how do we ever get any work done?

Wouldn't we start to lose focus or concentrate about twice every minute? This argument prompted researchers to look at a second phase of STM that is now referred to as Working Memory. Working Memory is the process that takes place when we continually focus on material for longer than STM alone will allow (Baddeley, 1992).

What happens when our short term memory is full and another bit of information enters? Displacement means that the new information will push out part of the old information. Suddenly some one says the area code for that phone number and almost instantly you forget the last two digits of the number. We can further sharpen our short term memory skills, however, by mastering chunking and using rehearsal (which allows us to visualize, hear, say, or even see the information repeatedly and through different senses). Finally, there is long term memory (LTM), which is most similar to the permanent storage of a computer. Unlike the other two types, LTM is relatively permanent and practically unlimited in terms of its storage capacity. Its been argued that we have enough space in our LTM to memorize every phone number in the U.S. and still function normally in terms of remembering what we do now. Obviously we don't use even a fraction of this storage space.

There are several subcategories of LTM. First, memories for facts, life events, and information about our environment are stored in declarative memory. This includes semantic memory, factual knowledge like the meaning of words, concepts, and our ability to do math (Lesch & Pollatsek, 1993, Rohrer et al., 1995) and episodic memory, memories for events and situations (Goldringer, 1996; Kliegel & Lindberger, 1993). The second subcategory is often not thought of as memory because it refers to internal, rather than external information. When you brush your teeth, write your name, or scratch your eye, you do this with ease because you previously stored these movements and can recall them with ease. This is referred to as nondeclarative (or implicit) memory. These are memories we have stored due to extensive practice, conditioning, or habits.

SHORT TERM MEMORY

There are typically six reasons why information is stored in our short term memory.

- *Primacy effect*: information that occurs first is typically remembered better than information occurring later. When given a list of words or numbers, the first word or number is usually remembered due to rehearsing this more than other information.
- *Recency effect*: often the last bit of information is remembered better because not as much time has past; time which results in forgetting.
- *Distinctiveness:* if something stands out from information around it, it is often remembered better. Any distinctive information is easier to remember than that which is similar, usual, or mundane.
- *Frequency effect:* rehearsal, as stated in the first example, results in better memory. Remember trying to memorize a formula for your math class. The more you went over it, the better you knew it.
- *Associations:* when we associate or attach information to other information it becomes easier to remember. Many of us use this strategy in our professions and everyday life in the form of acronyms.
- *Reconstruction:* sometimes we actually fill in the blanks in our memory. In other words, when trying to get a complete picture in our minds, we will make up the missing parts, often without any realization that this is occurring.

LONG TERM MEMORY

Information that passes from our short term to our long term memory is typically that which has some significance attached to it. Imagine how difficult it would be to forget the day you graduated, or your first kiss.

Now think about how easy it is to forget information that has no significance; the colour of the car you parked next to at the store or what shirt you wore last Thursday. When we process information, we attach significance to it and information deemed important is transferred to our long term memory.

There are other reasons information is transferred. As we all know, sometimes our brains seem full of insignificant facts. Repetition plays a role in this, as we tend to remember things more the more they are rehearsed. Other times, information is transferred because it is somehow attached to something significant. You may remember that it was a warm day when you bought your first car. The temperature really plays no important role, but is attached to the memory of buying your first car.

FORGETTING

You can't talk about remembering without mentioning its counterpart. It seems that as much as we do remember, we forget even more. Forgetting isn't really all that bad, and is in actuality, a pretty natural phenomenon. Imagine if you remembered every minute detail of every minute or every hour, of every day during your entire life, no matter how good, bad, or insignificant. Now imagine trying to sift through it all for the important stuff like where you left your keys.

There are many reasons we forget things and often these reasons overlap. Like in the example above, some information never makes it to LTM. Other times, the information gets there, but is lost before it can attach itself to our LTM. Other reasons include decay, which means that information that is not used for an extended period of time decays or fades away over time. It is possible that we are physiologically preprogrammed to eventually erase data that no longer appears pertinent to us.

Failing to remember something doesn't mean the information is gone forever though. Sometimes the information is there but for various reasons we can't access it. This could be caused by distractions going on around us or possibly due to an error of association (e.g., believing something about the data which is not correct causing you to attempt to retrieve information that is not there). There is also the phenomenon of repression, which means that we purposefully (albeit subconsciously) push a memory out of reach because we do not want to remember the associated feelings. This is often sited in cases where adults 'forget' incidences of sexual abuse when they were children. And finally, amnesia, which can be psychological or physiological in origin.

INTELLIGENCE

The assessment of human abilities dates back nearly 4000 years when China used written tests to rate applicants for civil service. Two-thousand years later, during the Hans Dynasty, civil service type exams were used in the areas of law, military, agriculture, and geography. In the early 1800s British diplomats observed the Chinese assessments and modified them for use in Britain and eventually the United States for use in civil service placement. Sir Francis Galton is a key figure in modern intelligence testing. As the first cousin of Charles Darwin, he attempted to apply Darwin's evolutionary theory to the study of human abilities. He postulate that intelligence was quantifiable and normally distributed. In other words, he believed that we could assign a score to intelligence where the majority of people fall in the average range and the percentage of the population decreases the farther from the middle their score gets.

The first workable intelligence test was developed by French psychologist Alfred Binet. He and his partner, Theodore Simon, were commissioned by the French government to improve the teaching methods for developmentally disabled children. They believed that intelligence was the key to effective teaching, and developed a strategy whereby a mental age (MA) was determined and divided by the child's chronological age (CA). This formula, stated as "MA/CA X 100." Another theorist, Raymond Cattell, described intelligence as having two distinct factors. The first he called Crystallized Intelligence, representing acquired knowledge, and second, Fluid Intelligence, or our ability to use this knowledge.

Sternberg (1988) argued that there are a number of ways to demonstrate intelligence or adaptive functioning. He proposed a model of intelligence referred to as the triarchic theory. According to this model there are three types of intelligence: (1) analytical, or the ability to solve a problem by looking at its components; (2) creative, the ability o use new or ingenious ways to solve problems; and (3) practical, referring to street smarts or common sense. While most IQ tests measure only analytical intelligence, they fail to include practical intelligence which is the most understandable to most of us Intelligence is not something we can see or hear, or taste. We can see the results of intelligence...sometimes.

Many argue that quantifying intelligence correctly is impossible and all that modern IQ tests do is test our knowledge and abilities. While it is true that a person can learn to improve his or her score, this can only occur if correct responses are taught to the person, which is highly unethical. We have also found that our individual IQ score remains quite consistent as we get older. Some argue, however, that modern IQ tests are prejudiced against certain ethnicities and cultures and tend to result in higher scores for others. Where this leaves us, however, is uncertain. As of today, these IQ tests are the best we have in our attempt to quantify the construct known as intelligence.

RELAXATION AND HYPNOSIS

Many internal and external factors affect how we think, feel, and behave. Although alcohol and drugs have been studied in great detail and have been shown to have both positive and negative effects on our state of mind, they will not be discussed in this section. For more information about these, follow the link above. In this section, we are going to focus primarily on the internal factors that influence our state of mind, particularly relaxation and hypnosis. These two terms are not foreign to most of us, but they can be highly misunderstood. Let's explore the concept of relaxation first.

RELAXATION

When studied in psychology, relaxation refers to a focusing on the mind and a relaxing of the body's muscles. Research has shown that being too tense and/or living with too much stress has a significant negative impact on our lives. It can lead to physical illnesses such as high blood pressure, ulcers, fatigue, and headaches and many psychological issues, including inappropriate or misdirected emotions, confusion, difficulty concentrating, and burn-out.

People utilize relaxation, in combination with stress management, to improve their quality of life, reduce the physical components of stress, and improve their psychological functioning. There are different forms of relaxation, including breathing exercises, deep muscle relaxation, progressive muscle relaxation, imagery, meditation, and yoga. Although each of these has different components, the main goal in each is to relax the body's muscles and focus the mind. Since the body and the mind cannot be separated, most agree that both of these components must be present for any relaxation technique to work.

HYPNOSIS

Hypnosis is very similar to relaxation in that the same two components of physical and mental must be addressed together. Most professionals agree that hypnosis is a very deep state of relaxation where your mind is more focused and the connection between your thoughts, emotions, and behaviors are more clear. Hypnosis is not magical; it can not cause you to do anything against your judgment or ethical beliefs; it can not make you 'cluck like a chicken.' What it can do it help you to focus on specific areas of your life with more clarity and teach you how to do this in a positive manner.

A hypnotherapist is typically a licensed professional who uses hypnosis as part of a treatment regimen for certain psychological disorders. It is rarely used as the primary treatment, but instead is most beneficial when used with relaxation and talk-therapy for a more rounded therapeutic approach. A hypnotist is a non-clinical term usually referring to an unlicensed individual who perform various forms of hypnosis for entertainment purposes. The two are quite different, the former is therapeutic and the latter is not designed to be so.

Most people are able to be hypnotized, although many factors play a role in your individual susceptibility. These factors include your belief in hypnosis, your trust for the therapist, your sense of safety, ability to concentrate and focus your mind, and the absence of external factors such as noise, uncomfortable temperature, and physical comfort. The key to successful hypnosis is your ability to focus on your body and mind and to trust and believe in your therapist. Without these hypnosis will not work, at least not to the fullest therapeutic value.

FORGETTING: SOME CONTRASTING ISSUES - FORGETTING AS A RESULT OF INTERFERENCE

Forgetting (retention loss) refers to apparent loss of information already encoded and stored in an individual's long term memory. It is a spontaneous or gradual process in which old memories are unable to be recalled from memory storage. It is subject to delicately balanced optimization that ensures that relevant memories are recalled. Forgetting can be reduced by repetition and/or more elaborate cognitive processing of information. Reviewing information in ways that involve active retrieval seems to slow the rate of forgetting. Forgetting functions (amount remembered as a function of time since an event was first experienced) have been extensively analyzed. The most recent evidence suggests that a power function provides the closest mathematical fit to the forgetting function.

One of the first people to study the mechanisms of forgetting was the German psychologist Hermann Ebbinghaus. Using himself as the sole subject in his experiment, he memorized lists of three letter nonsense syllable words—two consonants and one vowel in the middle. He then measured his own capacity to relearn a given list of words after a variety of given time period. He found that forgetting occurs in a systematic manner, beginning rapidly and then leveling off. Although his methods were primitive, his basic premises have held true today and have been reaffirmed by more methodologically sound methods.

THEORIES OF FORGETTING

The four main theories of forgetting apparent in the study of psychology as follows;

Cue-dependent Forgetting

Cue-dependent forgetting or retrieval failure, is the failure to recall a memory due to missing stimuli or cues that were present at the time the memory was encoded. It is one of five cognitive psychology theories of forgetting. It states that a memory is sometimes temporarily forgotten purely because it cannot be retrieved, but the proper cue can bring it to mind. A good metaphor for this is searching for a book in a library without the reference number, title, author or even subject. The information still exists, but without these cues retrieval is unlikely. Furthermore, a good retrieval cue must be consistent with the original encoding of the information. If the sound of the word is emphasized during the encoding process, the cue that should be used should also put emphasis on the phonetic quality of the word. Information is available however, just not readily available without these cues.

Trace Decay

Trace decay focuses on the problem of availability caused when memories decay. Hebb said that incoming information creates a pattern of neurons to create a neurological memory trace in the brain which would fade with time. Repeated firing causes a structural change in the synapses. Rehearsal of repeated firing maintains the memory in STM until a structural change is made.

Organic Causes

Forgetting that occurs through physiological damage or dilapidation to the brain are referred to as organic causes of forgetting. These theories encompass the loss of information already retained in long term memory or the inability to encode new information again. Examples include Alzheimer's, Amnesia, Dementia, consolidation theory and the gradual slowing down of the central nervous system due to aging.

INTERFERENCE THEORIES

Interference theory refers to the idea that forgetting occurs because the recall of certain items interferes with the recall of other items. In nature, the interfering items are said to originate from an over stimulating environment. Interference theory exists in two branches, Retroactive and Proactive inhibition each referring in contrast to the other. Retroactive interference is when the past memory interferes with the later memory, causing it to change in a particular extent. On the other hand, proactive interference is when the later memory interferes with the older memory, causing it to change.

DECAY THEORY

Decay theory states that when something new is learned, a neurochemical, physical "memory trace" is formed in the brain and over time this trace tends to disintegrate, unless it is occasionally used.

DEFINITIONS AND CONTROVERSY

Forgetting can have very different causes than simply removal of stored content. Forgetting can mean access problems, availability problems, or can have other reasons such as amnesia caused by an accident. A debatable yet popular concept is "trace decay", which can occur in both short and long-term memory. This theory, applicable mostly to short-term memory, is supposedly contradicted by the fact that one is able to ride a bike even after not having done so for decades. "Flashbulb memories" are another piece of seemingly contradicting evidence. It is believed that certain memories "trace decay" while others don't. Sleep is believed to play a key role in halting trace decay, although the exact mechanism of this is unknown.

FORGETTING AND RETRIEVAL INHIBITION MEMORY IN EVERYDAY LIFE

Retrieval-induced forgetting (RIF) refers to the finding that the successful retrieval of a memory trace apparently inhibits the retrieval of rival memory traces. Thus, when certain items from a particular category of words are practised, retrieval of the unpractised items in that same category is suppressed, so that they actually become harder to retrieve than similar items from a completely unpractised category. This phenomenon was first demonstrated by Anderson, Bjork, and Bjork (1994), who presented their participants with word pairs, each consisting of a category word and an example of an item from that category (e.g. fruit-banana). The list contained further items from the same category (e.g. fruit-apple), and others from different categories (e.g. drink-whisky).

Half of the items from certain categories (e.g. fruit) were subjected to retrieval practice. When retrieval was subsequently tested for all of the previously untested items, it was found that untested items from a tested category gave lower recall scores than those from an untested category. Anderson et al. (1994) concluded that the earlier retrieval of an item from a particular category had somehow inhibited the retrieval of other items from the same category. The RIF phenomenon has now been confirmed by a large number of studies. RIF has also been shown to occur in realistic settings involving meaningful items, such as revising for an examination and eyewitness memory for details of a crime.

A number of recent studies suggest that RIF works by inhibiting the retrieval of rival items, rather than merely reflecting the blocking of rival items by the strengthening of a cue-item association. In the first place, RIF is found to be cue-independent, in that its effects generalize to inhibit items semantically related to the cue but not tested with that cue. Moreover, it has been shown that RIF is observed only when retrieval has taken place, and is not brought about by passive study such as rereading the test items. It has also been found that RIF is dependent on interference, since an item will only produce RIF in a related item that interferes with it.

For example, Anderson et al. reported that little inhibition was observed when competing items were of low taxonomic frequency and therefore likely to cause low interference in view of their weak association with the category cue (e.g. fruit-guava). In contrast, high frequency items (e.g. fruit-banana) produced strong inhibition, presumably because they created more interference with other category members. This finding supports the view that the function of RIF is to overcome interference. Anderson (2003) argues that the function of RIF is to assist the selective retrieval of required items by inhibiting the retrieval of unwanted items. For example, remembering where you left your car in a large multi-storey car park would be extremely difficult if you had equally strong memories for every previous occasion on which you had ever parked your car. A mechanism that strengthens the most recent memory of parking your car, whilst inhibiting the memories of all previous occasions, would actually be very useful.

If RIF does indeed assist the retrieval process in some way, then it might be expected that some aspects of memory performance in everyday life might be related to the strength of the RIF effect. More specifically, it might be expected that individuals who show a relatively low level of RIF might be expected to suffer from poorer selective retrieval and thus more cognitive failures in everyday life. One well-established measure of cognitive failures in everyday life is the Cognitive Failures Questionnaire (CFQ), devised by Broadbent, Cooper, Fitzgerald, and Parkes (1982).

It includes such items as, 'Do you forget why you went from one part of the house to another?' and 'Do you forget where you put something like a newspaper or a book?'. Broadbent et al. (1982) reported that the CFQ is very reliable even across long test-retest intervals, and that factor analysis revealed no significant subscales. CFQ scores have been found to correlate with other measures of everyday memory and also with spouse ratings of cognitive failures. The present study investigates the relationship between RIF and CFQ scores to test the hypothesis that there will be a negative correlation between RIF and everyday forgetting.

Unit IV

Motivation and Emotion

THEORIES OF MOTIVATION: SOME MAJOR PERSPECTIVES

Some "Why" questions: Why do you go to class each day? Why did Cain kill Abel? Why do students study for hours (sometimes even days) to pass examinations (and don't say, "to pass examinations")? Why do professors teach students, and why do they test students? Why did you pick out those shoes or those pants to wear today? Each of these questions has an answer...there is some motive for engaging in those behaviors. We may define a motive (or motivation) as a need, want, interest, or desire that propels someone (or an organism) in a certain direction.

This motivating mechanism can be called many things—a habit, a belief, a desire, an instinct, a need, an interest, a compulsion, or a drive—but no matter what its label, it is this motivation that prompts us to take action. Indeed, the motivation comes from the verb "to move." Some Introductory Psychology books define the field of motivation as the study of goal-directed behaviour. With this definition in mind, are humans the only type of living organism that can have motivation?

THEORETICAL PERSPECTIVES

A) Instinct Theories

Many of the different theories of motivation are similar, except for the amount of emphasis they place on either biology or environment. Most include some level of both (some nature, some nurture). However, there is one theory that completely emphasizes biology...Instinct theory.

- Instinct Theory — states that motivation is the result of biological, genetic programming. Thus, all beings within a species are programmed for the same motivations.
  - At the heart of this perspective, is the motivation to survive - we are biologically programmed to survive. And, all of our behaviors and motivations stem from biological programming. Thus, are actions are instincts.

For example, a human mother, unlike many other species, will stay awake with a crying infant all night long trying to provide comfort. Why? Instinct theory suggests that she is programmed to behave in this manner - it is not due to learning or conditioning, not to being raised properly or poorly, not to having strong female role models or weak role models, or anything else, other that pure biology.

This perspective is very much the sort that was offered recently in the controversial article that stated, Parents don't matter that much in the development of their children.

- William McDougal (1908) - influential theorist who viewed instincts as behaviour patterns that are:
  (a) Unlearned
  (b) Uniform in expression
  (c) Universal in a species

For example, within a species of bird, all the members may build identical nests and work in the same ways. This is true even for those birds of that species born and raised in captivity and isolation, and thus could not have learned the appropriate nest building behaviour from other, experienced role model birds. McDougal carried it a step further by stating that humans are the same and have instincts for behaviors such as: parenting, submission, jealousy, mating, and more.

– Problems with this perspective

- Theorists have never been able to agree on a list of

instincts; Many instincts are NOT universal and seem to be more dependent on individual differences (for example, jealousy. Not all humans exhibit the same jealously levels, behaviors, etc.).

- Today - instinct theory has a more biological emphasis for specific motives and not all (like aggression and sex). But, there is still a strong instinct perspective in the study of animals (ethology)
  - Sociobiological Perspective (Sociobiology) — the study of genetic and evolutionary bases of behaviour in all organisms, including húmans. This view spawned from instinct theory, but it is not purely an instinct theory.
- Major Viewpoint - sociobiology states that natural selection favors social behaviors that maximize reproductive success. Thus, the primary motivating force for living organisms (including humans) is to pass on our genes from one generation to the next.

This theory, inspired by Charles Darwin, argues that in the last 15 million years the human species has evolved socially as well as physically. Through the process of natural selection, individuals who were even slightly predisposed to engage in adaptive social behaviors were the "fittest" and tended to survive longer and to be more successful in passing their genes along to future generations. Over countless generations, this selection process weeded out individuals who lacked these predispositions and those who possessed them prospered. Even though these tendencies may not enhance our fitness in today's world, eons spent in harsher environments have left us genetically predisposed to perform certain social behaviors when situational cues call forth ancient instincts.

Instinct theory argued that people try to survive, and that any quality that increases survival will eventually become genetically based. However, sociobiology has changed this view slightly by arguing that the organism's fundamental goal is not mere survival, or even the survival of its offspring. Rather, the fittest individual is the one that succeeds in passing the maximum number of genes on to the next generation. Why, for example, do animals go to all the trouble of breeding and raising offspring? Because having children is an extremely effective means of ensuring the survival of one's genes in a future generation. Caring for offspring may seem self-sacrificing, but these actions are prompted by the gene's selfish tendency to seek survival at all costs. Even if the parent perishes protecting its young, its genes will continue to flourish in its offspring. To Darwin, the fittest animal is the one that can survive longest. To Hamilton, the fittest animal is the one that maximizes the survival of its genes in future generations.

- This perspective can explain motives such as competition, aggression, sexual activity, and dominance.
- It can also explain differences in men and women's mating preferences. For example:

In one study an attractive man or woman (the researchers' accomplice) asked strangers of the opposite sex one of the following questions: "I have been noticing you around campus. I find you very attractive." The accomplice then asked one of the following questions, depending on the group the subject had been assigned to: (a) "Would you go out with me tonight"; (b) "Would you come over to my apartment tonight?" (c) "Would you go to bed with me tonight?"

The Results: None of the women agreed to the third request compared to the 75% hit rate for men. Is it possible that the differences were due to instincts or do you think they must be due to something else? In another example: Studies have shown that women are more likely to engage in extramarital affairs during ovulation, when they are more likely to get pregnant (the studies did NOT state or even insinuate that the women were making conscious efforts to get pregnant from a male other than their spouse or boyfriend, only that women were indeed more likely to be ovulating during the time they decided to have the extramarital affairs).

- Seems Selfish - this perspective may seem selfish, but it can also explain seemingly altruistic behaviors:

For example: A Blackbird will risk death to signal the flock that a hawk (a predator) is nearby? In so doing, the Blackbird increases its chance of getting killed, but also increases the chances of the other Blackbirds surviving and, therefore, increasing the odds that more genes will be passed on an organism will risk its own life to keep the possibility of passing on familial genes alive. Others of the same genetic strain will survive and keep the gene pool going even if that particular bird does not so this may be a selfish perspective, but it has the potential to produce remarkably unselfish behaviour.

- Drive Theories
  - A Drive is an internal state of tension that motivates an organism to engage in activities that should (hopefully) reduce this tension.
  - Most organisms seem to try and maintain Homeostasis - a state of physiological equilibrium.

For example, we have a homeostatic temperature of 98.6 degrees Farenheight. If this temperature begins to waiver enough you have a number of possible autonomic responses: if temperature increases, you perspire. If temperature decreases, you shiver.

So, when you experience a drive, you are motivated to reduce this state of tension and pursue actions that will lead to a drive reduction (reduce the state of tension).

For Example - hunger leads to physical discomfort (internal tension - drive), which leads to the motivation to get food, which leads to eating, which leads to a reduction in physical tension (drive reduction), which finally leads to the restoration of equilibrium.

- There are some problems:
  - Homeostasis seems irrelevant to some human motives - “thirst for knowledge”...what the heck is that?
  - Motivation may exist without a drive arousal. For example, humans do not eat only when they are hungry. Don’t believe me? Ever go out for a nice dinner, eat enough to be full, but then still decide to have that great chocolate desert anyway? I thought so.

- Incentive Theory

An incentive may be defined as an external goal that has the capacity to motivate behaviour. This does not mean that it will always motivate behaviour, only that it can. Now, we get to a situation in which we can see a difference with previous theories:

Drive theory acts by an internal state pushing you in a specific direction. However, incentive theory acts when an external stimulus pulls you in a certain direction.

This is directly related to Skinner. Here we can see a move away from biological influence toward the environment and its influence on behaviour. You attend class not because you were biologically programmed to become a student, but rather, because there is something external that is rewarding to you. Is it the grade you seek? Is it the desire to avoid going into the job market? Is it the desire to obtain a better job with a degree than possible without one? Regardless which it is, the idea is that the motivation is something external, not internal.

- Malsow's Need Hierarchy

This Humanistic perspective is a blend of biological and social needs and is a sweeping overview of human motivation. Because Maslow believed that all needs vary in strength, he arranged them in a pyramidal form to indicate which have more strength. The most basic needs (like shelter and food) are vital to daily survival, and are at the bottom, while needs that are less important to staying alive are higher on the pyramid.

We may define the Need Hierarchy as - a systematic arrangement of needs according to priority, which assumes that basic needs must be met before less basic needs are aroused. Thus, like stage theories, we must meet one need before we move on to the next.

Levels:

- Physiological - these include the need for food, water, and other vital components of life. If these needs are not met, the organism can't survive. Thus, these are the most basic and important.
- Safety and security - these needs refer more to the

long term survival than day to day needs. Humans tend to seek out order and have a desire to live in a world that is not filled with chaos and danger. As a result, they seek out stable lives with careers, homes, insurance, etc.

- Belongingness and love - after obtaining a safe environment to live and establishing some long term plans, people seek out love and affection from family members, friends, and lovers.
- Esteem - at this level, people become concerned with self-esteem which may be based on achievements that they earn, recognition from others for jobs they do, etc.
- Cognitive - needs at this level are based on acquiring knowledge and understanding of the world, people, behaviour, etc. If you are in college to learn (not simply to get a degree) then you are attempting to fulfill your cognitive needs.
- Aesthetic - aesthetic needs include beauty and order in life. Getting your life in order may provide a sense of comfort that people often lack. In addition, spending time finding and observing beauty in the world becomes an option and a desire as people do not have to struggle and fight to stay alive. Remember the episode of Star Trek: The Next Generation in which people from our century who had been frozen are found and thawed? These people could not understand that money was no longer important, that starvation had been abolished on Earth, and that people now had the opportunity and will to better themselves through learning about art, music, etc. Picard was preaching the aesthetic level of Maslow's hierarchy.
- Self-actualization - this is the highest and most difficult level to reach. In fact, according to Maslow, very few people actually reach this level. Self-actualization is the need to fulfill one's own potential. As Maslow stated, "What a man *can* be, he *must* be."

Interestingly, Maslow indicated that people will be frustrated if they can't pursue their true loves and talents. For example, if a person has a talent for painting, but they become a doctor, they will be forever frustrated because the need for self-actualization will be hindered.

ACHIEVEMENT MOTIVATION

Over the years, behavioral scientists have noticed that some people have an intense desire to achieve something, while others may not seem that concerned about their achievements. This phenomenon has attracted a lot of discussions and debates. Scientists have observed that people with a high level of achievement motivation exhibit certain characteristics. Achievement motivation is the tendency to endeavor for success and to choose goal oriented success or failure activities. Achievement motivation forms to be the basic for a good life. People who are oriented towards achievement, in general, enjoy life and feel in control. Being motivated keeps people dynamic and gives them self-respect. They set moderately difficult but easily achievable targets, which help them, achieve their objectives. They do not set up extremely difficult or extremely easy targets.

By doing this they ensure that they only undertake tasks that can be achieved by them. Achievement motivated people prefer to work on a problem rather than leaving the outcome to chance. It is also seen that achievement motivated people seem to be more concerned with their personal achievement rather than the rewards of success. It is generally seen that achievement motivated people evidenced a significantly higher rate of advancement in their company compared to others. Programs and courses designed, involves seven "training inputs." The first step refers to the process through which achievement motivation thinking is taught to the person. The second step helps participants understand their own individuality and goals.

The third assist participants in practicing achievement-related actions in cases, role-plays, and real life. A fourth refers to practicing of achievement-related actions in business and other games. A fifth input encourages participants to relate the achievement behaviour model to their own behaviour, self-image, and goals. The sixth programme facilitates participants to develop a personal plan of action. Finally, the course provides participants with feedback on their progress towards achieving objectives and targets. Achievement motivation as a branch of study has greatly established its prominence. A number of companies are now training their employees in the same.

EMOTIONS: THEIR NATURE, EXPRESSION AND IMPACT

EMOTIONS

We all have them, and yet most of us can't explain them. Do people really know why they have them, when they have them, how to control them, etc.? Like so many other aspects of our psychological makeup, emotions are comprised of several components. We will discuss emotions in terms of the cognitive, physiological, and behavioral components.

A. Cognitive Level (this is the label or name associated with the emotion)

- One key aspect of emotions, according to Woodworth & Sehlesberg, is that we have perceptions of them that usually ranges from:

Pleasantness-unpleasantness & weak-strong (this is the level of activation)

So, we perceive our emotions as having some level of pleasantness and strength. For example, if your boyfriend or girlfriend breaks up with you, you experience some type of emotion, like sadness. Then, you experience this emotion along the pleasantness and strength dimensions - if you loved this person, you may experience sadness that is very unpleasant and intense (strength).

- Usually, research on emotions involves a person's subjective report or experience of an experience. Aside from all of the normal problems associated with self-report data, there are a few others that occur with self report measures of emotions:

- There are over 400 words in the English language that refer to emotions. So how do we know exactly what is meant (how do we operationalize) when someone says, for example, they feel "sad"? What does that mean compared to all the other words?
- People can't turn emotions on and off so control over these for study is very difficult.
- As we know, emotions involve some type of personal evaluations that normally ranges from pleasant-unpleasant. However, we may have experiences that involve both. For example - getting a promotion = more money, but also more responsibility and more time away from others activities. So there are both pleasant and unpleasant emotions associated with this one experience.

- Physiological Level

Emotions are accompanied by physiological arousal, usually at an autonomic level (involuntary/automatic).

For example - have you ever had the experience of being in a car when it spins out of control on an icy road? Almost instantly upon the car spinning off track, you experience an increase in heart rate, blood pressure, breathing, your pupils dilate, etc. This occurs, at some level, with all emotions. The systems involved with this activity are:

- Central Nervous System (CNS): limbic system and cortex
- Peripheral Nervous System (PNS): somatic and autonomic, sympathetic and parasympathetic

But, very often physiological changes are too small to notice. In these cases, we rely on:

- Galvanic Skin Response (GSR) - measures fluctuations in electrical conductivity of the skin that occur when sweat glands increase activity.
- Polygraph - "lie detector" - used to measure the

subtle variations in muscle tension, heart rate, etc., associated with emotion that occurs very subtly.

- Behavioral Level: Nonverbal Expression

Very often organisms communicate without words. They may rely on smiling, frowning, clenching their fists, turning their backs, etc. Thus, we may communicate emotions nonverbally; through body language. One of the most influential and important researchers in the field of emotion, is Ekman. Here are a couple of examples from Ekman's work:

Ekman showed photos to people and asked them to identify what emotion was being expressed in those photos. He found that people from different cultures could recognize common facial features (people from different cultures all identified, for example, smiling as a sign of happiness).

He found 7 basic emotions most often identified from photos of facial expressions: happiness, sadness, anger, fear, surprise, disgust, and contempt. He also indicated that the use of facial expressions to communicate seems to be innate - people who have been blind from birth make many similar facial expressions.

THEORIES OF EMOTIONS

James-Lange Theory of Emotion

James and Lange (a Danish physiologist) proposed the same explanation of emotion at about same time - thus the theory was named for both of them.

A common sense idea about emotion would be:

Environmental influence (some event) —> Psychological experience —> Physiological state changes (emotion)

BUT: the James-Lange theory states:

Environmental influence (event) —> Physiological change —> Psychological experience

In other words, James and Lange would say, "I feel afraid because I tremble". If a person sees a bear while walking along in the woods, James and Lange would suggest that the person would tremble and then realise that, because they are trembling, they are afraid.

James stated:

"My theory ... is that the bodily changes follow directly the perception of the exciting fact, and that our feeling of the same changes as they occur is the emotion. Common sense says, we lose our fortune, are sorry and weep; we meet a bear, are frightened and run; we are insulted by a rival, and angry and strike. The hypothesis here to be defended says that this order of sequence is incorrect ... and that the more rational statement is that we feel sorry because we cry, angry because we strike, afraid because we tremble ... Without the bodily states following on the perception, the latter would be purely cognitive in form, pale, colorless, destitute of emotional warmth. We might then see the bear, and judge it best to run, receive the insult and deem it right to strike, but we should not actually feel afraid or angry."

Problems: later studies separated the internal organs that James said caused arousal from the CNS, but this did not eliminate emotional responding. So, perceptions of bodily changes could not be the only factor involved in emotions.

The Cannon-Bard Theory

Background: again two people had the same perspective at roughly the same time (although Cannon was considered to be the more influential one). This theory made use of information about physiological structures not available to James and Lange. Cannon's critique (1929) of James-Lange Theory - He indicated that some of the problems with the James-Lange theory were:

- People who show different emotions may have the same physiological (visceral) state - Example: cry when happy & sad
- Visceral changes are often too difficult to notice by a person having the experience to be used as cues
- Visceral changes are often too slow to be a source of emotions, which erupt very quickly. For example, when something bad happens to you, do you always cry before you feel sad? Or can you feel sad before crying?

- Physiological arousal may occur without the experience of an emotion:

For example: exercise —> increased heart rate —> no emotional significance

Back to common sense theory:

Emotion occurs when the thalamus sends signals to BOTH the cortex (which produces conscious experience of emotion) and autonomic nervous system (visceral arousal) at the same time. BUT - as we already know, the thalamus is not the only player involved in emotion. The limbic system, hypothalamus and others are all involved. So, this leads us to the Cognitive view.

Cognitive View: Schachter and Singer Two Factor Theory

- Schachter and Singer maintain that we don't automatically know when we are happy, angry, or jealous. Instead, we label our emotions by considering situational cues. We feel some emotion. To really understand what emotion we are having at that particular time, we use the cues in the environment at the time to help us determine the current emotion. This labeling process depends on two factors:
  - Some element in the situation must trigger a general, nonspecific arousal marked by increased heart rate, tightening of the stomach, and rapid breathing.
  - People search the situation/environment for cues that tell them what has caused the emotion.

The infamous Schachter-Singer study of emotion:

- Schachter and Singer told men who volunteered they were studying a vitamin supplement called Suproxin. The men were asked if they were willing to take the drug, and those who consented were injected with epinephrine or a placebo. Epinephrine, which is also called adrenaline, is released by our hormonal system whenever we face a stressful situation, and generally increases blood pressure, heart rate, and respiration. Thus the men who received the epinephrine were more physiologically aroused than those who received the inert placebo.

- Schachter and Singer manipulated subjects' interpretations of their physical sensations. They told some of the epinephrine-injected subjects that even though the drug wasn't harmful, side effects were quite common: they might feel flushed, their hands might shake, and their hearts might pound. The other subjects, in contrast, were given no information at all about the effects of the drug. Schachter and Singer reasoned that once the epinephrine kicked in, their subjects would begin to search for the cause of their arousal. People who had been told that the drug would arouse them should have assumed that the drug was causing their hands to shake and their heart to pound. But if they weren't warned about the drug's effects, then they would be more likely to interpret their arousal as an emotion.
- What kind of emotion would these uninformed subjects experience? Schachter and Singer believed that their reaction would depend on the available situational cues. They therefore manipulated this variable as well. They arranged for their subjects to wait for the Suproxin's effects in a small room with another person. This individual was one of Schachter and Singer's accomplices, and he was trained to behave in either a euphoric or angry fashion. The euphoric confederate clowned around during the 20 minutes, doodling on scratch paper, playing a game of "basketball" with wadded up balls of paper, making and flying a paper airplane, building a tower out of file folders, and playing with a Hula Hoop. The angry confederate, in contrast, became increasingly agitated during the 20 minutes. The subjects were asked to complete questionnaires that contained very personal questions. The accomplice,

after loudly criticizing questions that requested information about childhood diseases, father's income, and family members' bathing habits and psychiatric adjustment, flew into a rage at the question "How many times each week do you have sexual intercourse?"

- Schachter and Singer observed and coded the actions taken by each subject, and also asked them to describe their emotion state. As they had predicted, the physiologically aroused subjects who hadn't been told about the drug's side-effects responded with emotions that matched the confederate's actions. If they were aroused and hadn't been expecting the arousal, then they felt happy when their fellow subject was happy, but angry when their fellow subject was angry. Forewarned subjects and unaroused subjects who received a placebo, however, did not display any pronounced emotion. Also, the subjects in a special control condition—people who had been given epinephrine but had been misinformed about its possible effect – also displayed the emotions enacted by a euphoric confederate.

RELATIONSHIP BETWEEN EMOTION AND COGNITION

The relationship between cognition and emotion has fascinated important thinkers within the Western intellectual tradition. Historically, emotion and cognition have been viewed as largely separate. In the past two decades, however, a growing body of work has pointed to the interdependence between the two.Cognition refers to processes such as memory, attention, language, problem solving, and planning. Many cognitive processes are thought to involve sophisticated functions that may be unique to primates. They often involve so-called controlled processes, such as when the pursuit of a goal (e.g., maintaining information in mind) needs to be protected from interference (e.g., a distracting stimulus). A prototypical example of a neural correlate of a cognitive process is the sustained firing of cells in dorsolateral prefrontal cortex as a monkey maintains information *in mind* for brief periods of time.

With the advent of functional MRI (fMRI), it appears that cognitive processes engage cortical regions of the brain. Whereas there is relative agreement about what constitutes cognition, the same cannot be said about emotion. Some investigators use definitions that incorporate the concepts of drive and motivation: emotions are states elicited by rewards and punishers. Others favour the view that emotions are involved in the conscious (or unconscious) evaluation of events (i.e., appraisals). Some approaches focus on basic emotions (e.g., fear, anger), others on an extended set of emotions, including moral ones.

Strong evidence also links emotions to the body. Brain structures linked to emotion are often subcortical, such as the amygdala, ventral striatum, and hypothalamus. These structures are often considered evolutionarily conserved, or *primitive*. They are also believed to operate fast and in an *automatic fashion*, such that certain trigger features (e.g., the white of the eyes in a fearful expression) are relatively unfiltered and always evoke responses that may be important for survival. Accordingly, an individual may not be necessarily conscious of a stimulus that may have triggered brain responses in an affective brain region, such as the amygdala. Because of the inherent difficulty in providing clear definitions for both cognition and emotion, they will not be further defined here. We now turn to illustrating some of the interactions between emotion and cognition. Given the enormous scope of this topic, by necessity, this review will be relatively narrow in scope and will emphasize the brain systems involved in the interactions between emotion and *i*) perception and attention; *ii*) learning and memory; and *iii*) behavioral inhibition and working memory.

Other valuable sources include. A key conclusion from this review and from other current discussions of the relationship between cognition and emotion is that it is probably counterproductive to try to separate them. Instead, current thinking emphasizes their interdependence in ways that challenge a simple division of labour into separate *cognitive* and *emotional* domains. In particular, in the context of the brain, the general dichotomization alluded to above in terms of cortical-cognitive and subcortical-emotional brain areas is now viewed as largely simplified and breaks down rather quickly when more in-depth analyses are carried out; e.g.

Before proceeding, however, a brief historical note is in order. The emotion/cognition debate came into sharp focus with the report of the mere-exposure effect, which led to a strong belief that affect was primary to and independent of cognition.

It can be said that the mere-exposure effect and other behavioral findings shifted ongoing debates to focus on affect as being related to unconscious processing and subcortical activity, with cognition being related to conscious processing and cortical involvement. Interestingly, behavioral findings were interpreted in the context of the "low route" suggested by LeDoux (1996), which was purported to carry affective information subcortically. These early behavioral studies provided a strong impetus to the wave of neuroscience research in the late 1990s (and beyond) that investigated related phenomena.

Perception and Attention

Viewing emotion-laden visual stimuli is linked to heightened and more extensive visual system activation (Pessoa et al., 2002a; Vuilleumier, 2005). For instance, viewing faces with emotional expressions evokes increased responses relative to viewing neutral faces throughout ventral occipitotemporal visual cortex. Visual responses are also stronger when subjects view emotional scenes (e.g., a war scene) compared do neutral scenes (e.g., a lake scene). Increased visual activation is observed in both *late* visual areas, such as the fusiform gyrus and superior temporal sulcus, and early visual cortex in occipital cortex. Recent studies suggest that, in humans, even retinotopically organized visual cortex, including visual areas V1 and V2 along the calcarine fissure, are modulated by the affective significance of a stimulus.

Enhanced visual activation when viewing emotional stimuli is consistent with the observed improvements in behavioral performance in several visual tasks. For instance, angry and happy faces are detected faster in visual search tasks, and possibly other emotional stimuli, too, such as a snake or spider compared to neutral stimuli. Stronger evidence comes from studies of the *attentional blink* paradigm, in which subjects are asked to report the occurrence of two targets (T1 and T2) among a rapid stream of visual stimuli. When T2 follows T1 by a brief delay, participants are more likely to miss it, as if they had blinked (hence the name). The attentional blink is believed to reflect a capacity-limited processing stage, possibly linked to a process of consolidation of the detected item for conscious reports.

Interestingly, the attentional blink has been shown to be modulated by emotional stimuli, as subjects are significantly better at detecting T2 when it is an emotion-laden word (e.g., *rape*) than when it is a neutral word. Converging evidence for a link between perception, attention, and emotion comes from additional studies. For example, patients with unilateral inattention due to spatial hemineglect (often as a result of right hemisphere parietal lesions) are better at detecting happy or angry faces compared to neutral ones.

These findings are consistent with the notion that emotional faces may direct the allocation of attention. For instance, in one study, emotional faces were flashed at spatial locations that subsequently displayed low-contrast visual stimuli. They found that detection of the target was strongest when the fear face served as the spatial cue, suggesting that emotional stimuli can provide additional attentional guidance above and beyond a generic spatial cue. How is the increase in perceptual processing and attentional capture that are observed during the perception of affective stimuli mediated in the brain? Growing evidence links the amygdala, a subcortical region, with these effects.

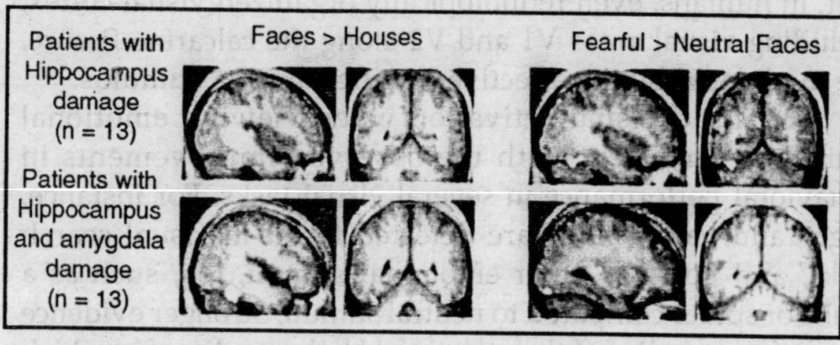

Fig. Functional brain imaging results in humans support a role of the amygdala in modulating visual responses to emotional stimuli.

Patients with medial temporal lobe sclerosis who have lesions involving the hippocampus alone (upper row) show normal activation of the fusiform cortex when contrasting fearful vs. neutral faces (right), as do healthy subjects (not shown). Patients with additional lesions involving the amygdala (lower row) show no effect of fear expression in visual cortex. However, fusiform cortex is still normally activated in both patient groups when they perform a task on faces relative to houses (left). These results suggest that amygdala damage can have distant functional consequences on the activity of visual cortex, selectively affecting emotional modulation. Adapted from Vuilleumier (2005), Trends Cogn Sci, How brains beware: neural mechanisms of emotional attention, copyright (2005), with permission from Elsevier. Original data from.

Thus, it appears that the amygdala may underlie a form of *emotional modulation* of information that in many ways parallels attentional effects that are observed with non-emotional information. There are several ways in which emotional modulation may be accomplished. First, it is possible that direct projections from the amygdala to visual processing regions enhance visual processing. The amygdala sends projections across all levels of the visual system, including anterior regions in temporal cortex and posterior regions in occipital cortex (including V1 and V2). Thus, the amygdala is well situated to modulate sensory processing according to the affective significance of a visual object.

A second possibility is that the amygdala interacts with other brain regions that are important for the control of attention, such as frontal and parietal regions, which, by their turn, modulate visual processing. In the latter scenario, the amygdala (possibly indirectly) would recruit attentional circuits so as to enhance the sensory processing of emotion-laden stimuli.

A final issue that should be addressed when considering interactions between emotion and perception/attention is whether the perception of emotion-laden stimuli is *automatic*, namely independent of attention and awareness. This question has received considerable attention because specific answers to this question (no or yes) suggest potentially different relationships between emotion and cognition (more or less independence between the two, respectively). Interestingly, evidence both for and against automaticity has been presented. For instance, emotional faces evoke responses in the amygdala even when attention is diverted to other stimuli.

Perhaps even more strikingly, amygdala responses are sometimes reported for emotional faces of which subjects are not conscious. Furthermore, cases of affective blindsight have been reported. These and other related findings suggest that at least some types of emotional perception occur outside of *cognitive* processing – and may rely on direct subcortical pathways conveying visual information to the amygdala. At the same time, recent findings have suggested that the perception of emotion-laden items requires attention, as revealed by attentional manipulations that consume most processing resources, leaving relatively few resources for the processing of unattended emotional items. Furthermore, it also appears that amygdala responses evoked by *unaware* stimuli depend somewhat on the manner by which awareness is operationally defined, such that no unaware responses are observed when awareness is defined, for instance, via signal detection theory methods. Overall, the automaticity debate remains unresolved and controversial.

Emotional content can change the formation and recollection of a memory event, consistent with findings in both human and animal studies. Compared to neutral items, humans remember better emotionally arousing information, including emotionally charged stories, film clips, pictures, and words. For instance, in one study participants viewed two videos, one composed of neutral film clips and another composed of emotional film clips. Although the two types of clips were taken from the same source and were equated in terms of levels of *understandability*, subjects were better at remembering emotional relative to neutral clips when tested approximately 3 weeks following the initial viewing of the films.

In another study, subjects viewed a large array of emotional and neutral pictures from the International Affective Picture System, a stimulus set that has been normed in terms of the dimensions of valence (positive/negative) and arousal (calm/excited). Participants initially rated the pictures along the dimensions of valence and arousal. An incidental free-recall test was administered both immediately and at one year following the rating sessions. Pictures rated as highly arousing were remembered better than all other pictures, including those rated as moderately arousing. Interestingly, the pattern of results was very similar when the subjects were tested a year later, namely, highly arousing pictures were better remembered.

In humans, the amygdala is known to be a critical structure for the enhancement of memory by emotion, consistent with both lesion and neuroimaging work. Recent studies have begun to delineate some of the specific functions of this structure. For instance, it appears that the right amygdala is more strongly involved in emotional memory formation, whereas the left amygdala is engaged by the retrieval of those memories, suggesting a potential hemispheric dissociation of amygdala involvement at different stages of emotional memory. In addition, amygdala responses are also linked to a novelty effect on memory tasks – i.e., the tendency to classify items as new as opposed to old.

In humans, there is some support for the notion that the enhancement of memory due to emotion is due mainly to the arousal dimension of emotional items and not valence (positive/negative) per se (Phelps, 2006), a notion that is more firmly established in nonhuman animal studies. In these studies, the effects of emotion on memory have been revealed by a vast array of experimental manipulations, including inhibitory avoidance training, contextual fear conditioning, cued fear conditioning, water-maze spatial and cued training, among others. Typically, the effects of emotion on memory are investigated via drug administration, including agonists and antagonists of specific brain receptors. For instance, in one experiment, rats were trained to swim to an escape platform after being placed in a water tank. To mimic the effects of arousal, a group of animals received an injection of d-amphetamine immediately after training; a control group received a saline injection.

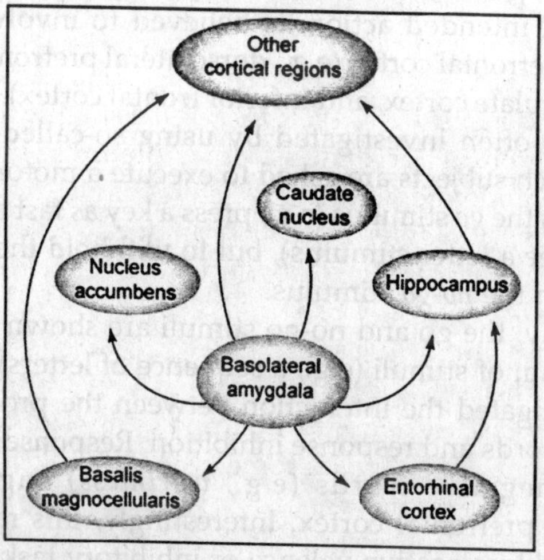

Fig. Projections from the basolateral complex of the amygdala to other brain areas involved in memory consolidation. Reprinted from McGaugh (2002), Trends Neurosci, Memory consolidation and the amygdala: a systems perspective, copyright (2002), with permission from Elsevier.

Behavioral testing revealed that d-amphetamine administration in the amygdala enhanced memory both on a spatial task and on a non-spatial cued task. A growing body of animal studies strongly supports a model in which emotion influences memory by modulating memory storage. In particular, the amygdala and the closely associated basal forebrain system involving the *stria terminalis* appear to play a major role in this modulatory process. These structures are thought to play a central role on memory consolidation by modulating activation in a network of brain regions, including the hippocampus, which is centrally involved in memory formation, but also additional brain structures, such as the nucleus accumbens, caudate nucleus, entorhinal cortex, in addition to other cortical regions.

BEHAVIORAL INHIBITION AND WORKING MEMORY

An important dimension of cognition involves *behavioral inhibition*. Response inhibition, namely the processes required to cancel an intended action, is believed to involve control regions in prefrontal cortex (e.g., dorsolateral prefrontal cortex, anterior cingulate cortex, and inferior frontal cortex). Response inhibition is often investigated by using so-called go/no-go tasks in which subjects are asked to execute a motor response when shown the *go* stimulus (e.g., press a key as fast as possible when you see a letter stimulus), but to withhold the response when shown the *no-go* stimulus.

Typically, the go and no-go stimuli are shown as part of a rapid stream of stimuli (e.g., a sequence of letters). A recent study investigated the interaction between the processing of emotional words and response inhibition. Response inhibition following negative words (e.g., *worthless*) engaged the dorsolateral prefrontal cortex. Interestingly, this region was not recruited by negative valence or inhibitory task demands *per se*; instead, the dorsolateral cortex was sensitive to the explicit interaction between behavioral inhibition and the processing of negatively valenced words.

Working memory, another important cognitive operation, involves the maintenance and updating of information in mind when the information is no longer available to sensory systems (e.g., when keeping a phone number in mind for a few seconds before dialing the number). Evidence for cognitive-emotional interaction comes from working memory studies, too. For instance, when participants were asked to keep in mind neutral or emotional pictures, maintenance-related activity in dorsolateral prefrontal cortex was modulated by the valence of the picture, with pleasant pictures enhancing activity and unpleasant pictures decreasing activity relative to neutral ones.

Interestingly, emotional pictures did not affect dorsolateral responses during a second experimental condition during which participants were *not* required to keep information in mind, indicating that the modulation of sustained activity by emotional valence was particular to the experimental context requiring active maintenance. In another study, participants watched short videos intended to induce emotional states (e.g., clips from uplifting or sad movies), after which they performed challenging working memory tasks. Bilateral lateral prefrontal cortex activity reflected equally the emotional and working memory task components. In other words, prefrontal activity did not stem from the working memory task alone or by the mood ensuing from the viewing of the video, but resulted from an interaction between cognition and emotion.

IMPACT OF COGNITION ON EMOTION

Although this short review focuses on the impact of emotional content on cognitive functions, here we briefly discuss another important line of studies that has investigated cognitive-emotional interactions, namely, cognitive emotion regulation. A particularly informative regulation strategy is "cognitive reappraisal", which involves rethinking the meaning of affectively charged stimuli or events in terms that alter their emotional impact. Reappraisal appears to depend upon interactions between prefrontal and cingulate regions that are frequently implicated in cognitive control and systems like the amygdala and insula that have been implicated in emotional responding.

Interestingly, having the goal to think about stimuli in ways that maintain or increase emotion may boost amygdala activity whereas having the goal to decrease emotion may diminish it. Furthermore, changes in emotional experience and autonomic responding may correlate with the concomitant rise or fall of prefrontal and/or amygdala activity. Although much of the work on the cognitive regulation of emotion has relied on a relatively strict separation between cognition and emotion, which are in this context viewed as engaged in tug-of-war for the control of behaviour, this framework is likely overly simplistic. As proposed by Ochsner and Gross (2008), a more fruitful approach will entail developing an integrated framework for specifying what combinations of interacting subsystems are involved in emotional responding, as individuals exert varying degrees and types of regulatory control over their emotions.

ANATOMICAL BASIS FOR COGNITIVE-EMOTIONAL INTERACTIONS

In attempting to understand the relationship between emotion and cognition, it is important to consider anatomical information. Advances in our understanding of brain connectivity suggest that a given brain region is only a few synapses away from every other brain region. Indeed, it appears that the brain is configured according to a small-world topology in which the path length between nodes is small – typically, cortical areas are connected directly or via just one or two intermediate areas – and nodes are highly clustered. Thus, a careful consideration of brain connectivity is informative in understanding potential cognitive-emotional interactions. In the past decade, several quantitative analysis of brain connectivity have been undertaken.

Not surprisingly, prefrontal areas are among those most distant from the sensory periphery, suggesting that they receive highly-processed and integrated sensory information. Such potential insulation of the prefrontal cortex from the periphery is thought to be a key anatomical feature of this region and presumably confers the primate brain with a greater degree of flexibility. Highly processed information would also be able to support more abstract processing that is required for cognition. Interestingly, the amygdala, a region often linked to emotional processing, appears to be equally removed from the sensory periphery – although in some species, direct sensory thalamic projections may be present. In addition, the amygdala makes very widespread projections. Overall, it appears that the amygdala is very well situated to integrate and distribute information.

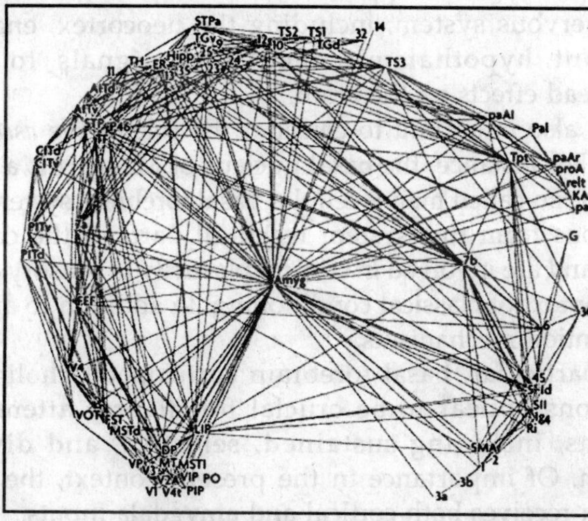

Fig. Brain connectivity graph. Quantitative analysis of brain connectivity reveals several clusters of highly interconnected regions (represented by different colors).

In this analysis, the amygdala was connected to all but 8 cortical areas. These connections involved multiple region clusters, suggesting that the amygdala is not only highly connected, but that its connectivity topology might be consistent with that of a *hub* that links multiple functional clusters. In this manner, the amygdala may be important for the integration of cognitive and emotional information.

It is also instructive to consider the connectivity of the hypothalamus, as it has been long recognized for its importance in emotional behaviours. In particular, via its descending connections that innervate brainstem motor systems, this structure is thought to play a key role in the implementation of goal-directed behaviors. Hypothalamic signals also can be conveyed to the cortex, mostly by way of the thalamus. Critically, prefrontal cortical territories project directly to the hypothalamus. Thus, the hypothalamus appears to be organized in such a way that it can generate both relatively reflexive behaviors and behaviors that are voluntarily triggered by inputs from the cerebral cortex. Overall, this structure appears to be connected with all levels of the nervous system, including the neocortex, enabling important hypothalamic regulatory signals to have widespread effects on the brain.

It is also important to consider the role of the *ascending systems*. For instance, the basal nucleus of Maynert is a major part of the so-called magnocellular basal forebrain system. The projections from this system reach all parts of the cortical mantle, and are involved in cortical plasticity in sensory cortex in the context of classical conditioning, in addition to arousal and attention mechanisms.

In particular, basal forebrain corticopetal cholinergic projections appear to be crucial for diverse attentional functions, including sustained, selective, and divided attention. Of importance in the present context, the basal forebrain receives both cortical and amygdala inputs.

Notably, recent anatomical evidence suggests the existence of specific topographically organized prefrontal-basal forebrain-prefrontal loops, so that specific prefrontal cortical targets of the basal forebrain connect back to sites from which the corticopetal fibers originate. Such loops provide a direct substrate for cognitive-emotional integration, for example by allowing amygdala signals to be broadcast widely, including to frontoparietal regions known to be important for the control of attention. More generally, the overall anatomical arrangement of the basal forebrain may involve multiple functional-anatomical *macrosystems* with wide-ranging effects on brain computations and important clinical implications. In summary, the picture that emerges from anatomical connectivity data suggests a remarkable potential for integration of information.

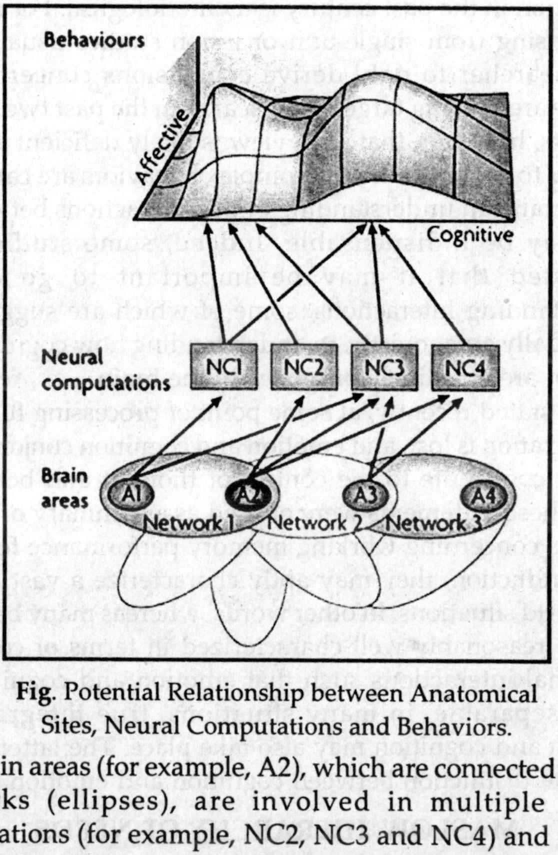

Fig. Potential Relationship between Anatomical Sites, Neural Computations and Behaviors.

Brain areas (for example, A2), which are connected to form networks (ellipses), are involved in multiple neural computations (for example, NC2, NC3 and NC4) and specific computations (for example, NC4) are carried out by several areas (for example, A2 and A3). Therefore, the structure–function mapping is both one-to-many and many-to-one; in other words, many-to-many. Multiple neural computations underlie behaviour. Each behaviour has both affective and cognitive components, indicated by the affective and cognitive axes. Note that the axes are not orthogonal, indicating that the dimensions are not independent from each other. Brain areas with a high degree of connectivity (*hubs*) may be especially important for regulating the flow and interaction of information between regions.

Historically, emotion and cognition have been viewed as separate entities. One factor that may have contributed for this separation in the past century is methodological. For instance, data arising from single-unit or lesion studies usually allow the researcher to only derive conclusions concerning the specific areas being targeted. Research in the past two decades suggests, however, that such view is likely deficient and that, in order to understand how complex behaviors are carried out in the brain, an understanding of the interactions between the two may be indispensable. Indeed, some studies have suggested that it may be important to go beyond understanding interactions, some of which are suggested to be mutually antagonistic, to understanding how cognition and emotion are effectively *integrated* in the brain.

As stated recently, at some point of processing functional specialization is lost, and emotion and cognition conjointly and equally contribute to the control of thought and behaviour. While these statements were offered as a summary of specific findings concerning working memory performance following mood induction, they may aptly characterize a vast array of real-world situations. In other words, whereas many behaviors may be reasonably well characterized in terms of cognitive-emotional interactions such that emotion and cognition are partly separable, in many situations, true integration of emotion and cognition may also take place. The latter further blurs the distinction between cognition and emotion.

MASLOW: HIERARCHY OF NEEDS

Maslow's hierarchy of needs is a theory in psychology, proposed by Abraham Maslow in his 1943 paper *A Theory of Human Motivation*, which he subsequently extended to include his observations of humans' innate curiosity. Maslow studied what he called exemplary people such as Albert Einstein, Jane Addams, Eleanor Roosevelt, and Frederick Douglass rather than mentally ill or neurotic people, writing that "the study of crippled, stunted, immature, and unhealthy specimens can yield only a cripple psychology and a cripple philosophy." Maslow also studied the healthiest one percent of the college student population. In his book, *The Farther Reaches of Human Nature*, Maslow writes, "By ordinary standards of this kind of laboratory research... this simply was not research at all. My generalizations grew out of my selection of certain kinds of people. Obviously, other judges are needed."

REPRESENTATIONS

Maslow's hierarchy of needs is predetermined in order of importance. It is often depicted as a pyramid consisting of five levels: the lowest level is associated with physiological needs, while the uppermost level is associated with psychological needs, particularly those related to identity and purpose. Deficiency needs must be met first. Once these are met, seeking to satisfy growth needs drives personal growth. The higher needs in this hierarchy only come into focus when the lower needs in the pyramid are met.

Once an individual has moved upwards to the next level, needs in the lower level will no longer be prioritized. If a lower set of needs is no longer being met, the individual will temporarily re-prioritize those needs by focusing attention on the unfulfilled needs, but will not permanently regress to the lower level. For instance, a businessman at the esteem level who is diagnosed with cancer will spend a great deal of time concentrating on his health (physiological needs), but will continue to value his work performance (esteem needs) and will likely return to work during periods of remission.

DEFICIENCY NEEDS

The lower four layers of the pyramid are what Maslow called "deficiency needs" or "D-needs": physiological, safety and security, love and belonging, and esteem. With the exception of the lowest (physiological) needs, if these "deficiency needs" are not met, the body gives no physical indication but the individual feels anxious and tense.

PHYSIOLOGICAL NEEDS

For the most part, physiological needs are obvious - they are the literal requirements for human survival. If these requirements are not met (with the exception of sex), the human body simply cannot continue to function.

Physiological needs include:

- Breathing
- Homeostasis
- Water
- Sleep
- Food
- Excretion
- Sex
- Clothing
- Shelter

SAFETY NEEDS

With their physical needs relatively satisfied, the individual's safety needs take over and dominate their behaviour.

These needs have to do with people's yearning for a predictable, orderly world in which injustice and inconsistency are under control, the familiar frequent and the unfamiliar rare. In the world of work, these safety needs manifest themselves in such things as a preference for job security, grievance procedures for protecting the individual from unilateral authority, savings accounts, insurance policies, and the like. For the most part, physiological and safety needs are reasonably well satisfied in the "First World."

The obvious exceptions, of course, are people outside the mainstream — the poor and the disadvantaged. If frustration has not led to apathy and weakness, such people still struggle to satisfy the basic physiological and safety needs.

They are primarily concerned with survival: obtaining adequate food, clothing, shelter, and seeking justice from the dominant societal groups.

Safety and Security needs include:

- Personal security
- Financial security
- Health and well-being
- Safety net against accidents/illness and the adverse impacts

SOCIAL NEEDS

After physiological and safety needs are fulfilled, the third layer of human needs is social. This psychological aspect of Maslow's hierarchy involves emotionally-based relationships in general, such as:

- Friendship
- Intimacy
- Having a supportive and communicative family

Humans need to feel a sense of belonging and acceptance, whether it comes from a large social group, such as clubs, office culture, religious groups, professional organizations, sports teams, gangs ("Safety in numbers"), or small social connections (family members, intimate partners, mentors, close colleagues, confidants).

They need to love and be loved (sexually and non-sexually) by others. In the absence of these elements, many people become susceptible to loneliness, social anxiety, and clinical depression. This need for belonging can often overcome the physiological and security needs, depending on the strength of the peer pressure; an anorexic, for example, ignores the need to eat and the security of health for a feeling of control and belonging.

ESTEEM

All humans have a need to be respected, to have self-esteem, self-respect. Also known as the belonging need, esteem presents the normal human desire to be accepted and valued by others. People need to engage themselves to gain recognition and have an activity or activities that give the person a sense of contribution, to feel accepted and self-valued, be it in a profession or hobby. Imbalances at this level can result in low self-esteem or an inferiority complex. People with low self-esteem need respect from others. They may seek fame or glory, which again depends on others. It may be noted, however, that many people with low self-esteem will not be able to improve their view of themselves simply by receiving fame, respect, and glory externally, but must first accept themselves internally. Psychological imbalances such as depression can also prevent one from obtaining self-esteem on both levels.

AESTHETIC NEEDS

The motivation to realise one's own maximum potential and possibilities is considered to be the master motive or the only real motive, all other motives being its various forms. In Maslow's hierarchy of needs, the need for self-actualization is the final need that manifests when lower level needs have been satisfied.

SELF-TRANSCENDENCE

Near the end of his life Maslow revealed that there was a level on the hierarchy that was above self-actualization: self-transcendence. "[Transcenders] may be said to be much more often aware of the realm of Being (B-realm and B-cognition), to be living at the level of Being... to have unitive consciousness and "plateau experience" (serene and contemplative B-cognitions rather than climactic ones) ... and to have or to have had peak experience (mystic, sacral, ecstatic) with illuminations or insights. Analysis of reality or cognitions which changed their view of the world and of themselves, perhaps occasionally, perhaps as a usual thing."

SUCCESS OF OFFSPRING

He stated that the achievements and success of his offspring were more satisfying than the personal fulfillment and growth characterized in self-actualization.

MARKETING

Maslow's hierarchy is often one of the first theories taught to marketing students as a basis for understanding consumers' motives for action.

Marketers have historically looked towards consumers' needs to define their actions in the market. By designing a product that meets a consumers' needs, they will more often choose that product than a competitor.

Whichever product better fulfills this void, will be chosen

more frequently, thus increasing sales. This makes the model relevant to Transpersonal business studies.

CRITICISMS

While Maslow's theory was regarded as an improvement over previous theories of personality and motivation, it had its detractors. For example, in their extensive review of research which is dependent on Maslow's theory, Wahba and Bridgewell found little evidence for the ranking of needs Maslow described, or even for the existence of a definite hierarchy at all.

Conducted in 2002, a recent study forwards this line of thought, claiming that "the hierarchy of needs is nothing more than a fool's daydream; there is no possible way to classify ever-changing needs as society changes." Chilean economist and philosopher Manfred Max Neef has also argued fundamental human needs are non-hierarchical, and are ontologically universal and invariant in nature - part of the condition of being human; poverty, he argues, is the result of any one of these needs being frustrated, denied or unfulfilled.

MCCLELLAND: ACHIEVEMENT MOTIVATION

McClelland said that most people possess and exhibit a combination of these characteristics. Some people exhibit a strong bias to a particular motivational need, and this motivational or needs 'mix' consequently affects their behaviour and working/managing style. Mcclelland suggested that a strong n-affil 'affiliation-motivation' undermines a manager's objectivity, because of their need to be liked, and that this affects a manager's decision-making capability.

A strong n-pow 'authority-motivation' will produce a determined work ethic and commitment to the organisation, and while n-pow people are attracted to the leadership role, they may not possess the required flexibility and people-centred skills. McClelland argues that n-ach people with strong 'achievement motivation' make the best leaders, although there can be a tendency to demand too much of their staff in the belief that they are all similarly and *highly* achievement-focused and results driven, which of course most people are not. McClelland's particular fascination was for achievement motivation, and this laboratory experiment illustrates one aspect of his theory about the affect of achievement on people's motivation. McClelland asserted via this experiment that while most people do not possess a strong achievement-based motivation, those who do, display a consistent behaviour in setting goals:

Volunteers were asked to throw rings over pegs rather like the fairground game; no distance was stipulated, and most people seemed to throw from arbitrary, random distances, sometimes close, sometimes farther away. However a small group of volunteers, whom McClelland suggested were strongly achievement-motivated, took some care to measure and test distances to produce an ideal challenge - not too easy, and not impossible.

Interestingly a parallel exists in biology, known as the 'overload principle', which is commonly applied to fitness and exercising, ie., in order to develop fitness and/or strength the exercise must be sufficiently demanding to increase existing levels, but not so demanding as to cause damage or strain. McClelland identified the same need for a 'balanced challenge' in the approach of achievement-motivated people.

McClelland contrasted achievement-motivated people with gamblers, and dispelled a common pre-conception that n-ach 'achievement-motivated' people are big risk takers. On the contrary - typically, achievement-motivated individuals set goals which they can influence with their effort and ability, and as such the goal is considered to be achievable. This determined results-driven approach is almost invariably present in the character make-up of all successful business people and entrepreneurs.

McClelland suggested other characteristics and attitudes of achievement-motivated people:

- Achievement is more important than material or financial reward.
- Achieving the aim or task gives greater personal satisfaction than receiving praise or recognition.

- Financial reward is regarded as a measurement of success, not an end in itself.
- Security is not prime motivator, nor is status.
- Feedback is essential, because it enables measurement of success, not for reasons of praise or recognition (the implication here is that feedback must be reliable, quantifiable and factual).
- Achievement-motivated people constantly seek improvements and ways of doing things better.
- Achievement-motivated people will logically favour jobs and responsibilities that naturally satisfy their needs, ie offer flexibility and opportunity to set and achieve goals, eg., sales and business management, and entrepreneurial roles.

McClelland firmly believed that achievement-motivated people are generally the ones who make things happen and get results, and that this extends to getting results through the organisation of other people and resources, although as stated earlier, they often demand too much of their staff because they prioritise achieving the goal above the many varied interests and needs of their people.

Interesting comparisons and relationships can be drawn between McClelland's motivation types, and the characteristics defined in other behavioural models, eg:

John Adair's Action-Centred Leadership model: Achievement-motivated managers are firmly focused on the Task, often to the detriment of the Individual and the Team. Affiliation-motivation people are Team and Individual centred.

Katherine Benziger'sThinking Styles model: Achievement-motivation is a double-frontal brain mode style; affiliation-motivation is right basal (rear); authority-motivation is arguably left basal (rear).

DISC (Inscape, Thomas International, etc) system: Achievement-motivated people are 'D' profiles - results-driven, decisive, dominant, etc. Affiliation-motivated people are I (proactive) and S (reactive) profiles.

Hersey/Blanchard's Situational Leadership® model:

Achievement-motivated people tend to favour the styles of the first and second modes ('telling' and 'selling'); affiliation-motivated people tend to favour the third mode ('participating'); and the authority-motivated people tend to favour the style of mode four ('delegating').

McGregor XY Theory: Achievement-motivated people tend towards X-Theory style, due to their high task focus; there are plenty of exceptions however, and training definitely helps the n-ach manager to see the value of employing Theory Y style. n-pow managers are definitely Theory X. n-affil are typically Theory Y and if not can relatively easily be trained to be so.

Herzberg motivators and hygiene factors: n-ach people are more responsive to the Herzberg motivators (especially achievement obviously) than n-affil and n-pow people.

CARL ROGERS: SELF- THEORY

Since the study of personality began, personality theories have offered a wide variety of explanations for behaviour and what constitutes the person. This essay offers a closer look at the humanistic personality theory of Carl Rogers. Rogers' theory of personality evolved out of his work as a clinical psychologist and developed as an offshoot of his theory of client-centered (later called person-centered) therapy. He was first and foremost a therapist, with an abiding respect for the dignity of persons and an interest in persons as subjects rather than objects. Rogers approach to the study of persons is phenomenological and idiographic. His view of human behaviour is that it is "exquisitely rational". Furthermore, in his opinion: "the core of man's nature is essentially positive", and he is a "trustworthy organism". These beliefs are reflected in his theory of personality.

To examine this theory more closely, a summary of the key features follows, with subsequent exploration of Rogers' view of self, his view of the human condition and his rationale for improvement of this condition. A brief overall assessment will conclude the discussion. While Rogers' humanistic conception of personality has both strengths and weaknesses, it is a valuable contribution to the study of persons, recognizing agency, free will and the importance of the self.

ACTUALIZING TENDENCY

Rogers (1959) maintains that the human "organism" has an underlying "actualizing tendency", which aims to develop all capacities in ways that maintain or enhance the organism and move it toward autonomy. This tendency is directional, constructive and present in all living things. The actualizing tendency can be suppressed but can never be destroyed without the destruction of the organism.

The concept of the actualizing tendency is the only motive force in the theory. It encompasses all motivations; tension, need, or drive reductions; and creative as well as pleasure-seeking tendencies. Only the organism as a whole has this tendency, parts of it (such as the self) do not. Maddi (1996) describes it as a "biological pressure to fulfill the genetic blueprint". Each person thus has a fundamental mandate to fulfill their potential.

SELF

The human organism's "phenomenal field" includes all experiences available at a given moment, both conscious and unconscious. As development occurs, a portion of this field becomes differentiated and this becomes the person's "self". The "self" is a central construct in this theory. It develops through interactions with others and involves awareness of being and functioning. The self-concept is "the organized set of characteristics that the individual perceives as peculiar to himself/herself". It is based largely on the social evaluations he/she has experienced.

SELF-ACTUALIZING TENDENCY

A distinctly psychological form of the actualizing tendency related to this "self" is the "self-actualizing tendency". It involves the actualization of that portion of experience symbolized in the self. It can be seen as a push to experience oneself in a way that is consistent with one's conscious view of what one is. Connected to the development of the self-concept and self-actualization are secondary needs (assumed to likely be learned in childhood): the "need for positive regard from others" and "the need for positive self-regard", an internalized version of the previous. These lead to the favoring of behaviour that is consistent with the person's self-concept.

ORGANISMIC VALUING AND CONDITIONS OF WORTH

When significant others in the person's world (usually parents) provide positive regard that is conditional, rather than unconditional, the person introjects the desired values, making them his/her own, and acquires "conditions of worth". The self-concept then becomes based on these standards of value rather than on organismic evaluation. These conditions of worth disturb the "organismic valuing process", which is a fluid, ongoing process whereby experiences are accurately symbolized and valued according to optimal enhancement of the organism and self.

The need for positive self-regard leads to a selective perception of experience in terms of the conditions of worth that now exist. Those experiences in accordance with these conditions are perceived and symbolized accurately in awareness, while those that are not are distorted or denied into awareness. This leads to an "incongruence" between the self as perceived and the actual experience of the organism, resulting in possible confusion, tension, and maladaptive behaviour. Such estrangement is the common human condition. Experiences can be perceived as threatening without conscious awareness via "subception", a form of discrimination without awareness that can result in anxiety.

FULLY FUNCTIONING PERSON AND THE SELF

Theoretically, an individual may develop optimally and avoid the previously described outcomes if they experience only "unconditional positive regard" and no conditions of worth develop. The needs for positive regard from others and positive self-regard would match organismic evaluation and there would be congruence between self and experience, with full psychological adjustment as a result. This ideal human condition is embodied in the "fully functioning person" who is open to experience able to live existentially, is trusting in his/her own organism, expresses feelings freely, acts independently, is creative and lives a richer life; "the good life".

It should be noted that; "The good life is a *process* not a state of being. It is a direction, not a destination". For the vast majority of persons who do not have an optimal childhood there is hope for change and development toward psychological maturity via therapy, in which the aim is to dissolve the conditions of worth, achieve a self congruent with experience and restore the organismic valuing process. In Rogers' view personality change is certainly possible and is further a necessary part of growth. However, he notes that self-acceptance is a prerequisite (1961). Rogers originally failed to recognize the importance of "self". When he began his work he had the "settled notion that the "self" was a vague, ambiguous, scientifically meaningless term which had gone out of the psychologist's vocabulary with the departure of the introspectionists".

However, through his work with clients he came to appreciate the importance of self. The "self" is described as:

the organized, consistent, conceptual gestalt composed of perceptions of the characteristics of the "I" or "me" and the perceptions of the relationships of the "I" or "me" to others and to various aspects of life, together with the values attached to these perceptions.

This gestalt is a fluid and changing process, available to awareness. By using the term "gestalt", Rogers points to the possibility of change describing it as "a configuration in which the alteration of one minor aspect could possibly alter the whole picture".

Rogers' conception of self is rather broad. He does describe a variation of self: the "ideal self" which denotes the self-concept the individual would most like to possess, but other explicit variations are not offered. Similarly, specific concepts related to identity and identity development are missing, although the self image is certainly revisable and undergoes change over the lifespan. Exactly when the differentiation of phenomenal field into self occurs is also not specified. Rogers concept of self-actualization is specifically related to the self and is thus different from Goldstein's use of the term (which matches the actualizing tendency) and also different from Maslow's which appears to incorporate both tendencies in one.

The actualizing tendency is fundamental to this theory. Rogers considers it "the most profound truth about man". He finds strong biological support for this tendency in many varied organisms. Rogers' conception of an active forward thrust is a huge departure from the beliefs of Freud and others who posit an aim for tension reduction, equilibrium, or homeostasis. Rogers (1977) notes that sensory deprivation studies support this concept as the absence of external stimuli leads to a flood of internal stimuli, not equilibrium.

While the idea of an actualizing tendency makes sense, Rogers never specifies what some of the inherent capacities that maintain and enhance life might be. Perhaps it is because doing so might violate Rogers' "intuitive sense of human freedom". Maddi further suggests that the belief in inherent potentialities may lie in this theory's position as an offshoot of psychotherapy where it is useful for both client and therapist to have a belief in unlimited possibilities. However, applying this idea to all human beings in a theory of personality sets up the logical requirement of precision regarding what the potentialities might be. The inherent potentialities of the actualizing tendency can suffer distorted expression when maladjustment occurs, resulting in behaviour destructive to oneself and others.

The actualization and self-actualization tendencies can be at cross purposes with each other when alienation from the true self occurs, so there is organismic movement in one direction and conscious struggle in another. Rogers (1977) revised his previous thinking concerning this incongruence, stating that while he earlier saw the rift between self and experience as natural, while unfortunate, he now believes society, (particularly Western culture), culturally conditions, rewards and reinforces behaviors that are "perversions of the unitary actualizing tendency." We do not come into the world estranged from ourselves, socialization is behind this alienation. Rogers (1961) finds the human infant to actually be a model of congruence. He/she is seen as completely genuine and integrated, unified in experience, awareness and communication. Distorted perceptions from conditions of worth cause our departure from this integration.

There is some empirical support for the hypothesis that congruence between self and experience leads to better personality adjustment and less defensiveness. Some research has also tended to support the idea of changes in self-concept occurring as a result of therapy. However, Maddi (1996) raises and interesting point regarding such studies. While it has been found that self-descriptions move toward ideals after counseling and one would assume the closer a person is to full functioning the smaller the discrepancy would be, statements of ideals may be operational representations of conditions of worth, which are socially imposed. Conditions of worth are to be dissolved rather than moved toward for full functioning in this theory! While Rogers sees the common human condition as one of incongruence between self and experience, this does not minimize his ultimate belief in the autonomy of human beings. Rogers sees the human being as: "capable of evaluating the outer and inner situation, understanding herself in its context, making constructive choices as to the next steps in life, and acting on those choices". This illustrates a belief in agency and free will.

While humans behave rationally, Rogers maintains that: "The tragedy for most of us is that our defenses keep us from being aware of this rationality so that we are consciously moving in one direction, while organismically we are moving in another." Unlike Freud, Rogers did not see conflict as inevitable and humans as basically destructive. It is only when "man is less than fully man", not functioning freely, that he is to be feared. The human capacity for awareness and the ability to symbolize gives us enormous power, but this awareness is a double-edged phenomenon : undistorted awareness can lead to full functioning and a rich life, while distortions in awareness lead to maladjustment and a multitude of destructive behaviors.

The "maladjusted person" is the polar opposite of the fully functioning individual (who was introduced early in this essay). The maladjusted individual is defensive, maintains rather than enhances his/her life, lives according to a preconceived plan, feels manipulated rather than free, and is common and conforming rather than creative. The fully functioning person, in contrast, is completely defence-free, open to experience, creative and able to live "the good life". Empirical support for the fully functioning person is somewhat mixed. The openness to experience characteristic has been supported. However, some studies have found that openness to experience and organismic trusting did not intercorrelate, contrary to expectations. Ryckmann (1993) notes that some studies have found non-defensive people are more accepting of others and Maddi (1996) cites numerous studies that indicate self-accepting people also appear to be more accepting of others.

It is somewhat puzzling given his humanistic emphasis on individuality, that Rogers describes only two extremes of people. Maddi (1996) suggests these extreme characterizations of only two types may be due to this personality theory being secondary to a theory of therapy. It is appropriate for a theory of psychotherapy to concern itself with the two extremes of fullest functioning and maladjustment. However, when theorizing about all people, two types are insufficient. Carl Rogers was most interested in improving the human condition and applying his ideas. His person-centered therapy may well be his most influential contribution to psychology. Rogers' pervasive interest in therapy is what clearly differentiates him from Maslow, despite some similarities in their ideas. The person-centered approach has had impact on domains outside of therapy such as family life, education, leadership, conflict resolution, politics and community health. Rogers greatest contribution may lie in his encouraging a humane and ethical treatment of persons, approaching psychology as a human science rather than a natural science.

LEVELS OF ASPIRATION AND ITS PSYCHOLOGICAL IMPLICATIONS

It is rare to find an educational mission statement today absent of some reference to student aspirations. Indeed, educators have long recognized the value of students who set ambitious goals, and who are inspired in the present to progress toward those goals. It is expected that students who set challenging goals learn to become task-oriented, feel a sense of purpose, and learn more. It is no surprise, then, that raising the aspirations of students is a universal priority. As with any social construct (e.g., achievement, anxiety), the term aspirations lends itself to a variety of definitions and interpretations. Does it refer to goals, expectations, or dreams? Intentions? Performance motivation? Should aspirations be viewed from a short term or long term perspective (or both)? Is it a general, overall measure or context-specific? Is it a value-laden or value-neutral concept?

For example, if one aspires to be an accomplished thief, is there a judgment to be made whether this is a good or bad thing? Clearly, "aspirations" embodies several different meanings, and thus deserves clarification. The construct of aspirations finds its origins in the experimental research on "level of aspiration" conducted in the early 1930s. Although work in this area contributed to our understanding of human behaviour, many of the findings were produced from "within the laboratory" and thus had few implications for students or schools. Research in level of aspiration faded in the late 1950s and achievement motivation emerged as a dominant theory of motivation. The motive to set goals and succeed at reaching those goals appears to be an acquired trait, one susceptible to intervention.

Lastly, social comparison theory indicates that within groups there are pressures toward uniformity. Given this phenomenon, it is not unreasonable to assume that the aspirations of students are influenced by standards implicitly or explicitly set by the school and/or peers. It is our belief that a definition of aspirations must be contextualized, and further, that it should address both present and future perspectives. For these reasons we hypothesize that a student with aspirations is one who is involved in various activities for both their inherent value and enjoyment and their connection to future goals.

LEVEL OF ASPIRATION

The concept of "level of aspiration" was first noted by Dembo (1931/1976) in an experiment designed to investigate anger. In an effort to evoke frustration and anger, subjects were asked to engage in tasks that were either very difficult or impossible to perform. An unintended consequence of the experiment was that subjects formulated their own, medial aim when the original objective was too difficult to attain. This transitional goal, although relatively easier to accomplish, represented a step toward the more challenging objective. Dembo called this intermediate goal the subject's "momentary level of aspiration". Early level of aspiration experiments explored the conditions for success and failure experiences.

In those instances, success and failure experiences were inferred from the general behaviour of the subjects. The next 2 decades witnessed investigations designed to quantify, for a given task, the levels at which individuals intended to perform. The attempt to operationalize the concept of aspirations was made through the quantification of such measures as height, rigidity/mobility, and responsiveness. These all represented specific goal-setting behaviors, such as the number of times the level of aspiration moved in the same direction as the preceding performance (i.e., responsiveness). In 1931 the first major psychological experiment related to level of aspiration was conducted by Hoppe.

He examined factors that influenced goal-setting behaviour by measuring the effect of success and failure on individuals' decisions to raise or lower their level of aspiration.

Hoppe assessed individuals' aspiration level on the basis of three criteria: (1) the spontaneous remarks of the subject, (2) the occurrence of success and failure experiences, and (3) the way in which the subject "goes at" the task. Hoppe's research introduced the notion that experiences of success and failure were indicative of intermediate goal attainment. Specifically, a success experience is conditional upon a performance that exceeds the momentary level of aspiration.

And, conversely, a failure experience results when the performance falls below the intermediate objective. Hoppe concluded that "the experience of a performance as a success or failure does not depend alone on its objective goodness, but on whether the level of aspiration appears to be reached or not reached". Also among Hoppe's findings was that individuals' level of aspiration exhibited a lack of stability during the course of an activity, and that there appeared to be disparities among individuals in terms of their level of aspiration: Such differences, he thought, were suggestive of personality differences in the areas of ambition, prudence, courage, and self-confidence.

Like other researchers during this time, Hoppe defined level of aspiration within the context of a specific task. He construed level of aspiration to be the "totality of ... expectations or aspiration for the future performance achievement of a person, a totality which shifts after each achievement, and which is sometimes vague and sometimes precise". It was generally recognized that Hoppe's technique of measuring aspiration level lacked the degree of objectivity and validity called for by experimental research standards.

In response, Jucknat (1937) proposed a less subjective measure. He required subjects to choose among a series of progressively difficult tasks (mazes). Although this design was thought to offer a more objective indicator of level of aspiration, it was not immune to social bias. Subjects were asked to reveal their intended performance on some task in the presence of the researcher, which clouded their "true" intentions. Attempts to develop even more precise measures of level of aspiration were undertaken. Prior experiments had required subjects to reveal their intended performance on one dimensional, rarely executed tasks without the knowledge of how they would perform.

Frank asked subjects how well they intended to do on a task after telling them how they did on the previous trial (e.g., how well in relation to others, how well without references to others, and so on). This shift in methodology in a sense re-defined the construct of level of aspiration. Frank described level of aspiration as "the level of future performance in a familiar task which an individual, knowing his level of past performance in that task, explicitly undertakes to reach".

Later, Frank reported that the relation of level of aspiration to the level of past performance "at any time depends primarily on the relative strength of the following three needs:

- The need to keep the level of aspiration as high as possible (i.e., above the level of past performance),
- The need to make the level of aspiration approximate the level of future performance, and
- The need to avoid failure, where failure is defined as a level of performance below the level of aspiration (this need tends to drive the level of aspiration below the level of past performance).

Further, both environmental and personal facts appeared to affect the relative strength of these three needs. Such personal factors, he postulated, could partially explain the degree and direction of the difference between level of aspiration and performance. Four profiles were delineated:

- The person who tends to keep "his feet on the ground" would demonstrate the need to maintain a level of aspiration close to his level of past performance,
- The person with his "head in the clouds" would hold his level of aspiration to unrealistically high levels,
- The "cautious" per- son would keep his aspiration level below his level of past performance and
- The "ambitious" individual would consistently set his level of aspiration at reasonably high levels.

Frank (1935b) also identified two psychological

determinants of the level of aspiration. The first is the desire to avoid failure, or the need to keep the aspiration level below the level of past performance. The second, and more prevalent, is the need to maintain a high aspiration level irrespective of performance. The ego-level, as defined by Hoppe (1931/1976), underlies these two needs. Hoppe described the ego-level as the "wide-embracing goals of the person which extend far beyond the single tasks ... [and] are related to the self-regard."

In other words, people desire to do well, not only for the sake of doing well, but to enhance their social status. The desire to avoid failure and the need to keep aspirations unrealistically high are thus mediated by the ego-level. During the 1940s the definition of level of aspiration underwent further refinement. While still regarded as "the level of future performance in a familiar task which an individual explicitly undertakes to reach" the notion that culture played a role emerged. Indeed, comparisons of the adequacy of performance to the task were supplemented by references to the performance of the group.

Success and failure experiences were manifest through the social environment. Frank (1941) found that level of aspiration may take on different meanings, depending upon contextual and individual factors. Two mechanisms through which level of aspiration moderates behaviour were proposed. First, it may be used as an incentive to improve performance. This can occur in two ways: a level of aspiration that is above the level of past performance can provide a goal to strive toward, or, a level of aspiration that is lower than past performance can reduce tension/performance anxiety, both of which presumably foster high(er) levels of achievement.

Second, keeping the level of aspiration (unreasonably) high can serve to protect the ego from the effects of failure. Poor performance relative to the goal is deemed insignificant (by others and by the individual), not taken seriously, thus preserving self-esteem. Ultimately, Frank (1941) viewed level of aspiration as the "final integration of complex and constantly shifting personal and situational factors." Some of these factors have been identified in the literature. For instance, the level of aspiration situation was thought to pose a threat to self- esteem. To deal with this perceived threat, individuals employ two strategies: they try to do well and they manipulate their level of aspiration.

In this sense, level of aspiration characterized "a compromise between the subject's evaluation of his ability with respect to the difficulty of the task and his desire to achieve a high level of performance-that is, between a judgment and a goal". Level of aspiration experiments has significantly contributed to subsequent interpretations of the concept of aspirations; however, they were of limited scope and direction. Numerous investigations during that era attempted to quantify aspiration level by engaging subjects in a variety of tasks and questioning them in a multitude of ways as to their intended performance.

Frank (1941) recognized that statistical analyses of this nature were "clearly too superficial to cast much light on the dynamics of the level of aspiration." He reported that the "significance of [these] studies of the level of aspiration lies in their demonstration of a promising experimental approach to problems of success and failure, of the formation of goals, and the genesis of the 'self' and its relations to personality structure, achievement, and the social environment." Social and cultural factors undoubtedly influence level of aspiration. Studies that attempted to tease out group effects revealed an interesting trend: the tendency among members to aspire to the collective level of aspiration of the group.

Achievement Motivation During the late I940s, as interest in level of aspiration research waned, achievement motivation emerged as an established theory of motivation. Achievement motivation can be defined as the conscious or unconscious drive to do well in an achievement-oriented activity. The 1950s and 1960s were known as the "Golden Age" of achievement motivation research. Research in achievement motivation addressed a variety of areas. McClelland focused on the social origins of achievement motivation and its role in economic development (e.g., cross-cultured studies).

Atkinson and his colleagues created several quantitative models designed to predict behaviour in success and failure situations. The past two decades have seen cognitive-based frameworks being applied to explain the drive to achieve (e.g., locus of control, attribution theory). Although McClelland and Atkinson (1949) were largely responsible for the development of the theory of achievement motivation, they were heavily influenced by Murray's (1938) research on personality. According to Murray, human behaviour is essentially goal-directed, and the most important information to know about a person is the direction and intensity of his or her aspirations. Murray identified a two-tiered list of human needs that account for behaviour.

Among his list of secondary needs, or those needs acquired and modified during socialization, is the desire to achieve. Considerable evidence suggests that achievement motivation is an acquired trait, one that is formed at an early age and remains constant over time. Nonetheless, McClelland (978) showed that achievement motivation can be distended. He compared a group of businessmen from a small community in India that underwent achievement motivation training to an analogous group. Over a 2- year period the experimental group created more new businesses and registered over twice as many employees as the control group. Kolb (1965) conducted a related study with underachieving male students from a variety of socioeconomic backgrounds.

He found that school grades improved for all groups; however, the lower- class students did not maintain these higher achievement levels. This was interpreted to suggest that achievement motivation is a product of the social environment. Individuals high and low in achievement motivation appear to differ in a number of ways. On complex tasks, those high in achievement motivation start at the same level as those with low achievement motivation but do progressively better as they proceed. Persons high in achievement motivation prefer activities of moderate difficulty, whereas those low in achievement motivation choose tasks of either extreme difficulty or easiness.

Mahone (1960) and Morris (1966) reported that students high in a measure of achievement motivation selected occupations commensurate with their level of ability while students who exhibited fear of failure tendencies did not. The expectations and standards of the group significantly impact the aspirations of its members regardless of their level of achievement motivation. In other words, the aspiration level of individual group members is buoyed by the prevailing group standard. Thus, even those with an inner drive to achieve limit their accomplishments to the success level of the group; they fear being ostracized or alienated from the group.

This tendency toward uniformity is more pronounced the more isolated the culture. Social Comparison Theory Within a particular culture there is an inherent pressure toward uniformity. Festinger (l942/1989b) explicated his social comparison theory via nine hypotheses. The first four are addressed here. People have a need to assess their beliefs and level of ability. When objective evidence is largely absent, people tend to use others of similar ability and opinion as a source of comparison. There is a general desire to improve one's ability (i.e., get better at something), but one cannot improve one's beliefs. Efforts to reach agreement are based primarily on pressures toward uniformity, and this can run counter to attempts to achieve.

The result is that group members strive to do well but only proximally better than the members of the group. Social comparison theory can help explain individual differences in level of aspiration. The group serves as a powerful anchor that limits the level of aspiration, particularly when the group is cut off from other groups ... [people tend to use others who are similar or have similar levels of abilities as a source of social comparison. The threat of ostracism tends to restrict the performance of those with high ability, and performance levels are typically anchored somewhere around the mean.

Although related, achievement motivation and level of aspiration do not represent exactly the same concept. Level of aspiration typically refers to the task-specific assessment of the degree to which an individual intends to perform, with reference to past performance and social milieu. It is more an effect or result. Achievement motivation can affect level of aspiration, and influence how we think and process information. It is a cause as well as a trait. Moreover, achievement motivation emphasizes the interaction between stable personality factors and transient environmental influences.

It serves to explain the goal-directed behaviour of individuals with respect to their motives, expectations about the consequences of their actions, and values placed on the expected consequences. The Hypothesis Using prior research on aspirations, achievement motivation, and social comparison theory as a basis, we suggest an integrated schema for conceptualizing aspirations. Aspirations can be defined as a student's ability to identify and set goals for the future, while being inspired in the present to work toward those goals. This construct of aspirations has two major underpinnings: inspiration and ambitions. Inspiration reflects that an activity is exciting and enjoyable to the individual and the awareness of being fully and richly involved in life here and now. It is depicted by an individual who becomes involved in an activity for its intrinsic value and enjoyment.

An individual with a high level of inspiration is one who believes an activity is useful and enjoyable. Ambitions represent the perception that an activity is important as a means to future goals. It reflects individuals' perceptions that it is both possible and desirable to think in future terms and to plan for the future. This way of viewing student aspirations is unique in that it combines the motivational components of the present (inspiration) with the future (ambitions). Individuals' perceptions may reflect only one of the dimensions, however. For example, some students may be thoroughly engaged in activities in the present, but have no future goals nor see their value.

In contrast, other students may set long term goals yet do little or nothing in the present to accomplish those future goals. Ideally-and by our definition-an individual with aspirations must exhibit behavioral traits reflective of both ambitions and inspiration. That is, they must have the ability to identify and set goals for the future while being motivated in the present to progress toward those goals. Moreover, the inspiration and ambitions dimensions occur within particular contexts, and as such are subject to varying value judgments. For example, if someone's goal is to be a wealthy drug dealer and this individual is currently inspired to sell drugs to one's peers for a substantial income, by our definition this person could be characterized as someone with aspirations.

Obviously, this is not the intent of schools who promote student aspirations. Therefore, it is imperative as we define aspirations we do not look at this concept void of cultural differences and expectations. Although our work began with its focus on educational goals, through our historical analysis and experience in schools, we see the concept of aspirations being played out in virtually all arenas of personal growth. Specifically, aspirations can and must be recognized not only with respect to educational attainments, but vocational and perhaps, most importantly, quality of life issues as well.

Implications for Students and Schools The inspiration/ ambitions conceptual design of aspirations has implications for students and schools. This manner of perceiving student aspirations takes into account the interaction of the students in their environment. It forces educators and researchers to answer the questions: How does school climate influence student aspirations? What conditions, if any, appear to effect changes in the way students view the work they do in school and the goals they set for their future?

Such questions lead to the need to identify the conditions in school which will affect the student's ability to think about the future, while at the same time being inspired in the present. McClelland's work on achievement motivation has provided evidence that the drive to achieve is acquired and subject to certain influence. He showed that the achievement motivation and hence achievement levels of groups could be raised. Perhaps the drive to achieve (and to aspire) among school cultures and subcultures can be improved, which could lead to overall achievement gains.

Social comparison theory indicates that within groups there exist inherent pressures toward uniformity. Schools should be aware of this tendency and challenge it by fostering an environment that encourages diversity, excellence, and risk-taking among their students. Students who perform exceedingly well in an activity (i.e., better than everyone else) are put in a position where they are different from others. Educators can combat the tendency toward uniformity by making it acceptable for students to excel and aspire to try different things. While schools are in a position to help foster aspirations, students are not absolved of all responsibility.

To the contrary, students must take responsibility and be held accountable for their present and future situations. They, too, have to speak out and work with educators to create an environment that promotes empowerment, a sense of belonging, sensible risk-taking opportunities, and engaging activities. Implications for Research We have presented a new manner in which to perceive the construct of aspirations. Prior research, adhering to the framework described above, our field research, and anecdotal evidence have logically lead to this theoretical perspective.

We iterate that it is currently an hypothesis. Further research must be invested to confirm or disconfirm its validity. There are many questions to be answered. Among them, are there indications that students who set future goals and who are motivated in the present to achieve those goals "better off?" And if so, are there distinct properties of goals (in terms of their specificity, level of difficulty, and proximity) that appear to align themselves more than others regarding our definition of students' aspirations? The early research helped us understand aspirations as an expression of the desire to achieve and improve.

We have drawn and learned from two key areas of research. Level of aspiration research has shown that aspirations are qualified by the nature of the activity or goal, by experiences of success and failure, and by social pressures to aim high and do well. Measuring the intention to do or be something is scarcely amenable to the mechanistic process of quantification. To be sure, measuring a "true" aspiration level is an inexact, if not possible, task. This is hardly surprising when one considers the dynamic nature and vast complexities underlying human behaviour. Research in achievement motivation has contributed through its identification of the trait to want to achieve and through its illumination that such a trait can be acquired and modified.

Moreover, achievement motivation of entire groups appears to be malleable. Given that people's inner drive to achieve influences their aspiration level, improvements in the former should lead to improvements in the latter. Assuming that students' aspirations can be impacted in some way, and assuming that the best way to go about that is to do so indirectly via changes in whole group aspirations, there are enormous implications for schools (e.g., create an environment which fosters aspirations). Finally, social comparison theory has taught us that cultural standards bear upon individuals' expectations. Group pressures toward uniformity place a ceiling on performance (and perhaps aspirations).

Schools can learn from and challenge this tendency. For a child to dream is such a heralded notion. But how often do we as educators encourage students to dream yet overlook what it will take in the present to realise those dreams? Likewise, how often do we become so concerned with the present that we ignore the future? To neglect the present is to sabotage the future. We propose a view of aspirations that incorporates both the present and the future. It emphasizes the need for individuals to look at what they are doing now and recognize its relevance to their future. Only then, we suggest, do they truly have aspirations.

Unit V

Cognitive Processes

THINKING

Thought and thinking are mental forms and processes, respectively ("thought" is both). Thinking allows beings to model the world and to deal with it according to their objectives, plans, ends and desires. Words referring to similar concepts and processes include cognition, sentience, consciousness, idea, and imagination. *Thinking* involves the mental manipulation of information, as when we form concepts, engage in problem solving, reason and make decisions. Thinking is a higher cognitive function and the analysis of thinking processes is part of cognitive psychology.

BASIC PROCESS

The basic mechanics of human brain cells reflect a process of pattern matching or rather recognition. In a "moment of reflection", new situations and new experiences are judged against recalled ones and judgements are made. In order to make these judgements, the intellect maintains present experience and sorts relevant past experience. It does this while keeping present and past experience distinct and separate. The intellect can mix, match, merge, sift, and sort concepts, perceptions, and experience. This process is called reasoning. Logic is the science of reasoning. The awareness of this process of reasoning is access consciousness. Thinking is not merely a process occurring in animals and humans. AI (artificial intelligence) focuses on machine thinking.

Aids to thinking:

- Use of models, symbols, diagrams and pictures.
- Use of abstraction to simplify the effort of thinking.
- Use of metasyntactic variables to simplify the effort of naming.
- Use of iteration and recursion to converge on a concept.
- Limitation of attention to aid concentration and focus on a concept. Use of peace and quiet to aid concentration.
- Goal setting and goal revision. Simply letting the concept percolate in the subconscious, and waiting for the concept to re-surface.
- Talking with like-minded people. Resorting to communication with others.
- Working backward from the goal.
- Desire for learning.

BASIC ELEMENTS OF THOUGHT: CONCEPTS, PROPOSITIONS, IMAGES

It is difficult to find in the writings of Plato or Aristotle a clear endorsement of propositions in our sense. Plato's most challenging discussions of falsehood, in *Theaetetus* (187c-200d) and *Sophist*, focus on the puzzle (well-known to Plato's contemporaries) of how false belief could have an object at all. Thinking that Theaetetus flies would seem to require thinking the non-existent flying Theaetetus. Were Plato a propositionalist, we might expect to find Socrates or the Eleactic Stranger proposing that false belief certainly has an object — in fact, the same sort of object as true belief — and that this object is the primary bearer of truth-value.

But it seems no such proposal is seriously considered. In both dialogues, it is suggested that thought is a kind of inward dialogue carried on in the mind itself (*Theaetetus* 189e-190a and *Sophist*263e), and that judgment results when the two inward voices affirm the same thing. Plato is standardly understood as explaining false belief (*doxa*) in terms of the assertion of a false statement (*logos*). But it is far from clear that he takes the objects of belief to be statements rather than simply the ordinary concrete objects (e.g., Theaetetus) and forms (e.g., *flying*) which the statement is about, and still less clear that he takes statements to be *sharable* between minds. Statements, for Plato, might simply be tokens of inner speech, as Nuchelmans suggests.

Aristotle expends great energy in investigating what in reality makes true statements true, but less investigating the nature of truth-bearers themselves. In his most significant discussions of truth and falsehood, he seems not to take a clear stand on the question of propositions. In *On Interpretation* 1 16a, for instance, Aristotle remarks that falsity and truth require combination and separation, whether of names and verbs in speech, or of elements in thought. However, it is unclear whether the resulting combination of thought elements is anything other than a token thought, as opposed to something which is the content of the token thought and which could be thought by others, could be denied, asserted, etc.

Arguably, the first employment in the western philosophical tradition of the notion of proposition, in roughly our sense, is found in the writings of the Stoics. In the third century B.C., Zeno and his followers, including Chrysippus especially, distinguished the material aspects of words from that which is said, or *lekta*. Among *lekta*, they distinguished the complete from incomplete (or deficient), the latter corresponding roughly to the meanings of predicates, the former to the meanings of sentences. Among complete *lekta* they included *axiomata*, or the meanings of declarative sentences. For the Stoics, only *axiomata*, and not the words used to articulate them, were properly said to be true or false. *Axiomata* were therefore the proper subject matter of Stoic logic.

Lekta posed a problem for Stoic materialism, according to which everything real is corporeal. For the Stoics, the real was limited to that which can act or be acted upon, and therefore to the bodily. *Lekta*, however, were thought to be incorporeal. Seneca explains:

For instance, I see Cato walking; the sense of sight reveals this to me and the mind believes it. What I see is a material object and it is to a material object that I direct my eyes and my mind. Then I say 'Cato is walking'. It is not a material object that I now state, but a certain affirmation about him... (Epistulae morales, 117, 13)

The notion of a proposition can also be found in the works of Medieval philosophers, including especially Abelard (1079-1142) and his followers, but also among later scholastic philosophers in England, including Adam Wodeham (d. 1358) and Walter Burleigh (1275-1344). Abelard distinguishes between *dicta* or what is said and acts of assertion (or thinking), the former being the fundamental bearers of truth-value. While Abelard himself seems to have had little to say about the nature or identity conditions of *dicta,* his successors took up the subject with vigour. Are *dicta* particular acts of thinking, concrete events or facts, or entities having the same sort of being as universals? Each of these views is considered and evaluated in the treatise *Ars Meliduna,* of unknown authorship.

A similar debate raged among the English scholastics in the fourteenth century. Against Ockham's nominalistic account, under which the object of assent is a complex token mental sentence, Adam Wodeham, for example, maintained that the object of assent is not any sort of mental entity, nor even a *thing* at all, properly speaking, nor of course a *nothing* but rather a *being the case.*

When we turn to the early modern period, it is not easy to find, at least in the writings of major philosophers, an unabashed assertion of the reality of propositions. Unsurprisingly, one looks in vain in the writings of the British empiricists. As for Descartes, particular acts of judgments serve as the primary bearers of truth-value (although there is considerable debate about the status of his eternal truths). Leibniz's *cogitato possibilis* have some of the characteristics of propositions. These *possible* thoughts seem to play the role of thought-contents and the fundamental bearers of truth-value. However, it is a matter of debate whether they are accorded real ontological status.

Propositionalists were by no means rare in the 19th century, Gottlob Frege being the best known example. The

Czech philosopher and mathematician Bernard Bolzano also deserves special mention. In his *Wissenschaftslehre*, or *Theory of Science*, published in 1837, he argued for the existence of what he called '*Sätze an sich*,' or sentences in themselves, which he clearly distinguished from linguistic items or mental phenomena. They are the fundamental bearers of truth and falsity, and the objects of the attitudes. It is the goal of every science, including mathematics, is to state the fundamental true sentences in themselves pertaining that subject matter. (This marks a clear departure from the psychologizing approaches of many of Bolzano's contemporaries.) Like Frege after him, Bolzano conceived of propositions as complexes composed of wholly abstract mind-independent constituents (*vorstellungen an sich*). Bolzano's work has had a profound influence on Husserlian phenomenology and the development of modern logic.

Arguably, the three figures whose work has most shaped the framework for contemporary Anglophone work on propositions are Gottlob Frege, G.E. Moore, and Bertrand Russell. We will give short summaries of their thought on the matter. In 1892, Frege published his classic paper "On Sense and Reference". This chapter contains his first formulation of the distinction between sense (*Sinn*) and reference (*Bedeutung*). Roughly speaking, the sense of an expression is the mode of presentation of its referent, or the cognitive value of its referent. Expressions were said to *express* their senses. Sentences, too, had both referents and senses, according to Frege. The referent of a sentence is its truth-value. Its sense is a thought, not a token thought, but a thought in the sense of a proposition: a sharable content. Thus, in Fregean jargon, meaningful sentences express thoughts.

Frege conceived of thoughts as structured complexes of senses. The thought expressed by 'The evening star is bright' consists of the sense of 'the evening star' and the sense of 'is bright'. (It should be noted that this claim about structure does not strictly follow from the fact that sense is compositional, i.e., that the sense of a whole is fixed by the senses of its constituent parts and their syntactic mode of arrangement.)

In his late masterpiece, "The Thought" (1922), Frege is explicit about the nature of thoughts. They are not part of the outer realm, which consists of those entities perceivable by the senses. This Frege thinks is obvious. Nor are they part of the inner realm, which consists of ideas. Unlike ideas, thoughts do not require an owner (i.e., they exist even if not present in any mind), and can be present to more than one mind. A third realm must be recognized, he tells us — a realm of abstract eternal entities which we can *grasp* by virtue of our power of thinking. However, Frege is explicit that thoughts do act:

Thoughts are not wholly unactual but their actuality is quite different from the actuality of things. And their action is brought about by a performance of a thinker; without this they would be inactive, at least as far as we can see. And yet the thinker does not create them but must take them as they are. They can be true without being grasped by a thinker; and they are not wholly unactual even then, at least if they *could* be grasped and so brought into action.

This is perhaps the *locus classicus* for platonism in the modern sense of that term, that is, for the doctrine that there exist mind-independent abstract entities. In their early writings, Russell and Moore endorse propositionalism. In his 1903 book *The Principles of Mathematics*, Russell affirms the existence of propositions, taking them to be complexes of ordinary concrete objects (the referents of words) rather than of Fregean senses. Propositions so conceived are now standardly called *Russellian*, and propositions conceived as complexes of senses or abstract entities are called *Fregean*. In his 1899 paper, "The Nature of Judgment," Moore affirms the existence of propositions, taking them to be broadly Fregean in nature (in particular as being complexes of mind-independent Platonic universals which he calls concepts).

Russell and Moore later grow suspicious of propositions (although Russell seems to have accepted them later as a kind of derived or immanent entity). Interestingly, Moore's thinking on the matter seems to have changed dramatically during the winter of 1910-11, as his published lectures *Some Main Problems of Philosophy* reveal. Before Christmas, Moore claims:

In the one case *what* is apprehended is the meaning of the words: Twice two are four; in the other case *what* is apprehended is the meaning of the words: Twice four are eight... Now by a proposition, I mean the sort of thing which is *apprehended* in these two cases.... I hope it is plain that there certainly are such things as propositions in this sense.

After Christmas, Moore is more skeptical. While the theory of propositions is admittedly simple and natural, there are good reasons to reject it. He specifies two problems, both having to do with *facts*, a topic he avoided in his earlier lectures. The first is that the theory of propositions suggests the "primitivist" theory of truth, previously held by Moore and also Russell, according to which truth is a simple unanalyzable property of propositions. Primitivism, Moore now claims, requires the claim that facts consist in the possession by a proposition of the simple property of truth. This Moore now finds unacceptable. The second problem is simply that the theory seems intuitively false:

...if you consider what happens when a man entertains a false belief, it doesn't seem as if his belief consisted merely in his having a relation to some object which certainly *is*. It seems rather as if the thing he was believing, the *object* of his belief, were just *the* fact which certainly is *not* — which certainly is not, because the belief is false.

Russell echoes similar sentiments in essays after *Principles*. In 1910 he writes that "we feel that there could be no falsehood if there were no minds to make mistakes", and in the 1918 he remarks that a person with "a vivid instinct as to what is real" cannot "suppose that there is a whole set of false propositions about ".

These doubts led Russell (1912) to propose a multiple relation theory of judgment, to replace the standard two-place relational theory. To use Russell's example, in judging that Desdemona loves Cassio, Othello stands, not in a binary relation to a proposition, but rather in a multiple or many-placed relation to Desdemona, loving, and Cassio. Othello's judgment is true when there is a fact of Desdemona loving Cassio and otherwise false. This theory, and its contemporary incarnations, is discussed in a supplementary document. Moore's doubts led him to postulate what appear to be merely possible facts as the objects of the propositional attitudes. When a subject believes that x is F and x is not F, the object of belief is the non-existent but possible fact that x is F.

ROLES FOR PROPOSITIONS: MODALITY

If there are propositions, they would appear to be good candidates for being the bearers of alethic modal properties (necessary and possible truth), as well as the relata of *entailment*. And if propositions stand in entailment relations, then there would seem to be maximal consistent sets of them. Prima facie, such sets seem to be good candidates for possible worlds (Adams 1974; 1981). A proposition will be true in a possible world (at a maximal consistent set of propositions) iff it is a member of that world.

If possible worlds are understood in this way, however, it is important to distinguish two meanings for talk of 'the actual world'. This may refer either to the totality of what exists, to what Lewis calls I and all my surroundings, or to the maximal consistent set which includes all the true propositions. The latter is part of I and all my surroundings, but only a proper part.

ROLES FOR PROPOSITIONS: SEMANTICS

The Relational Analysis

By our stipulation, 'proposition' is used to pick out the objects of the attitudes and the bearers of truth and falsity. One would therefore expect that if there are propositions, they would figure importantly in the semantics of attitude- and truth-ascriptions. One would expect, in particular, that in 'S believes that p', and in 'that p is true', the *that*-clauses would refer to propositions. One might doubt whether *that*-clauses could really *refer*, if reference is understood on the model of proper names. For, *that*-clauses are not proper names, nor are they noun phrases. Still, because propositions are the objects of the attitudes and the bearers of truth, mustn't they somehow be semantically associated with ascriptions of attitudes and of truth? Following Jeffrey King (2002), we will use the term 'designate' as a catch-all covering any sort of semantic association between a linguistic item and an entity. We follow standard terminology in using the word 'express' to pick out the relation between a predicate and the property which is its sense or semantic content. An attitude ascription '*S V*s that *p*' is true iff '*S*' designates a person who stands in the attitude relation expressed by '*V*' to the proposition designated by 'that *p*' (and false iff '*S*' designates a person who doesn't stand in such relation to such a proposition).

Analogously, there is the *Property Analysis* of truth-ascriptions:

'That *p* is true' or 'it is true that *p*' is true if the proposition designated by 'that *p*' has the property expressed by 'true'.

One of the great advantages of these analyses – the combination of which we will simply call *The Relational Analysis* – is the smooth explanation of the validity of certain inferences. Consider, for example:

Charles believes everything Thomas said.
Thomas said that cats purr.
So, Charles believes that cats purr.

Something Barbara asserted is true.
Nothing John denied is true.
So, something Barbara asserted John did not deny.

John believes that every even is the sum of two primes.
Goldbach's Conjecture is that every even is the sum of two primes.
So, John believes Goldbach's Conjecture.

These inferences are valid if they have the following simple logical forms:

For all *x* such that Thomas said *x*, Charlie believes *x*.
Thomas said *A*.
So, Charlie believes *A*.

Some *x* such that Barbara asserted *x* is true.
No *x* such that John denied *x* is true.
So, some *x* such that Barbara asserted *x* is such that John did not deny *x*.

MEANINGS OF SENTENCES

Propositions are also commonly treated as the meanings or, to use the more standard terminology, the *semantic contents* of sentences, and so are commonly taken to be central to semantics and the philosophy of language. However, there is room for doubt about whether propositions are the right sort of entity for the job. Here is why. Note that a sentence would appear to contribute the same content regardless of whether it occurs as a proper part of a larger sentence. So, a sentence such as 'in the past, Reagan was president' would seem to be true depending on whether the content of 'Reagan is president' is true at some past time. But this would seem to imply that this content must lack temporal qualification — that it can change in its truth-value over time.

Similarly, it seems there are locative sentential operators 'in Chicago, it is raining'. If so, then by a similar argument, it would seem that the content of 'it is raining' would have to lack spatial qualification. The problem is this: it seems *propositions,* being the objects of belief, cannot in general be spatially and temporally unqualified. Suppose that Smith, in London, looks out his window and forms the belief that it is raining. Suppose that Ramirez, in Madrid, relying on yesterday's weather report, awakens and forms the belief that it is raining, before looking out the window to see sunshine. What Smith believes is true, while what Ramirez believes is false. So they must not believe the same proposition. But if propositions were generally spatially unqualified, they would believe the same proposition. An analogous argument can be given to show that what is believed must not in general be temporally unqualified.

If these worries are well-taken, then the meanings or contents of sentences are not in general propositions. Appealing to recent work in linguistics, Jeffrey C. King (2003) presents evidence against one of the crucial assumptions of the above arguments, that there are no genuine locational or temporal operators in English. King claims that 'somewhere' and 'sometimes' are better regarded as quantifiers over locational and temporal entities (i.e., either locations or times themselves or locational or temporal properties of events). Thus, 'somewhere, it is raining' would have the logical form 'there is some location *L* such that it is raining at *L*'.

King further argues that tenses are best analyzed as quantifiers over times rather than temporal operators. 'John flunked chemistry', thus, would have the form 'there is some time *t* within *I* such that John flunks chemistry at *t*', where the interval *I* is contextually supplied. These analyses, of course, requires the controversial claim that predicates like 'is raining' and 'flunks ' include extra argument places for locations and times. King emphasizes that his argument is thoroughly empirical. It relies on results from empirical linguistics. If King is right, however, the view that the contents of sentences are propositions can be maintained.

ARGUMENTS FOR PROPOSITIONS

One Over Many

One familiar argument for propositions appeals to commonalties between beliefs, utterances, or sentences, and infers a common entity. Thus, it has been suggested, less in print perhaps than in conversation, that propositions are needed to play the role of being what synonymous sentences have in common, what a sentence and its translation into another language have in common, etc. Arguments of this sort are typically met with the following reply: commonalties do not necessarily require common relations to a single entity. Two red things have something in common, in that they are both red, but it does not *follow* that they bear a common relation to a single entity, the universal of redness.

Similarly, two sentences, in virtue of being synonymous, can be said to have something in common, but that fact alone does not entail they are commonly related to a proposition. When a relation *R* is symmetric and reflexive with respect to a certain domain, it may be useful to speak of the things in the domain which bear *R* to one another as "having something in common", but nothing of ontological significance follows. Thus, the conclusion is drawn: we need an argument for thinking that commonalties require common relations to a single entity.

METALINGUISTIC ARGUMENTS

One standard sort of argument for propositions is metalinguistic. Thus, many argue that propositions are needed as the designata of *that*-clauses in order to explain how certain arguments are valid and in fact sound. More generally, it has been argued that the assumption of propositions simplifies semantics.

THE METAPHYSICS 101 ARGUMENT

Our focus here will be on a different sort of argument. Here is a speech the basic character of which should be familiar to undergraduate students of metaphysics:

When someone has a belief, we can distinguish *what she believes* from *her believing it*. I have a belief that Bush is the US president, for example. We can distinguish *what I believe* in believing that Bush is the US president — the content of my belief — from *my believing that Bush is the US president*. What I believe in believing this is something you believe, too. What we both believe is the proposition that Bush is the US president. This same proposition may be asserted, doubted, etc. And, in fact, this proposition is true: Bush is the US president. So, there are propositions, and they are the contents of beliefs and other attitudes and they are the bearers of truth and falsity.

One might attempt to regiment these remarks, somewhat artificially, to take the form of an argument, which we will dub the *Metaphysics 101* argument:

- With respect to any belief, there is *what is believed* and *the believing of it*, and these are distinct.
- What is believed is something that may be rejected, denied, disbelieved, etc. by multiple subjects, and is something that may be true or false.
- There are beliefs.
- So, there are propositions (i.e, sharable objects of the attitudes and bearers of truth-values).

Further tinkering might improve the argument in certain ways. Our concern, however, is whether the argument goes seriously awry. The Metaphysics 101 Argument is not metalinguistic. It does not rely on premises about English. This can be verified by noting that the argument looks just as good after it is translated into other languages. Nevertheless, it might be claimed that the argument derives its apparent force from a seductive mistake about how English (and other languages) function. Perhaps this is another case of what Wittgenstein called "language on holiday."

LINGUISTIC PROBLEMS

How might one reply to the arguments for propositions just discussed? One might reply, of course, by arguing for the opposite conclusion.

Thus, many have argued, on broadly naturalistic grounds, that we ought not accept propositions. Any such argument will involve controversial claims about the nature and status of propositions.

These issues are discussed in section 7. However, one increasingly popular reply to arguments for propositions is to argue, (1), that they presuppose the Relational Analysis, and (2), that the Relational Analysis does a poor job of accounting for certain linguistic data.

THE SUBSTITUTION PROBLEM

The problem here is quite simple. If, as the Relational Analysis entails, attitude-ascriptions of the form '*S V*s that *p*' assert relations to propositions, then we should be able to replace 'that *p*' with 'the proposition that *p*' without affecting truth-value. But in general we can't do this. Therefore, the Relational Analysis is false. Here are some examples of failed substitutions:

- I insist that it will snow this year. (TRUE)
- So, I insist the proposition that it will snow this year.
- I imagine that it will snow this year. (TRUE)
- So, I imagine the proposition that it will snow this year. (FALSE)

- I remember that combustion produces phlogiston. (FALSE)
- I remember the proposition that combustion produces phlogiston. (TRUE).

The class of attitude verbs for which substitution problems arise — the "problematic" attitude verbs — can be divided into two subclasses: one consisting of verbs which do not grammatically tolerate substitutions (e.g., intransitive verbs such as 'insist', 'complain', 'say', and VPs of the form 'Aux Adj', such as 'is pleased', 'was surprised'); the other consisting of verbs which grammatically tolerate substitutions but for which truth-value is not necessarily preserved (e.g., 'expect', 'anticipate', 'bet', 'gather', 'judge', 'claim', 'maintain', 'hold', 'judge', 'feel', 'remember', 'know', 'recognize', 'find').

THE OBJECTIVIZATION EFFECT

Closely related to the Substitution Problem is what Moltmann calls the *Objectivization Effect*, or objectivization. Substitutions in some cases seem to force a new reading for the verb, an *object* reading rather than a *content* reading. Thus, in 'I imagine that it will snow this year,' 'imagine' has the content reading (this is, by stipulation, what the content reading is!), whereas in 'I imagine the proposition that it will snow this year,' 'imagine' takes an object reading — it expresses the same relation that holds between subjects and garden variety objects such as those designated by NPs like '19th-century Wessex' and 'my college roommate'. The problem here can be described as follows. If the Relational Analysis is true, then propositional attitudes are relations to propositions; but then it seems very odd that we should be unable to retain the content meaning by substituting 'the proposition that p' for 'that p'.

THE AMBIGUITY RESPONSE

The relationalist might claim *that*-clauses are ambiguous, and in particular that they pick out different kinds of entities depending on which attitude verb they complement. How do we tell what kinds of entities are picked out? We look at substitution failures. Thus, it might be argued the truth of '*S* remembers that *p*' requires that the subject bear the remembering relation to a fact, rather than a proposition. After all, 'remember' shows substitution failures for 'the (true) proposition that *p*' but not for 'the fact that *p*'.

However, there are obstacles to this response. For one thing, some attitude verbs seem not to permit substitutions no matter which nominal complement is chosen. King (2002) gives the example of 'feel'. What sorts of entities, then, do that-clauses designate when they complement 'feel'? No answer is possible. Is the Relational Analysis therefore false of such verbs? Perhaps even more damaging, there are verbs which are near synonyms of 'believes', at least in attitude ascriptions, and which grammatically take NP complements, but which exhibit substitution failures and objectivization. 'Feel' is one example, as are 'maintain', 'hold', 'judge', 'expect', and 'suspect'. How could 'believes' designate a relation to propositions in attitude ascriptions but these verbs not? (Consider also the near-synonyms 'assert' and 'claim'.)

Even if the ambiguity hypothesis cannot provide the propositionalist with a general solution to the *Substitution Problem* and the *Objectivization Effect*, it may help in explaining other linguistic phenomena, such as the distributional differences between various nominal complements ('the fact that *p*', 'the proposition that p', 'the possibility that *p*', etc.).

THE SYNTAX RESPONSE

Next, following Jeffrey King (2002), the propositionalist might give a purely syntactic answer to the problems. King claims, first, that there is a very simple syntactic explanation for the substitution failures that produce ungrammaticalities: such verbs don't take NP complements at all, and so it doesn't take nominal complements, which are NP complements. (A verb can take *that*-clause complements without taking NP complements, because *that*-clauses are not NPs.) One might say something similar, for example, about why we cannot substitute descriptions for names in apposition (e.g., 'The philosopher Plato believed in universals' is true but 'the philosopher the teacher of Aristotle believed in universals' is not true.)

King claims, second, that the other class of failures are explained by shifts in verb meanings (i.e., because of objectivization). These shifts are due to syntactical matters, in particular the syntactic category of the verb complement. If the complement is an NP, the verb has an object meaning. If it is a *that*-clause, it has the content meaning. King recognizes the need for qualifications: verbs in the problematic class can have the content reading with certain special NPs, e.g., quantifiers ('everything Bush holds, Frist holds'), and anaphoric pronouns ('I hold that, too'.). In the final analysis, King claims only that all the syntactic properties of the complement (and not just its general syntactic category) determine the verb's meaning when taking that complement.

SUBSTITUTION AND OBJECTIVIZATION PROBLEMS FOR EVERYONE

Although the dominant view in the literature is that the *Substitution Problem* and the *Objectivization Effect* are problems principally for defenders of the Relational Analysis, it is intriguing to ask whether some version of these problems arise for *everyone* — friend or foe of the Relational Analysis, friend or foe of propositions. As noted above, there are near-synonyms which are alike in taking nominal complements but which differ with respect to substitutions. This seems to be a fact that everyone must explain. It is hard to think that the very slight differences in meaning between 'hold' and 'believe' as they occur in '*S V*s that *p*', could explain the substitutional differences.

Nor, as we saw above, does the ambiguity hypothesis seem helpful here. It seems likely that the substitutional differences must be explained in terms of shifts in verb meaning. Because substitution does not affect the meaning of 'believe', it must affect the meaning of 'hold', and, intuitively, it does. This does leave the question of how the *Objectivization Effect* itself is to be explained. But one might hope that a broadly syntactic solution — perhaps like King's — would be available to anyone, regardless of one's stance on propositions. If these problems are problems everyone faces, some heat is taken off the relationalist, and the propositionalist generally.

That said, the relationalist may have to take account of other linguistic puzzles. She will need to explain why it sounds so peculiar, e.g., to talk of "my believing what you desire, or my dreading what the thermometer indicated." And, even with purely cognitive attitude verbs, similar puzzles arise: the mild peculiarity of "I doubt/assert what you contemplate/entertain," for example, will require explanation.

MODIFYING/REPLACING THE RELATIONAL ANALYSIS

Let us suppose, for the sake of argument, the linguistic problems discussed above undermine the Relational Analysis. Some modifications of the Relational Analysis do not avoid the linguistic problems. For instance, it is not enough to claim that attitude verbs designate *three*-place relations between subjects, propositions, and modes of presentation.

One possibility is to deny that attitude verbs designate relations when complemented by *that*-clauses, and to claim that they rather make a syncategorematic semantic contribution. Under one approach, *that*-clauses in attitude ascriptions designate propositions which serve to "measure" attitudes conceived of as mental particulars. It is not clear that this view will be immune to substitution and objectivization problems.

Another possibility is to abandon the Relational Analysis altogether, in favour of a version of Bertrand Russell's "multiple relation" theory. Following Russell, Newman (2002) and Moltmann (2003; 2004), have recently argued that *that*-clauses in attitude ascriptions do not designate propositions but rather provide a number of entities as terms of a "multiple" attitude relation. These philosophers nonetheless do accept propositions, and use them to explain sentences in which 'proposition' explicitly occurs, e.g., ('Some proposition that John believes is true', 'John believes the proposition that snow is white'). The basic idea is that there are propositions, but they have the status of "derived objects" — derived from our attitudes, which themselves are not relations to propositions.

REASONING: TRANSFORMING INFORMATION TO REACH CONCLUSIONS

Most of us are not aware that there is a battle raging in what seems to us the normal goings-on of living. From the moment we wake up until the time we lay down after a day's work and leisure, we are subjected to propaganda from various sides. Indeed, most information available to us is in one way or another slanted to make us believe what the provider of that information thinks we should believe. Ultimately, the fight seems to be over whether we shall become (or continue to be) a docile work force, slaving for the benefit of a few, or whether we shall be able to grow spiritually and make our own decisions, to take charge of our own lives. No need to say, the author tends to believe we should choose the second option. But make no mistake, there are plenty of 'authorities' who will tell you in all earnest that controls are necessary, that too much freedom would be damaging to our own well-being.

Controls, so we are told, are for the good of each one of us, and is it not a small price to pay to give up some of our freedom (such as being continuously searched in airports, having our movements tracked by a "big brother" central data bank, having our communications analysed for possible subversive content) if we want to be protected from terrorism? But what is terrorism to begin with? It is a clever strategy supported by the most powerful of 'government' intelligence forces, put into action for the purpose of making us accept a continuous erosion of freedom at the hands of 'protective' police and anti-terrorist forces. As always, the end is supposed to justify the means. But wait a minute that argument is false because there really is no *end*. There are only *means*. Let me explain this a bit more clearly.

When someone says (or implies) that the end justifies the means, that presupposes that the end be something we know and have agreed upon. Now if our world is full of propaganda, which I think is quite easy to demonstrate, and if we often do not know what to think of the present time, how could we then possibly be agreeing as to an *end* which is a future state of affairs? We have no way to know. We cannot even predict the weather for more than a few days in advance, much less are we able to predict a future state of human affairs. Logically therefore, there can be no *end* which could justify any *means.* The *means* however, often have a direct and very negative effect on our lives and there is really nothing that could justify any means which diminish our individual right of choice or any other rights or freedoms. But let us get back, after this digression, to the theme of our discussion, which is data or information. Information is the ammunition used in the battle that is raging underneath the surface, the projectiles that endanger our sanity. Therefore it is important that we grasp what that substance is and how to treat (evaluate) it, in order to keep our sanity and our ability to make decisions.

In order to better understand what we are about to discuss, we need to get through a few basic definitions of terms:

- Information - this is a description, more or less factual, of past or present events or of existence. Data is a synonym. Information is intended to form, in the recipient's mind, a picture or an idea of what happened or what exists or existed in the past. Information is different from knowledge and it may reach various degrees of perfection in it's description of reality.
- Reality - that which actually exists or existed in the past, and that which is actually happening or has happened. Another way to define reality is to say it is that to which different people agree.
- Truth - is a perfect description of reality. Absolutes are unattainable in this world of physical existence. Truth is no exception to this rule. Therefore, absolute truth can be approached depending on the quality and factualness of the description of reality, but no description can ever be absolutely false or absolutely true.

- Knowledge - is based on information and/or insight. Knowledge is the product of the evaluation of information and depends on the individual's capability of reasoning and insight. It is the best conclusion which the mind of the individual is capable of reaching, based on the available information. Knowledge is individual certainty but is subject to revision as more or different information becomes available. Just as there is no such thing as absolute truth, there is no final knowledge within the confines of physical existence.
- Disinformation - is information with deliberately introduced imperfections, such as omissions of bits of data, falsehoods, too much emphasis on some unimportant aspect or not enough emphasis on some important part of the information. Generally, disinformation is provided with the intention of forming, in the mind of the recipient, a false perception of reality, leading to decisions or opinions that are favourable to the hidden plans of it's supplier. This should not be confused with misinformation, which is the mere passing on of false information without intention to deceive.
- Logic - is needed in order to correctly evaluate information. It is the faculty which allows us to transform information into knowledge. Logic is basically comparative. Past experience and knowledge is compared to current information in order to reach conclusions or to form opinions. Just as absolute truth and absolute knowledge are unattainable, logic is not a matter of 'black and white'. The true/false logic of computer fame is not flexible enough to allow for efficient evaluation of data. Logic must allow for gradients, it must be 'fuzzy', indistinct, to start evaluating more efficiently.

THE MECHANISM OF MIND

The mind is a sort of computer, a 'logic machine', owned

by each person and constantly engaged in a search for knowledge. The data banks of this computer contain every piece of information that has come to our notice, as well as every experience we have had during this (and former) lifetimes. Storage capacity is way above that of currently available computer memory. The stored information and experience is used at various levels of consciousness to facilitate the making of decisions. When the mind works well, it will have readily available for our inspection and evaluation all acquired information, sorted by relative importance, sorted by subject, tagged for it's reliability or lack of it and combined with cross-references to other similar bits of information. Ideally, the mind should at any moment reach the best conclusions that can be reached, given the available information. There are however several kinds of obstacles that can get into the way of correct evaluation.

OBSTACLES

The first one of these obstacles is distorted perception. Pain is a sort of distraction to the mind, emotions may cloud perception, disinformation may be mistakenly acted upon, believing it to be valid information. Another obstacle is memory loss or distortion. Drugs, both the official medical kind (tranquillisers and other psychoactive substances) and the illegal drugs sold on the streets (especially LSD and other hallucinogenic goodies) wreak havoc with the memory of a person. But memory can also be 'blanked out' by past pain and unconsciousness such as in accidents, surgical operations and experiences containing violence. A further block to the operation of the mind is overwhelm. This may occur because of too forceful an associate (family member, boss, teacher, etc.) or it may come about through passive acceptance of data from a source (such as television), which does not give the individual time to think about what was received.

And finally another block: illogic or inability to evaluate, generally acquired by education. Such an inability comes about through false 'knowledge' received through education, which acts as a bug in the person's mental software, causing wrong evaluation of data and in consequence wrong decisions. Fixed ideas would be in this category. Knowledge, by the way, can not be taught in schools or universities. All that may be taught with profit is the ability to acquire information and evaluate it, using sound reasoning. Generally, our schools do not put emphasis on developing these skills but insist on instilling masses of data into the minds of the unfortunate student. In many cases fixed (and often false) 'knowledge' is hammered in, resulting in an impaired ability to think for oneself.

OPERATION OF THE MIND

Having examined some of the possible obstacles to the mind's correct function, let's try and see how the mind does work when it is not led astray by false or missing data or by an illogical mode of operation. It seems that man has not so far been able to establish the mechanism of the mind's operation to any degree of satisfactory approximation, although certainly not for lack of trying. "Artificial Intelligence" has been around for years and it is an attempt to copy human thinking, but it has a long way to go before being able to duplicate the workings of our mind. The mind does not think in terms of 'true' and 'false'. It weighs the evidence and assigns a rating of probability to any given piece of information.

The human mind's thinking may be likened to a web of possibilities and probabilities made up of all the various elements that work together to form our knowledge and our opinions. These elements, each and everyone of them, have assigned to them what we might call a certainty rating that may go all the way from 'very improbable' to 'possible', 'probable' and 'almost certain', with a great number of intermediate steps. This is a gradient scale of probabilities, with 50/50 in the middle (undecided) and degrees of probability up to 'almost certain', as well as degrees of possibility down to 'almost certainly not'. The elements that form that network are, in order of importance from lowest to highest:

- Second hand information. This includes data obtained from records (books and other written works, films, videos, sound recordings), in short, any information based on the observations or the recordings of others.

- Conventional knowledge ('certainties' of others that may be introduced with education or schooling). These are the 'natural laws' and the 'scientific truths' we are taught in the first twenty-some years of our lives.
- First hand information (observations or experiences directly made by the person). Films, videos or sound recordings do not qualify as 'first hand', because they are too easily falsified.
- Individual knowledge (certainties that have been arrived at by the individual through evaluation of information and conventional knowledge, or through enlightenment).

Enlightenment is defined in this context as a spiritual experience of the individual, which can lead to a high degree of certainty. None of the parts of this mental 'web of knowledge' are absolutes. Knowledge and information are subject to continuous re-evaluation in the light of new observations. The mind could be described as a three dimensional spider web, with data of various kinds and various degrees of certainty at the crossin points. It is as if hanging in mid-air, fastened provisionally here and there to some relatively stable points of knowledge, each part interconnected with all the others. In addition to the subdivision given above into relative importances, information and knowledge are sorted in the mind into various themes or areas of pertinence. The data are heavily cross-referenced and cross-checked within each area of pertinence and somewhat less heavily between one theme and another.

The commanding consciousness, the will of the person her/himself is able to override and to (temporarily) 'force' probability ratings so as to play through possible alternative ways of looking at things. This is where insight, inspiration and ideas come into play. The creative and intuitive powers of consciousness allow for a very efficient mode of continuous re-evaluation, which is the basis of invention and creative work. Superior logic and genius are a result of several factors: Access to information, ability to evaluate information, absence of hampering educational preconceptions and other blocks to mental function, capacity of elaboration, and drive (necessity) to continuously re-evaluate, as well as the natural intuitive capabilities of the individual consciousness, the person him/herself.

In general, we can say that today's education is not conductive to making a genius out of anyone. The reason for this is, that often pre-conceptions, which have also been identified above as 'conventional knowledge', are considered more important than the individual student's knowledge. Questioning such educationally induced pre-conceptions is actively discouraged in schools and universities, as is doubting the information given by teachers. This creates a block on a student's mental abilities. Education is generally missing techniques that would enable the student to evaluate information.

THE FORMATION OF KNOWLEDGE

Knowledge is really a very personal thing. As said above, it cannot be instilled from the outside, through information, education, or otherwise. Even what we have identified as 'conventional knowledge' is not really knowledge for the individual, until taken apart, evaluated and re-assembled in the individual's own terms. Conventional knowledge may have been genuine knowledge for someone else, but for our student, it becomes information that has to be evaluated in order to be transformed into real knowledge.

Genuine knowledge is based on an evaluation, by the individual, of the data of experience, which leads to various gradations of certainty. Paradoxically, it seems that the highest degree of certainty is obtained from a 'religious' or 'spiritual' experience, an experience of things that do not pertain to physical existence. Next in order are first hand observations of physical world occurrences and lowest on the scale of values are experiences related to us by others, either directly or through some sort of record. Experience (data, information) must be evaluated against other, similar previous experiences and against what we have already acquired as knowledge.

Historically, man has lived (and developed his mental faculties) in a relatively 'honest' environment. When there was war, you knew there was war, and when peace reigned, that was quite obvious also. Messages travelled at a very slow pace and so disinformation, if there was any, travelled very slowly as well and reached comparatively few people.

It was possible to evaluate the truth of any message with two simple tests: First, comparing a piece of information with other information already known, looking for incompatibilities and second, looking for other pieces of information that would confirm the first one.

This is how our minds have been accustomed to function and the method was successful enough. Today, we must look for a better way to evaluate information, because data are routinely being manipulated and misinformation is quite prevalent.

Information is being made to suit the most diverse interests, it is being tailored to sway our thinking one way or another. The advent of the socalled 'information society' makes the development of a new weapon of mental self-defence a prime necessity.

The mind evaluates the truth of information by comparison. It keeps bits of information 'in suspension', so to say, until another bit of comparable information comes along which either confirms or contradicts the first bit. This is what we could call evaluation by 'multiple source'. If we hear the same thing from various different sources, that increases it's believability value. As explained above, this was workable in the past, but it has become an achilles heel in today's environment. Propaganda parallels exactly the mind's way of evaluation, and it exploits a basic weakness of our thinking. Some story may end up becoming 'common knowledge', just because it is being repeated by so many different sources. But objectively, two or more false reports do not make a fact. They make it more difficult to know the truth.

EVALUATION BY ILLOGIC

What are we to do, how can we find out what is really correct and what has been slanted? How can we discard the numerous 'multiple source' falsehoods posing as fact? We must make use of the points that make something illogical, in order to evaluate the truth-content of data. This is not something that comes easily, make no mistake.

It takes some training to find the illogics in information but once you do, you will never see the world with the same eyes.

Some of the salient points of illogic are:

- Conflicting reports: John says one thing and Mary says another. What does that mean? One *or both* are not telling the truth. We cannot just choose which one of them to believe. We must treat both reports as worthless, until we are able to find out for ourselves, to confirm or discard the information.
- Omissions: A newspaper reports that a poor country just received 30 million dollars in "development aid" and shows the extreme poverty reigning in the capital city of that country, accusing the local government of mismanagement of international aid. The report omits that the country is paying 7O million dollars a year of interest on foreign loans and that the "aid" will go straight to the creditor banks paying that interest, instead of being spent on bettering the economic conditions of the local population. Omissions are very hard to spot, and they may completely change the meaning of some piece of information.
- Falsehoods: Politician says "inflation is down" when in fact the statistics are 'adjusted' to make the government look good. It takes practice to catch falsehoods. Normally the figures are 'corrected' later, when no one remembers the first claim any more.
- Wrong emphasis: Long article in the newspaper. A mind blowing detail is reported in the last paragraph, which people normally do not get to, unless they are

very disciplined in their reading and very interested in the whole story.

- Out of sequence: "We spent 3 million dollars on a new construction project. - It was found that the project was not feasible." It seems that public administrations often do things out of sequence. In the meantime, 3 million dollars have gone lining someone's pockets.

There are of course an infinity of variations and combinations of these points of illogic. Others may exist. What is important for us is, to start using these illogics in our evaluation of information. Every time we see one of these points of illogic - and there is really no scarcity of them in the information we are given each day - we must look at it consciously and try to follow it down. Do not just shake your head and go on your way. Investigate. One thing leads to another. Pretty soon you will see through the veneer of what passes for information these days and will be able to make up your own mind as to the intentions of the providers of that information. You will also understand many of the things that go on around you and that just don't quite seem to make sense.

As I said in the beginning of this chapter, the stakes of the game are high. If you enjoy being a slave, just absorb all the information that is being offered, without critical analysis. Take your holidays once a year, to get away from it all, then come back and buckle down for another year ... If you value your freedom, start paying attention to the illogics in information. Start doubting everything unless you can yourself confirm it with personal observation and form your own personal knowledge. You will find that life takes on a completely new outlook.

PROBLEM-SOLVING: FINDING PATHS TO DESIRED GOALS

Every educator is familiar with the term "problem solving," and most would agree that the ability to solve problems is a worthy goal of education. But what is problem solving? Its meaning is actually quite straightforward: problem solving is the process of moving toward a goal when the path to that goal is uncertain. We solve problems every time we achieve something without having known beforehand how to do so. We encounter simple problems every day: finding lost keys, deciding what to do when our car won't start, even improvising a meal from leftovers. But there are also larger and more significant "ill-defined" problems, such as getting an education, becoming a successful person, and finding happiness. Indeed, the most important kinds of human activities involve accomplishing goals without a script.

Problem solving is a ubiquitous feature of human functioning. Human beings are problem solvers who think and act within a grand complex of fuzzy and shifting goals and changing means to attain them. This has always been true, but it is doubly so today because we live in a time of unprecedented societal transformation. When circumstances change, old procedures no longer work. To adapt is to pursue valued goals even when circumstances - and perhaps the goals themselves - are in flux. Because the pace of societal change shows no signs of slackening, citizens of the 21st century must become adept problem solvers, able to wrestle with ill-defined problems and win. Problem-solving ability is the cognitive passport to the future.

There is no formula for true problem solving. If we know exactly how to get from point A to point B, then reaching point B does not involve problem solving. Think of problem solving as working your way through a maze. In negotiating a maze, you make your way toward your goal step by step, making some false moves but gradually moving closer toward the intended end point. What guides your choices? Perhaps a rule like this: choose the path that seems to result in *some* progress toward the goal. Such a rule is one example of a *heuristic*. A heuristic is a rule of thumb. It is a strategy that is powerful and general, but not absolutely guaranteed to work. Heuristics are crucial because they are *the* tools by which problems are solved.

By contrast, algorithms are straightforward procedures that are guaranteed to work every time. For example, you have in your long-term memory algorithms that enable you to tie your shoelaces, to start up your car, and perhaps even to cook an omelet. Barring broken shoelaces, a dead battery, and rotten eggs, these algorithms serve you very well. An algorithm may even be so automatic that it requires very little conscious processing as you carry out the procedure.

Now here is an important consideration: what constitutes problem solving varies from person to person. For a small child, tying shoelaces will indeed require problem solving, just as cooking an omelet entails problem solving for many adults. Thus problem solving involves an interaction of a person's experience and the demands of the task. Once we have mastered a skill, we are no longer engaged in problem solving when we apply it. For a task to require problem solving again, novel elements or new circumstances must be introduced or the level of challenge must be raised. Some problem solutions, however, can never be reduced to algorithms, and it is often those problems that constitute the most profound and rewarding of human activities. The necessity of problem solving to all that is important about being a person cannot be overstated.

In addition, problem solving is not an advanced process that is reserved solely for mature learners. Indeed, people of all ages can and must be solvers of problems. Perhaps young children are the most natural problem solvers. Because they continually face circumstances that are novel, they must adapt. It's their "job." And they are amazingly good at it. Moreover, young children don't fret about failure the way that school-age children and adults tend to do. They take detours and setbacks in stride because they know intuitively that such obstacles are a part of the problem solving process. Still, we need to encourage problem solving in children. Whenever possible, this involves letting children find their own ways of reaching their goals. Good parents and other caregivers know when to stand back and let a child figure things out and when to step in and offer the right amount of help.

Armed only with our heuristics, then, we engage in a process of *heuristic search*. Like finding one's way through a maze, we move closer, haltingly, to where we want to be. We can't be sure of what lies around the next corner or that the direction that once seemed so promising will pay off. Progress toward important goals is incremental, and each move is informed by our repertoire of heuristics. Because of the possibility of false moves, we need to monitor our progress continually and switch strategies if necessary.

THE POWER OF HEURISTICS

If heuristics are the problem solver's best guide, it makes sense to elucidate them as much as possible. First, each learner must know what heuristics are and must be aware of their power. Second, each learner must have both general and specific heuristics at his or her disposal. General heuristics are cognitive "rules of thumb" that are useful in solving a great variety of problems. They are usually content-free and apply across many different situations. Specific heuristics are used in specialized areas, often specific subject domains or professions. Probably the most powerful general heuristic, alluded to in the maze example, is "means-ends analysis." Essentially, the heuristic is this: form a subgoal to reduce the discrepancy between your present state and your ultimate goal state. Phrased more colloquially: do something to get a little closer to your goal.

Problems defy one-shot solutions; they must be broken down. Means-ends analysis accepts incremental advancement toward a goal. The method is not fail-safe, of course, because positive results are not guaranteed with any heuristic. However, if all goes well, this heuristic will help move you incrementally toward your ultimate goal. You apply it again and again, trying to reduce the discrepancy further. By means of this less-than-direct path, you find your way to the ends you seek. Such a search is not simply a process of trial and error, because the steps taken are not blind or random. Rather, the application of a series of tactical steps leads you ever closer toward the goal. Mistakes made along the way must be accepted as inextricable from the problem-solving process.

The benefits conferred by means-ends analysis may be as

much emotional as intellectual. If a large and complex problem seems daunting as a whole, perhaps one can summon the will to accomplish a small piece of it. And that success can motivate one to persist. Thus starting a task can make the effort self-sustaining. Sometimes when we tackle a difficult project, it's as if we are trying to start a car on a cold winter morning. We encounter resistance. Once begun, however, the task becomes marginally easier and doesn't require a constant exertion of will to sustain it. At some point, we "cross the Rubicon" - we reach the point where it seems more difficult to stop than to carry on to completion. That is when a problem-solving activity becomes self-sustaining and bears us along by its momentum. "Just do it!" is not solely a great marketing slogan; it can also be seen as a directive to disregard the ominous hulking problem that looms ahead and simply take the first step.

Heuristics are usually picked up incidentally rather than identified and taught explicitly in school. This situation is not ideal. A curriculum that encourages problem solving needs to provide more than just practice in solving problems; it needs to offer explicit instruction in the nature and use of heuristics. Herbert Simon has written:

In teaching problem solving, major emphasis needs to be directed toward extracting, making explicit, and practicing problem-solving heuristics - both general heuristics, like means-ends analysis, and more specific heuristics, like applying the energy conservation principle in physics.

What are some other heuristics? One that is probably familiar to most readers goes by the name of "working backward." First, consider your ultimate goal. From there, decide what would constitute a reasonable step just prior to reaching that goal. Then ask yourself, What would be the step just prior to that? Beginning with the end, you build a strategic bridge backward and eventually reach the initial conditions of the problem. An illustration of the use of this approach can be taken from the Tower of Hanoi problem.

The rules are simple. Only one disk can be moved at a time, and a larger disk may never be placed on top of a smaller disk. The goal is to move the entire stack of disks from the first peg to the third. Working backward helps us understand that at some point we must find a way to place the largest disk at the bottom of the third peg. Working backward from there, we would infer that all the smaller disks would eventually need to be placed on the middle peg, according to the rules, so that the largest disk is free to move. That step also has logical precursors, and so on. Working backward makes the problem more manageable and its solutions much more efficient than following a less reasoned approach.

Or take another example. My daughter came home from school with a story about a provocative exchange between a teacher and a student:

Teacher: What do you want to be when you are an adult?
Student: I want to be rich.
Teacher: No, but what do you want to be?
Student: I don't care. I just want to be rich.

This student certainly had a clear goal in mind, though some might question its value independent of the means for achieving it. In any case, the student has some serious "working backward" to do. If his goal is to be rich, what kind of career might allow him to achieve it? Becoming a movie star? A Wall Street investor? An entrepreneur? A criminal? Some combination of these? If an entrepreneur, that might imply that majoring in business in college would be in order. In turn, that goal might suggest that tonight the student should study his mathematics a little harder than is his custom. Working backward makes "next steps" plainer than simply wishing and hoping that dreams will materialize.

A third heuristic seeks to solve problems through "successive approximation." Initial tries at solving a problem may result in a product that is less than satisfying. Writing is a good example. Few accomplished writers attempt to write perfect prose the first time they set pen to paper (or fingertips to keyboard). Rather, the initial goal is a rough draft or an outline or a list of ideas. Over time, a manuscript is gradually molded into form. New ideas are added. Old ones are removed. The organization of the piece is reshaped to make it flow better. Eventually, a polished form emerges that finally approximates the effect that the author intended.

Given time and effort, what started out as rough and approximate can become art. In fact, successive approximation seems to be an important heuristic in producing outstanding creative works of all kinds. This model is relevant to many pursuits other than writing. Inventions, theories, stories, recipes, and even personal and group identities start out rough but are restructured and refined over time. Think of the bicycle, whose various designs over the decades have metamorphosed toward greater efficiency and lighter weight. Successive approximation accepts the design process as problem solving, a series of zigs and zags toward something better. Not only is such a process compatible with human information processing, but awareness of the principle can sustain a halfbaked idea that initially seems raw, wild, and foolish but is just possibly the germ of an eventual marvel.

George Polya's advice was "Draw a figure." In that spirit, I offer a fourth and final example of a heuristic: portray the problem at hand in an explicit "external representation." List, describe, diagram, or otherwise render the main features of a problem. This heuristic has several important features. First, it allows us to represent more complexity than we can hold in mind at once. Depicting a problem on paper, whiteboard, or computer screen relieves short-term memory of the burden of representing the problem and allows the processing capacity of our brains to be directed toward solving it. An incidental benefit is that often the very attempt to represent the problem explicitly forces a problem solver to be clear about what it is he or she is trying to do and about what stands in the way. A clearer representation of goals and obstacles may by itself greatly simplify solution of the problem.

Another benefit of external representation is that the medium chosen to portray a problem may help the solver see the problem in a new way. In our heads we may understand a problem in words. On paper, we may discover that a picture makes more sense. Sometimes words can distort the more direct pictorial representations and so hinder problem solving.

Pictorial representations are used by experts in many fields and can be of considerable help. Finally, an external representation, unlike a mental representation, is potentially a "public document." The fact that other people can see it might help a group reach consensus about the nature of a problem. An obstacle that is prohibitive to one person might seem trivial or irrelevant to another. Likewise, a common representation might allow one participant to point out a significant opportunity that is unseen by other members of the group.

METACOGNITION

All heuristics help break down a problem into pieces. The problem as a whole is thus transformed. It is no longer a chaotic mass, like a ton of cooked spaghetti. Rather, through the creation of various subgoals, each of the pieces becomes manageable. The problem does become more complex in one sense because the pieces themselves must somehow be borne in mind. If a large goal is broken down into subgoals, then one cognitive challenge becomes goal management - keeping track of what to do and when. Goal management is probably a major aspect of intelligent thought. Patricia Carpenter, Marcel Just, and Peter Shell regard goal management as a central feature of problem solving.

A key component of analytic intelligence is goal management, the process of spawning subgoals from goals, and then tracking the ensuing successful and unsuccessful pursuits of the subgoal on the path to satisfying higher-level goals.... The decomposition of complexity ... consists of the recursive creation of solvable subproblems.... But the cost of creating embedded subproblems, each with [its] own subgoals, is that they require management of a hierarchy of goals.

The importance of monitoring subgoals is an example of a more general phenomenon: one common feature of problem solving is the capacity to examine and control one's own thoughts. This self-monitoring is known as metacognition. Metacognition is essential for any extended activity, especially problem solving, because the problem solver needs to be aware of the current activity and of the overall goal, the strategies used to attain that goal, and the effectiveness of those strategies. The mind exercising metacognition asks itself, *What* am I doing? and *How* am I doing? These self-directed questions are assumed in the application of all heuristics. However, in practice, teachers cannot simply assume that students will engage in metacognition it must be taught explicitly as an integral component of problem solving.

Problem solving requires both the vigilant monitoring and the flexibility per misted by metacognition. When solving problems, means shift continually depending on one's position relative to desired goals. Even goals change as old goals are superseded by new and better ones. Maintaining flexibility is essential. Too often we feel wedded to a chosen strategy and continue to apply that strategy even if it lead us wildly astray. When this happens, it is usually wrong to conclude that we must start over. The important question is always "What do I do *now*, given my goal, my current position, and the resources available to me?" Getting off course along the way is fully expected. Cool-headed reappraisal is the best response - not mindless consistency, panic, or surrender.

In pursuit of the goal of improving problem-solving ability, I have advocated the use of heuristics and have suggested a few. There are countless others. Some are general and apply to many problem situations, but most are specific and apply in specialized fields. Heuristics are vital, but they are not necessarily the most important aspect of problem solving. Perhaps more powerful than any heuristic is an understanding that, *by its very nature, problem solving involves error and uncertainty*. Even if success is achieved, it will not be found by following an unerring path. The possibilities of failure and of making less-than-optimal moves are inseparable from problem solving. And the loftier the goals, the more obvious will be the imperfection of the path toward a solution. The necessity of uncertainty is recognized implicitly whenever we commend someone for being a risk taker. It is not the taking of risks itself that is commendable; rather, taking risks is a means to an end. What we actually applaud is the courage to adopt a difficult and commendable goal and then to enter the thorny thicket of problem solving where the only way out is through heuristic search and nerve.

The willingness to suspend judgment - to accept temporary uncertainty-is an important aspect of thinking in general. John Dewey linked tolerance of uncertainty to reflective thinking:

Reflective thought involves an initial state of doubt or perplexity.... To many persons both suspense of judgment and intellectual search are disagreeable; they want to get them ended as soon as possible.... To be genuinely thoughtful, we must be willing to sustain and protract the state of doubt, which is the stimulus to thorough inquiry.

How then is it possible to improve problem-solving ability? First, we need to recognize when we are engaged in problem solving and accept as natural, normal, and expected the stepwise and discursive path toward a goal through the application of general and specific heuristics.

Second, we must not let anxiety take hold. Anxiety is a spoiler in the problem-solving process. It stalks right behind uncertainty, ready to pounce.

Demanding and uncertain environments, the seedbeds of all problems solving, are fertile ground for anxiety. Uncertainty is an integral part of the business of solving problems. Those who cannot bear situations in which it is impossible to see the way clearly to the end are emotionally ill-prepared to solve problems.

Errors are part of the process of problem solving, which implies that both teachers and learners need to be more tolerant of them. If no mistakes are made, then almost certainly no problem solving is taking place. Unfortunately, one tradition of schooling is that perfect performance is often exalted as an ideal. Errors are seen as failures, as signs that the highest marks are not quite merited. Worse still, errors are sometimes ridiculed or taken as ridiculous. Mistakes and embarrassment often go hand in hand. Perfect performance may be a reasonable criterion for evaluating algorithmic performance (though I doubt it), but it is incompatible with problem solving.

What so often counts most in schools is the important but incomplete cognitive resource of *knowledge*. Fixed knowledge and algorithms are easier to teach, learn, and test than is the tangled web of processes that make up problem solving. Typically, it is not before graduate school that problem solving really becomes the focus of an educational programme. Even in graduate school a student may not get to wrestle with the true problems of a field of study until the dissertation. What can reverse this sorry state of affairs?

A better understanding of the nature of problem solving is a place to start. Ultimately, we will have to change the culture of schooling. In the workplace as well, we need to revise our attitude toward errors - at least toward those that are a reasonable consequence of significant problem solving. (Errors in balancing the books don't count.) But if a job requires fluid intelligence-the ability to operate within the flux of continually changing demands and challenges-even the corporate culture must accept and deal with the multitude of paths toward solutions and the necessary existence of error.

For educators to accept errors, uncertainty, and indirect paths toward solutions is itself a difficult problem because doing so contradicts our ingrained beliefs and expectations about teaching and learning. But problem solving must be understood and promoted if the next generation is to be prepared for the unprecedented challenges (i.e., problems) that it will face. Yet great things are accomplished when great things are attempted, and in our efforts we do not face total uncertainty. We have, in fact, our experience and its dividend, our knowledge, to support us.

Heuristics and knowledge are what Herbert Simon has called the "two blades" of effective professional education, and he reminds us that "twobladed scissors are still the most effective kind." I would add that what is good for professional education is good for education of all kinds at all levels. By combining what we *do* know with our understanding of the problem-solving process, we can move toward our goals - perhaps not unerringly, but by the sort of wending progress that is the signature of problem solving.

METHODS OF STUDYING COGNITIVE PROCESSES

The investigation of how people use electronic information resources is important as a means of understanding how to make systems more usable and as a means of understanding information-seeking behaviour. Important developments have been the use of transaction logging data and of protocol analysis. However a trend in understanding information-seeking behaviour and in information system evaluation has been the move from controlled experiments to the study of information seeking in a natural setting.

The collection of transaction logging data of end users searching full text electronic information sources in a natural setting poses numerous challenges and raises methodological concerns. This chapter explores the challenges and describes a novel approach that was developed to address the limitations of traditional quantitative methodologies as applied to CD-ROM databases. The transaction logs for the research project were required to provide more qualitative data, capturing the search from start to finish as experienced and seen by end users.

The paper discusses transaction log analysis and protocol analysis as methods of data collection before outlining the novel methodology in detail, illustrating its operation with some examples of the data collected and concluding with a brief discussion on its use in a number of projects. The intention of the paper is to concentrate on the methodology itself rather than report results of specific research. Appendices are included which provide system requirements/technical detail and contact information of suppliers.

TRANSACTION LOG ANALYSIS

A useful definition of Transaction Log Analysis has been provided by Peters *et al.* (1993) who characterise it as:

...the study of electronically recorded interactions between on-line information retrieval systems and the persons who search for the information found in those systems.

Furthermore noting that its use as a research methodology

is relatively new, they have divided its development into three phases:

- Mid 1960s to mid 1970s - emphasis placed on evaluating system performance, rather than on user behaviour and performance, Meister and Sullivan's (1967) evaluation of user reactions being one of the first uses of transaction log analysis;
- Late 1970s to mid 1980s - first applications of transaction log analysis to the study of on-line catalogue systems, equal interest in how the system was used and in the searching behaviour of end users; and
- Late 1980s to date - diversification of transaction log application, usually focusing on use of operational information retrieval systems by end users.

Peters *et al.* have identified a variety of uses of transaction log data namely:

- Improving an information retrieval system;
- Improving human utilisation of the system;
- Improving human (and system) understanding of how the system is used by information seekers;
- Identification of how a system is being used by end users; and
- Study of prototype systems or potential system improvements.

Transaction-logging systems are usually a feature of automated library systems, which can be classified into two broad categories:

- Systems which count transactions as they occur; and
- Systems which store the text of the transactions.

Whilst systems of the first type may provide useful management information to librarians, it is only systems of the latter type which provide useful data for researchers because they capture and store users' entries and provide for retrieval of the stored data. Additionally some systems will also record information about the response returned by the system. Flaherty identifies typical transaction log data elements as:

- Patron's entry;
- Date and time;
- Terminal identification;
- Search file;
- Number of hits; and
- System response (not all systems).

Blecic *et al.* (1998) define transaction log analysis as "the detailed and systematic examination of each search command or query by a user and the following database result or output by the OPAC". According to this definition transaction log systems which do not record the system response to the user input are not true transaction logging systems.

Transaction logging systems have limitations. Hancock-Beaulieu *et al.* (1990) noted that whilst transaction logs could provide useful diagnostic evidence of procedural and conceptual problems, they also had specific limitations. These limitations include a lack of "information or the right type of data to inform adequately on how or why users searched in the way they did".

Other restrictions include:

- Not all systems have logging facilities;
- Problems in identifying individual search sessions;
- System response not always recorded; and
- Volume of data generated causes difficulties for analysis.

Having identified the limitations of existing systems, Beaulieu *et al.* (1990) developed a PC-based transaction logging software package, OLIVE. This system logged the user-host dialogue, condensed and summarised the data, played back the logon screen, acted as an agent in a three-way exchange by intercepting the user-host dialogue, and was able to include pre- and post-search questionnaires. This could be adapted for use across different OPACs. This system concentrated more on "screen logging rather than a transaction logging focus".

Kurth (1993) noted that,...students of transaction log data have begun to ask as many questions about what the transaction logs cannot reveal as they have asked about what transaction logs can reveal.

According to Kurth these limitations fall into four categories:

- System factors;
- User/search process factors;
- Data analysis factors; and
- Ethical and legal factors .

System factors, which impede the collection of transaction log data, are divided by Kurth into:

- Mechanical;
- Temporal;
- Spatial; and
- Intersystem factors.

Mechanical limitations include such elements as complex programming requirements and immense data size. Other system factors are determined by the fact that "on-line systems are unique entities which exist in time and space". Thus, changes to a bibliographic database, modifications to commands, indexing and displays will impact on the researcher's ability to replicate searches, and the same system on the same day will behave differently over a network. Intersystem factors are concerned with the development of transaction logging subsystems which vary widely, making comparisons across different on-line systems difficult.

A major "user/search process" limitation identified by Kinsella and Bryant (1987) is the inability to isolate and characterise individual users of on-line systems in order to describe the pattern of their use. Users' perceptions of their searches are not recorded, transaction logs cannot measure the information needs that users' are unable to express in their search statements (input), and they cannot reflect users' satisfaction with search results (output). As Kurth states, "[the fact] that transaction logs are unable to address such cognitive aspects of on-line searching behaviour is a true limit of the methodology". Supplementary research, such as questionnaires, protocol analysis and interviews, must be undertaken in order to build a fuller picture of searching behaviour, success and satisfaction. Kurth identifies data analysis issues as being threefold:

- Execution;
- Conception; and
- Communication.

Execution creates collection, storage and analysis problems related to the large size and complexity of the data set. Conceiving a method of analysis that is appropriate to both the data analysed and the research question asked is also crucial to the success of the study. The limitations discussed above combine to create a large number of variables to control when developing a methodology for analysing transaction log data. Communication problems arise when researchers:

- Fail to sufficiently define terms and measurement tools upon which their transaction log analysis will depend; and
- Fail to provide descriptions of their methodologies in sufficient detail to allow other researchers to test and verify their results.

Whilst transaction log analysis has considerable value as a data collection method, it has its limitations and it is best used in conjunction with a method which captures data regarding users' real information needs, comments and reactions whilst using a system and satisfaction with the system.

PROTOCOL ANALYSIS

Protocol analysis has been widely used across many research areas and has stimulated considerable debate about its merits and limitations as a method of eliciting information from the participant. There has been significant development and use of verbal protocol analysis in educational psychology and as such it is relevant to consider lessons from this area. However, think-aloud protocols have been used increasingly in information retrieval research.

Hancock-Beaulieu *et al.* have argued that Ericsson and Simon's (1980) paper on verbal reports as data "has led to the use of protocols or spoken thoughts in task analysis and decision making processes in a number of ... areas". Ericsson and Simon's central proposal is that verbal reports are data and, as such, require explication of the mechanisms by which the reports are generated, and the ways in which they are sensitive to experimental factors.

As a method for understanding the cognitive processes of subjects, doubts had been raised about the validity of verbal reports. Ericsson and Simon sought to evolve a methodology for verbal reporting which would address the limitations that had discredited it by proposing a move away from informal analysis of verbalised information toward objective procedures for collection and analysis. The model they propose for the verbalisation processes of subjects is based upon the theoretical framework of human information processing theory. Ericsson and Simon conclude that,...verbal reports, elicited with care and interpreted with full understanding of the circumstances under which they were obtained, are a valuable and thoroughly reliable source of information about cognitive processes.

Long and Bourg report on three areas of research where verbal protocol analysis provides unique information:

- The study of inferential processing during text comprehension;
- The study of individual differences in comprehension performance; and
- The study of conversational discourse and storytelling.

Long and Bourg's major premise is that readers do not provide a veridical report of their underlying mental processes when they 'think aloud' ... rather, they construct a text representation and then use it to 'tell a story' about their understanding".

Further, Long and Bourg in discussing Magliano and Graesser's work (1991) state that "verbal protocols are an important component of the three-pronged method [for studying inferential processing during comprehension]". They put forward that verbal protocols provide a rich and detailed database that can be used to generate hypotheses about what knowledge-based inferences occur during reading and that verbal protocols can be used to identify the knowledge structures that supply inferences. In the opinion of Long and Bourg:

verbal protocol analysis is ideal for identifying those inferences that involve access to world knowledge and those that involve access to prior text information. We are somewhat less convinced that verbal protocols provide valuable information about the memory operations that underlie these inferences."

The second area of study often utilising protocol analysis is the study of individual differences. Here, verbal protocols are used to investigate individual differences in readers' text representations and comprehension strategies. Long and Bourg examined several studies in this area and concluded that verbal protocol analysis led to interesting hypotheses about differences in the text representations constructed by individuals, who vary in reading skill and memory capacity. Further they noted that verbal protocols also lead to hypotheses about individual differences in learning strategies and production skills.

Research into the affect of learning styles and cognitive styles on successful information retrieval may be informed by this second approach. The third research area discussed by Long and Bourg is that of conversational discourse. Long and Bourg posit that "readers use their text representation to tell a story about their understanding of a story" and, as such, verbal protocols may provide useful information about some of the principles involved in conversational discourse.

As long ago as 1978, protocol analysis was used to describe the searching behaviour of a group of experimental searchers. Keen and Wheatley conducted an experiment in which five different kinds of printed subject indexes were searched and, from transcripts of the verbalised tape-recordings, evidence of the way the entries were processed by the user was found. The test focused on one user and was designed to contrast this with two other methods for capturing a comprehensive record of the search. The two other methods under investigation were the use of detailed record sheets and marking the index copies. Keen and Wheatley concluded that "as an analogy to recording searching, verbalised recorded indexing be used as a tool for exploring the indexing process and studying indexing aboutness". Keen has used the think-aloud methodology in subsequent studies.

Markey (1984) utilised protocol analysis to study manual searching of a library catalogue. With minimal prompting, users were encouraged to talk aloud as they searched. Their statements were recorded onto an audio tape and transcribed to produce a flow chart of the different steps of the complete search. From these protocols, patterns of searching behaviour emerged and models of different types of searches were identified. Transcription and coding was, however, a time consuming task.

Hancock-Beaulieu *et al.* (1990) identified the main limitations of protocol analysis as being two-fold:

- Fears that a direct approach would interfere and possibly distort the search process; and
- Transcription and subsequent coding is time consuming and cumbersome.

To minimise these problems Hancock (1987) devised a combined observation and talk aloud technique to study searchers using a microfiche catalogue. Subjects were encouraged to talk aloud as they searched to give an indication of what they were looking for and to confirm whether or not they succeeded. The direct observation of searchers' actions provided Hancock with the framework of the activity and in this way the searchers' actions confirmed what they said they were doing. The verbal protocol data provided details which could not be easily observed or which were not observable.

A NEW METHODOLOGICAL APPROACH

The foregoing analysis indicates that whilst there has been considerable methodological innovations in the study of user system interaction, there is scope for further improvement. Ideally we believe that transaction log analysis ought to have the following features:

- Show real time;
- Show elapsed time;

- Show mouse movement of end user;
- Show input of end user;
- Show response of the system, e.g. error messages, retrieved items;
- Be unobtrusive;
- Give control to the researcher;
- Synchronise transaction log with verbal protocols; and
- Be used across different interfaces.

We believe that the method outlined here meets these criteria and therefore constitutes a considerable step forward. The approach can utilise either of two types of technology. The first consists of a PC to video converter, called Grand Art, produced by Imagine Graphics.

This equipment consists of hardware and software that was connected between a PC and monitor and a standard VHS video recorder. Once the software is installed, the screen output is unobtrusively re-routed to the video and recorded, and simultaneously displayed on the monitor to the end user. The second is Lotus ScreenCam software that, once loaded, records all screen activity onto disc in the form of a film. Lotus ScreenCam is the authors preferred option as it records directly to PC.

With both of these systems the end result is a real time film of the searching session. Each of these technologies is able to record the search session from start to finish in real time, showing pauses, movements made by mouse, input by participants, system responses (for example, error messages, retrieved results lists, instructions and prompts etc.) as well as a user's comments and as they work through their search session. Importantly, use of different electronic resources can be logged without any changes to the system. These films can be played back for analysis at a later date through a standard video player and television set or viewed directly on a PC. This method of recording the end users' interactions with electronic resources can also be described as "screen logging" and provides a more qualitative observational approach to transaction logging.

ATTENTION - THEORIES OF ATTENTION

Before launching into a detailed analysis of the three most influential bottleneck theories which emerged in the late 1950s and early 1960s, it would be helpful to establish a perspective from which to make the comparison. As a start, therefore, it does not seem unreasonable to ask a fundamental question: What is attention? Without a good idea of what attention is, and especially its relationship to perception and consciousness, we are in a poor position to compare theories.

A very early definition is that of William James over 100 years ago:

"It is the taking possession in the mind, in clear and vivid form, of one out of several simultaneous possible objects or trains of thought. Focalization, concentration of consciousness is of its essence. It implies withdrawal from some things in order to deal effectively with others".

James's definition neatly exposes a problem that dogs the field of attention: the relationship between attention and consciousness. Dixon (1981) is almost a lone voice in squarely confronting this issue, noting that one legacy of behaviourism is that the conscious mind is virtually a taboo subject. Add to this the idea that the effects of attention are largely preconscious, hence dangerously close to the 'unconscious' of psychoanalytic theory, and one has a double taboo whammy that makes many uneasy and obscures much that is important and interesting.

One outcome of this unease is the varying ways in which researchers in the field conceptualise 'attention' and 'consciousness', often doing so in order to skirt around some of the fundamental problems just described. As we shall see later, when comparing Deutsch and Deutsch (1963) theory with the rest, the tangled notions and vague definitions of attention, awareness, mental effort/concentration and consciousness can lead to severe problems, not least that researchers, coming from different conceptual frameworks, seem at times to be talking different languages. Some theorists have made an explicit differentiation between attention and consciousness. For example, Johnston and Heinz (1968) view attention as "the systematic admission of perceptual data into consciousness ... the process whereby perception is biased toward or against specific inputs".

This seems a compelling idea, and especially fits with the bottleneck theories of selective attention, unfortunately there are some problems with it. Firstly, there is the problem that attention seems sometimes to be under conscious volition and at other times (often annoyingly) not. This raises the key question: under what circumstances is attention under conscious control? A second problem is that the view of attention as a kind of selection process before ideas are allowed into consciousness (where, presumably, most high level semantic processing, planning and decision making is performed) does not fit with certain empirical findings, especially in the field of subliminal perception.

Dixon (1981) in a major review of the field, proposes a model of the mind as an information processor in which there are two separate systems; one involving consciousness/awareness, and the other involving preconscious (or unconscious) processing. If we ally this to the popular view of attention as "the concentration and focusing of mental effort", then we have a notion of attention which can be quite separate to consciousness. In other words, if attention is a concentration of mental effort, and mental effort can be exerted unconsciously, then attention, at least in part, acts separately to consciousness. As an alternative, attention can be viewed in the highly restrictive sense of only being necessary for information that is novel and important.

This introduces the ideas of acquisition of skill and automaticity which are performed without conscious control. As we shall see later, this has important implications for the efficacy of the ubiquitous dichotic listening paradigm. Treisman (1988) takes this view, seeing attention as being necessary for the integration of perceptual features that form objects i.e. it is required to combine otherwise separate features that we have not already "chunked" (to borrow a word from memory research) together by previous repeated exposure. The third problem with the Johnston and Heinz definition is more practical, in that not everybody has adopted it. This may seem an obvious point, but introduces an important and often overlooked idea: that different theories/models of attention necessarily entail different definitions of what attention is. It is all too easy to impose one's own conceptualisations on certain words (e.g. "attention", "awareness" and "consciousness") and compare theories using language which severely distorts the original theorist's conceptualisations. It is as if one were to compare and contrast a Jackson Pollock with a Raphael on one's own notions of "beauty", "meaning" and "harmony".

THEORIES OF ATTENTION

From issues associated with a defintion of "attention", let me now move on to compare the clearest and the most influential bottleneck theories of selective attention: those of Broadbent (1958), Treisman (1960), and Deutsch and Deutsch (1963). At a basic level, these theories appear to explicitly show that the locus of the bottleneck in a person's information processing system is either 'early' (perceptual limitations) or 'late' (response limitations). We shall see later that this may be too crude an assessment, and shall also briefly consider other possibilities that arise from the work of Johnson and his colleagues which have been seen as resolving this 'early' verses 'late' problem. For both historic and conceptual reasons, the easiest way to start a comparison of the three theories is to look at them in two pairs: firstly Broadbent and Treisman; secondly Treisman and Deutsch & Deutsch.

COMPARING BROADBENT'S AND TREISMAN'S THEORIES

Comparing Broadbent's and Treisman's theories is a relatively straightforward affair since Treisman's model is a direct amendment of Broadbent's. Let me firstly give an brief outline of each model. Broadbent's model: Incoming stimuli, briefly held in a sensory register, undergo preattentive analysis by a selective filter on the basis of their physical characteristics. Those stimuli selected pass along a (very) limited capacity channel to a detection device where semantic analysis takes place. Those stimuli not selected ('filtered' out) are not analysed for meaning and do not reach consciousness. This is, therefore, an early selection theory, and an 'all or nothing' view of perception.

Treisman's model: Incoming stimuli, briefly held in a sensory register, undergo preattentive analysis by an attenuation filter on the basis of crude physical characteristics (the information resulting from this analysis is available to conscious perception and for reporting by the subject, regardless of what happens to the message beyond this point). Those stimuli selected (attended to) pass along a limited capacity channel to a detection device (a pattern recognizer, comprising a number of 'dictionary' units) where semantic analysis takes place.

Unattended stimuli are attenuated (the signal strength is lowered) before passing along the limited capacity channel to the detection device, where they are semantically processed if they meet certain criteria.

This is, therefore, an early selection theory, and an attenuation model of attention.

These theories have far more ideas in common than they do differences, yet it is the differences which are the key aspects. The two major differences are outlined in the following two paragraphs.

- Broadbent's filter is all-or-nothing (it does not allow through unattended messages), whereas Treisman's filter allows unattended messages through, but in an attenuated form. Treisman proposed this amendment to account for a number of empirical findings which were not explained by Broadbent. For instance, Moray (1959) had found that "subjectively 'important' messages such as a person's own name can penetrate the block [the all-or-nothing filter]: thus a person will hear instructions if they are presented with his own name as part of the rejected message". A similar finding by Oswald et al (1960) found that a person's own name and critical names presented to a sleeping subject elicited a clench response which had been previously conditioned. Treisman (1960), using a dichotic listening with shadowing procedure, found that if different sentences in the two ears are suddenly switched, then the subject shadows one or two words of the unattended message before reverting back to shadow the attended ear. Clearly, certain unattended messages can be processed semantically, hence the need to modify the physical characteristics filter.

Broadbent's is a simple single filter model, whereas Treisman's can be thought of as a two-stage filtering process: firstly, filtering on the basis of incoming channel characteristics, and secondly, filtering by the threshold settings of the dictionary units. Treisman's explanation as to the way these threshold settings perform a filtering operation explains the findings of Moray, Oswald and Treisman described above, and many other similar findings. The dictionary units have the two mportant properties of having thresholds that differ, and which are variable. Some units, those which respond to biologically (or emotionally) important signals, have permanently lowered thresholds. Hence, even very attenuated signals (because they are not being attended to) can trigger a unit which is 'tuned' to that signal. This explains the reason why one's own name can attract one's attention in a previously unattended message. On a more biological level, this explains the sensitivity that mothers have for the noises their babies make, even when virtually out of earshot. In addition to these semi-permanent threshold differentials, there is the transient variation in thresholds due to the expectations of the subject i.e. the context. The occurrence of a particular signal will, if it triggers a dictionary unit, lower the threshold for other signals which in the past have been associated with it.

COMPARING TREISMAN'S MODEL AND DEUTSCH AND DEUTSCH'S MODEL

Let us move on to a more problematical task: comparing Treisman's model with that of Deutsch and Deutsch (1963). There are two key points to consider. Firstly, Deutsch and Deutsch's theory is based on the same empirical data as Treisman's theory, but is reinterpreted from a different perspective. Secondly, Deutsch and Deutsch saw Treisman's model as being flawed in that the dual filtering process is redundant - why have the lower level filter, if the same job can be done by suitably controlling the thresholds of the dictionary units? Let me briefly outline Deutsch and Deutsch's theory.

Deutsch and Deutsch: Almost every incoming message in a sensory register reaches "the same perceptual and discriminatory mechanisms whether attention is paid to it or not; and such information is then grouped or segregated by these mechanisms". Discriminatory (or classifying) mechanisms become excited by particular attributes of the incoming message depending on preset weightings of importance. The discriminatory mechanism with the highest weighting will transfer this weighting to the other classifying mechanisms with which it has been grouped or segregated.

Since there will normally be activity in a number of classifying mechanisms, a "diffuse and non-specific system is necessary" which takes up a level, at any one time, corresponding with the level of the 'highest' discriminatory mechanism. This highest level sets a criterion by which all other levels are compared. Hence, only the discriminatory mechanism with the highest level activates the appropriate outputs (storage, motor response) and inhibits the outputs associated with the other discriminatory mechanisms. Further, the general level of arousal will alter access output systems. Hence, for a low level of arousal (e.g. sleep), only very high level messages will be able to alter storage/motor response.

At first sight, and accounting for major differences in terminology, this looks very similar to Treisman's theory. The 'discriminatory mechanisms' with their 'weightings of importance' look remarkably similar to Treisman's 'dictionary units' and 'thresholds'. One obvious difference is that Deutsch and Deutsch have no low level (physical characteristics) filter. Another difference is that all the 'discriminatory mechanisms' (including physical and semantic classifying structures) in Deutsch and Deutsch's theories are triggered, whereas Treisman has only those 'dictionary units' with signals above a threshold being triggered. However, since Deutsch and Deutsch have only the highest level being capable of further processing (output response), this amounts to the same idea as Treisman, whose threshold settings are altered depending on those units being triggered. So what is all the fuss about? Apart from the lack of a separate low level filter, both models have pattern recognition units/mechanisms that select one or two highly salient signals dependent on bottom-up (physical) and top-down (contextual) features which are then passed on to the appropriate response mechanisms.

The question then is: Why is Treisman's theory seen as typifying 'early' selection and Deutsch and Deutsch's as typifying 'late' selection? Support for the idea that both theories are basically the same comes from Moray (page 35, 1969) who in reviewing early and late selection theories, quotes a personal communication with J. A. Deutsch in 1968, in which: "Deutsch does not agree that their model is a response selection model, but regards it as selecting incoming signals in the same sense in which Treisman's model does". So why this misinterpretation in analysing the two theories. I believe the problem stems from the fact that the two theories come from different areas of psychology, and consequently are couched in the different language and conceptualisations. Treisman is wholeheartedly a cognitive psychologist using the tricks of the trade (dichotic listening, shadowing, reaction times, memory tests) to tease out the way different units in the mind process information.

Deutsch and Deutsch, on the other hand, are from the biological school (and I believe have never touched a pair of dichotic listening headphones in their lives). To use an artificial intelligence analogy, one could say that Treisman favours a traditional serial processing approach, whereas Deutsch and Deutsch are from the connectionist school of parallel distributed processing and neural networks.

The difference is highlighted when one reads their original papers. Whereas Treisman is written in "information processing speak", Deutsch and Deutsch's language is in terms of organisms, behaviours and neurophysiology (in fact their original paper contains a substantial section on the neurophysiological evidence relevant to their ideas). It is an astonishing, and little known, fact that Deutsch and Deutsch original (1963) paper on attention contains neither the word "consciousness" nor the word "conscious".

The conceptual rift between Treisman and Deutsch & Deutsch is clearly demonstrated in two papers printed in 1967, in which they, themselves, appear to be talking different languages. In the first, "Selective attention: perception or response?"

Treisman and Geffen seem to demonstrate by means of a dichotic listening task with shadowing and finger tapping instructions that "the main limit is perceptual".

In the second paper, "Comments on 'Selective attention: perception or response?'", Deutsch and Deutsch take a completely different reading of this experiment opening with the statement "We cannot understand why Treisman and Geffen (1967) think their experiment argues against our theory". To add insult to injury, Deutsch and Deutsch go on to criticise Treisman's amendment of Broadbent's theory, by arguing that the reduced signal-to-noise ratio of unattended messages rather than reducing the load on the signal-recognition system would actually increase it, since signal detection theory says that the noisier the signal, the more analysis is required to extract it. No doubt Treisman, Deutsch and Deutsch are highly intelligent and knowledgeable people, and it is not my place to try and resolve their differences. Suffice to say (if I am not labouring the point) that it is their different conceptualisation and definitions of 'attention', 'awareness', 'perception' and 'consciousness' that, I believe, is causing the problems.

PROBLEMS FOR BOTTLENECK THEORIES

Let me end by briefly looking at two analyses that have a significant bearing on the bottleneck theories of attention. Firstly, a problem that a number of researchers believe is inherent with the major paradigm involved in providing empirical evidence for selective attention theorists: i.e. dichotic listening with shadowing. The usefulness of this technique, I believe, was twofold: it clearly demonstrated the direction of attention, and it required so much mental effort that none is available to allow even a brief switch of attention to other directions. However, this technique is seen as being so mentally effortful to the experimental subject that it precludes studying the affect of attention under the more real-life circumstances where attention is rarely overloaded to such an extent and, therefore, can be switched and interwoven with the many parallel activities that can be performed without conscious attention (i.e. automatic skills).

Another objection is that dichotic listening may still allow for switches of attention for instance, Mowbray (1964) found that memory for 'unattended' events was associated with a temporary shift of attention away from the primary message. A major advance in experimental technique was introduced around 1970 with inferential methodologies. This led to research that showed that at least under conditions below information-overload, a capacity model of attention was probably more applicable than bottleneck theories.

The second idea, I feel is appropriate to end with, comes from work by William Johnston and his colleagues: e.g. Johnston & Heinz (1978); Johnston & Wilson (1980). This work appeared to demonstrate that there is no single bottleneck in the information processing system, but that there are a series of filters so that incoming stimuli can be processed both 'early' or 'late' depending on the situation: i.e. "the unattended message is processed according to task demands". This is, therefore, a *flexible* theory of selective attention.

One of the strongest empirical evidence which, it is claimed, supports this hypothesis is that of Johnston and Wilson (1980). In this study, subjects were aurally presented with a series of simultaneous word pairs, one of which was occasionally an instance of a predetermined category (e.g. animals) that the subject had been instructed to 'listen out' for. These words were always homonyms (e.g. bear) so that the simultaneous paired word could be appropriate (e.g. hibernate), inappropriate (e.g. naked) or neutral (e.g. luck).

The first part of the experiment was carried out with binaural presentation (i.e. both words to both ears), with the finding that "detection of targets can be facilitated by appropriate nontargets and inhibited by inappropriate ones. Thus, non-targets can influence the way in which targets are semantically represented".

In the second part, presentation was dichotic with the subject precued as to the ear that the target word would appear in. Under these conditions, the effects found in the first part of the experiment did not occur.

The overall conclusion being that "precueing appears to curtail the perceptual processing of nontargets. The data run counter to theories that claim that focused attention does not entail the perceptual suppression of nontargets".

A close examination of the actual words used in the experiment reveals that appropriate nontarget words are almost invariably words that would normally be associated with the targets (e.g. hair-comb, blocks-wooden, duck-quacking), whereas the majority of inappropriate nontargets (23 out of 36 words) are synonyms of the inappropriate categorisation (e.g. hair-rabbit, blocks-barricades, duck-dodge).

It seems to me that rather than there being facilitation by semantic processing of the nontarget word in the binaural case, it was a simple association (a precategorical perceptual grouping) between the target and nontarget.

For example, one has heard the words hearing the simultaneous presentation of the word blocks and wooden would trigger a 'dictionary unit' that 'looks out' for "wooden block", as if this was a single word. I believe this seriously questions the validity of the results.

PERCEPTION - THEORIES OF PERCEPTION

In philosophy, psychology, and the cognitive sciences, perception is the process of attaining awareness or understanding of sensory information. It is a task far more complex than was imagined in the 1950s and 1960s, when it was predicted that building perceiving machines would take about a decade, a goal which is still very far from fruition. The word comes from the Latin words *perceptio, percipio,* and means "receiving, collecting, action of taking possession, apprehension with the mind or senses." Perception is one of the oldest fields in psychology. The oldest quantitative law in psychology is the Weber-Fechner law, which quantifies the relationship between the intensity of physical stimuli and their perceptual effects.

The study of perception gave rise to the Gestalt school of psychology, with its emphasis on holistic approach. What one perceives is a result of interplays between past experiences, including one's culture, and the interpretation of the perceived. If the percept does not have support in any of these perceptual bases it is unlikely to rise above perceptual threshold. Two types of consciousness are considerable regarding perception: phenomenal (any occurrence that is observable) and psychological. The difference everybody can demonstrate to him- or herself is by the simple opening and closing of his or her eyes: phenomenal consciousness is thought, on average, to be predominately absent without sight. Through the full or rich sensations present in sight, nothing by comparison is present while the eyes are closed. Using this precept, it is understood that, in the vast majority of cases, logical solutions are reached through simple human sensation.

The analogy of Plato's Cave was coined to express these ideas. Passive perception (conceived by René Descartes) can be surmised as the following sequence of events: surrounding '! input (senses) '! processing (brain) output (re-action). Although still supported by mainstream philosophers, psychologists and neurologists, this theory is nowadays losing momentum. The theory of active perception has emerged from extensive research of sensory illusions, most notably the works of Richard L. Gregory. This theory, which is increasingly gaining experimental support, can be surmised as dynamic relationship between "description" (in the brain) "! senses "! surrounding, all of which holds true to the linear concept of experience.

Basic physical truths such as cause and effect and vagrant patterns imposed upon the perceived laws of creation similarly support this dualistic appreciation of reality-perception.

Additional types include:

- Amodal perception
- Colour perception
- Depth perception
- Visual perception
- Form perception
- Haptic perception
- Speech perception
- Perception as Interpretation
- Numeric Value of Perception
- Pitch perception
- Harmonic perception
- Rhythmic perception

In the case of visual perception, some people can actually see the percept shift in their mind's eye. Others, who are not picture thinkers, may not necessarily perceive the 'shape-shifting' as their world changes. The 'esemplastic' nature has been shown by experiment: an ambiguous image has multiple interpretations on the perceptual level. The question, "Is the glass half empty or half full?" serves to demonstrate the way an object can be perceived in different ways. Just as one object can give rise to multiple percepts, so an object may fail to give rise to any percept at all: if the percept has no grounding in a person's experience, the person may literally not perceive it. The processes of perception routinely alter what humans see.

When people view something with a preconceived idea about it, they tend to take those preconceived ideas and see them whether or not they are there. This problem stems from the fact that humans are unable to understand new information, without the inherent bias of their previous knowledge. A person's knowledge creates his or her reality as much as the truth, because the human mind can only contemplate that to which it has been exposed. When objects are viewed without understanding, the mind will try to reach for something that it already recognizes, in order to process what it is viewing. That which most closely relates to the unfamiliar from our past experiences, makes up what we see when we look at things that we don't comprehend.

This confusing ambiguity of perception is exploited in human technologies such as camouflage, and also in biological mimicry, for example by Peacock butterflies, whose wings bear eye markings that birds respond to as though they were the eyes of a dangerous predator. Perceptual ambiguity is not restricted to vision. For example, recent touch perception research Robles-De-La-Torre & Hayward 2001 found that kinesthesia based haptic perception strongly relies on the forces experienced during touch. Cognitive theories of perception assume there is a poverty of stimulus. This (with reference to perception) is the claim that sensation are, by themselves, unable to provide a unique description of the world. Sensations require 'enriching', which is the role of the mental model.

A different type of theory is the perceptual ecology approach of James J. Gibson. Gibson rejected the assumption of a poverty of stimulus by rejecting the notion that perception is based in sensations. Instead, he investigated what information is actually presented to the perceptual systems. He and the psychologists who work within this paradigm detailed how the world could be specified to a mobile, exploring organism via the lawful projection of information about the world into energy arrays. Specification is a 1:1 mapping of some aspect of the world into a perceptual array; given such a mapping, no enrichment is required and perception is direct perception. The brain, with which one perceives the world, is made up of neurons "buzzing" at 50 cycles a second, while the world as it exists in reality is made up of electro-magnetic radiation oscillating at 500 trillion cycles a second.

This means that the human brain cannot nearly keep up with the 'realness of reality.' To compensate, the brain takes a preconceived idea about the object, then uses those preconceived ideas to see whether or not they are there. The problem with attaining an accurate perception of reality stems from the fact that humans are unable to understand new information, without the inherent bias of their previous knowledge. The extent of a person's knowledge creates his or her reality as much as the truth, because the human mind can only contemplate that to which it has been exposed. When objects are viewed without understanding, the mind will try to reach for something that it already recognizes, in order to process what it is viewing. That which most closely relates to the unfamiliar from a person's past experiences makes up what he or she sees when he or she looks at things that he or she does not comprehend.

PERCEPTION-IN-ACTION

The ecological understanding of perception derives from Gibson's early work is perception-in-action, the notion that perception is a requisite property of animate action; without perception action would not be guided and without action perception would be pointless. Animate actions require perceiving and moving together. In a sense, "perception and movement are two sides of the same coin, the coin is action." One aspect of Gibson's approach has been questioned however: it is his implicit belief that singular entities, which he calls 'invariants', already exist in the real and that all that the perception process does is to home in upon 'them'. A view known as social constructionism regards the continual adjustment of percept and action to the external input as precisely what constitutes the 'entity,' which is therefore far from being 'invariant.'

In human communication, according to the theory, a running hypothesis that there is an 'invariant', a target to be homed in upon, is a pragmatic necessity to allow an initial measure of understanding to be established prior to the updating a statement aims to achieve, but it does not and need not represent an actuality. It is added that, after all, it is extremely unlikely that what is desired or feared by an organism will never suffer change—indeed, radical change—as time goes on; the social constructionist theory thus allows for the needful evolutionary adjustment.

A mathematical theory of perception-in-action has been devised and investigated in many forms of controlled movement by many different species of organism, General Tau Theory. According to this theory, tau information, or time-to-goal information is the fundamental 'percept' in perception.

THEORIES OF PERCEPTION

- McClelland's and Rumelhart's Interactive Activation Model
- Anne Triesman's Feature Integration Theory

The feature integration theory, developed by Treisman, a professor at Princeton University's Department of Psychology, and Gelade since the early 1980s, posits that different kinds of attention are responsible for *binding different features into consciously experienced wholes*. The theory has been one of the most influential psychological models of human visual attention. According to Treisman, in a first step to visual processing, several primary visual features are processed and represented with separate feature maps that are later integrated in a saliency map that can be accessed in order to direct attention to the most conspicuous areas.

- Treisman distinguishes two kinds of visual search tasks, feature search and conjunction search. Feature search can be performed fast and pre-attentively for targets defined by primitive features. Conjunction search is the serial search for targets defined by a conjunction of primitive features. It is much slower and requires conscious attention. She concluded from many experiments that colour, orientation, and intensity are primitive features, for which feature search can be performed.
- It was widely speculated that the saliency map could be located in early visual cortical areas, e.g. the

Primary Visual Cortex (V1), though this is controversial. Wolfe's popular Guided Search Model offers a more up to date theory of visual search but is also problematic.

- Evidence for this theory comes from the phenomenon of illusory conjunctions, popout of primitives in visual search (making them easily identifiable regardless of number of distracters) and the fact that participants can often remember the presence of an object, but not its location, during a fast visual search.
- Irving Biederman's Recognition-by-Components Theory

The Recognition-by-components theory, or RBC theory, was proposed by Irving Biederman to explain object recognition. According to RBC theory, we are able to recognize objects by separating them into *geons*. Geons can be composed of various shapes (i.e. cylinders, cones, etc.) that can be assembled in various arrangements to form a virtually unlimited amount of objects.

STRENGTHS OF THE THEORY

Utilizing geons as structural primitives results in two key advantages. Because geons are based on object properties that are stable across viewpoint ('viewpoint invariant'), and all geons are disciminable from one another, a single geon description is sufficient to describe an object from all possible viewpoints. The second advantage is that considerable economy of representation is achieved: a relatively small set of geons form a simple "alphabet" that can combine to form complex objects. For example, with only 24 geons, there are 306 billion possible combinations of 3 geons, allowing for all possible objects to be recognised.

Experimental evidence:

- Participants show a remarkable ability to recognise objects despite visual noise provided that the geons are visible
- Removal of feature-relation information (relations between geons) impairs object recognition

- No visual priming if different geons are used between trials

Theoretical Evidence

The RBC theory is supported by the transversality principle from geometry.

WEAKNESSES

RBC theory is not in itself capable of starting with a photograph of a real object and producing a geons-and-relations description of the object; the theory does not attempt to provide a mechanism to reduce the complexities of real scenes to simple geon shapes. RBC theory is also incomplete in that geons and the relations between them will fail to distinguish many real objects. For example, a pear and an apple are easily distinguished by humans but lack the corners and edges needed for RBC theory to recognize they are different. However, Irving Biederman has argued that RBC theory is the "preferred" mode of human object recognition, with a secondary process handling objects that are not distinguishable by their geons. He further states that this distinction explains research suggesting that objects may or may not be recognized equally well with changes in viewpoint.

Unit VI

Intelligence and Creativity

NATURE OF INTELLIGENCE: GARDNER'S THEORY OF MULTIPLE INTELLIGENCES

The theory of multiple intelligences was proposed by Howard Gardner in 1983, to more accurately define the concept of intelligence and address whether methods which claim to measure intelligence (or aspects thereof) are truly scientific.Gardner's theory argues that intelligence, particularly as it is traditionally defined, does not sufficiently encompass the wide variety of abilities humans display. In his conception, a child who masters multiplication easily is not necessarily more intelligent *overall* than a child who struggles to do so. The second child may be stronger in another *kind* of intelligence, and therefore may best learn the given material through a different approach, may excel in a field outside of mathematics, or may even be looking through the multiplication learning process at a fundamentally deeper level that hides a potentially higher mathematical intelligence than in the one who memorizes the concept easily.

DEVELOPMENT OF THE THEORY

"Howard Gardner, multiple intelligences and education" by given field (child prodigies, autistic savants);

- Neurological evidence for areas of the brain that are specialized for particular capacities (often including studies of people who have suffered brain damage affecting a specific capacity);
- The evolutionary relevance of the various capacities;

- Psychometric studies; and
- Susceptibility to encoding in a symbol system or notation (e.g. written language, musical notation, choreography).
- An identifiable core operation or set of operations.
- A distinctive development history, along with a definable set of 'end-state' performances.

Gardner originally identified seven core intelligences: linguistic, logical-mathematical, spatial, bodily-kinesthetic, musical, interpersonal and intrapersonal. In 1997 at the symposium "MIND 97" (Multiple Intelligences New Directions) he added an eighth, the "Naturalist" Intelligence. Investigation continues on whether there are Existentialist (existential) and Spiritualist (spiritual) Intelligences. The theory has been widely criticized in the psychology and educational theory communities.

The most common criticisms argue that Gardner's theory is based on his own intuition rather than empirical data and that the intelligences are just other names for talents or personality types. Despite these criticisms, the theory has enjoyed a great deal of popularity amongst educators over the past twenty years. There are several schools which espouse MI as a pedagogy, and many individual teachers who incorporate some or all of the theory into their methodology. Many books and educational materials exist which explain the theory and how it may be applied to the school of IFSS.

GARDNER'S CATEGORIES OF INTELLIGENCE

The categories of intelligence proposed by Gardner are:

Bodily-kinesthetic

This area has to do with bodily movement. In theory, people who have Bodily-kinesthetic intelligence should learn better by involving muscular movement, i.e. getting up and moving around into the learning experience, and are generally good at physical activities such as sports or dance. They may enjoy acting or performing, and in general they are good at building and making things. They often learn best by doing something physically, rather than reading or hearing about it. Those with strong bodily-kinesthetic intelligence seem to use what might be termed muscle memory - they remember things through their body such as verbal memory or images.

Careers that suit those with this intelligence include athletes, dancers, actors, surgeons, doctors, builders, and soldiers.

Although these careers can be duplicated through virtual simulation they will not produce the actual physical learning that is needed in this intelligence.

Interpersonal

This area has to do with interaction with others. In theory, people who have a high interpersonal intelligence tend to be extroverts, characterized by their sensitivity to others' moods, feelings, temperaments and motivations, and their ability to cooperate in order to work as part of a group.

They communicate effectively and empathize easily with others, and may be either leaders or followers. They typically learn best by working with others and often enjoy discussion and debate. Careers that suit those with this intelligence include sales, politicians, managers, teachers, and social workers.

Verbal-linguistic

This area has to do with words, spoken or written. People with high verbal-linguistic intelligence display a facility with words and languages. They are typically good at reading, writing, telling stories and memorizing words along with dates. They tend to learn best by reading, taking notes, listening to lectures, and discussion and debate. They are also frequently skilled at explaining, teaching and oration or persuasive speaking. Those with verbal-linguistic intelligence learn foreign languages very easily as they have high verbal memory and recall, and an ability to understand and manipulate syntax and structure. This intelligence is highest in writers, lawyers, philosophers, journalists, politicians, poets, and teachers.

LOGICAL-MATHEMATICAL

This area has to do with logic, abstractions, reasoning, and numbers. While it is often assumed that those with this intelligence naturally excel in mathematics, chess, computer programming and other logical or numerical activities, a more accurate definition places emphasis on traditional mathematical ability and more reasoning capabilities, abstract patterns of recognition, scientific thinking and investigation, and the ability to perform complex calculations.

It correlates strongly with traditional concepts of "intelligence" or IQ. Many scientists, mathematicians, engineers, doctors and economists function in this type of intelligence.

NATURALISTIC

This area has to do with nature, nurturing and relating information to one's natural surroundings. This type of intelligence was not part of Gardner's original theory of Multiple Intelligences, but was added to the theory in 1997. Those with it are said to have greater sensitivity to nature and their place within it, the ability to nurture and grow things, and greater ease in caring for, taming and interacting with animals. They may also be able to discern changes in weather or similar fluctuations in their natural surroundings. Recognizing and classifying things are at the core of a naturalist. They must connect a new experience with prior knowledge to truly learn something new.

"Naturalists" learn best when the subject involves collecting and analyzing, or is closely related to something prominent in nature; they also don't enjoy learning unfamiliar or seemingly useless subjects with little or no connections to nature. It is advised that naturalistic learners would learn more through being outside or in a kinesthetic way. The theory behind this intelligence is often criticized, much like the spiritual or existential intelligence, as it is seen by many as not indicative of an intelligence but rather an interest. Careers that suit those with this intelligence include scientists, naturalists, conservationists, gardeners and farmers.

INTRAPERSONAL

This area has to do with introspective and self-reflective capacities. Those who are strongest in this intelligence are typically introverts and prefer to work alone. They are usually highly self-aware and capable of understanding their own emotions, goals and motivations.

They often have an affinity for thought-based pursuits such as philosophy. They learn best when allowed to concentrate on the subject by themselves. There is often a high level of perfectionism associated with this intelligence. Careers that suit those with this intelligence include philosophers, psychologists, theologians, writers and scientists.

VISUAL-SPATIAL

This area has to do with vision and spatial judgment. People with strong visual-spatial intelligence are typically very good at visualizing and mentally manipulating objects. Those with strong spatial intelligence are often proficient at solving puzzles.

They have a strong visual memory and are often artistically inclined. Those with visual-spatial intelligence also generally have a very good sense of direction and may also have very good hand-eye coordination, although this is normally seen as a characteristic of the bodily-kinesthetic intelligence. Some critics point out the high correlation between the spatial and mathematical abilities, which seems to disprove the clear separation of the intelligences as Gardner theorized. Since solving a mathematical problem involves reassuringly manipulating symbols and numbers, spatial intelligence is involved in visually changing the reality.

A thorough understanding of the two intelligences precludes this criticism, however, as the two intelligences do not precisely conform to the definitions of visual and mathematical abilities. Although they may share certain characteristics, they are easily distinguished by several factors, and there are many with strong logical-mathematical intelligence. Careers that suit those with this intelligence include artists, engineers, and architects.

MUSICAL

This area has to do with rhythm, music, and hearing. Those who have a high level of musical-rhythmic intelligence display greater sensitivity to sounds, rhythms, tones, and music. They normally have good pitch and may even have absolute pitch, and are able to sing, play musical instruments, and compose music. Since there is a strong auditory component to this intelligence, those who are strongest in it may learn best via lecture. In addition, they will often use songs or rhythms to learn and memorize information, and may work best with music playing in the background. Careers that suit those with this intelligence include instrumentalists, singers, conductors, disc-jockeys, orators, writers (to a certain extent) and composers and sales reps.

OTHER INTELLIGENCES

Other intelligences have been suggested or explored by Gardner and his colleagues, including spiritual, existential and moral intelligence. Gardner excluded spiritual intelligence due to what he perceived as the inability to codify criteria comparable to the other "intelligences". Existential intelligence (the capacity to raise and reflect on philosophical questions about life, death, and ultimate realities) meets most of the criteria with the exception of identifiable areas of the brain that specialize for this faculty. Moral capacities were excluded because they are normative rather than descriptive.

SAVANT SYNDROME

Gardner used case studies of autistic savants as part of his theory on multiple intelligences. On one hand they have severe mental disabilities and thus impaired social skills, but on the other they have some extraordinary mental abilities not found in most people. The Savant Syndrome skills involve striking feats of memory and often include arithmetic calculation and sometimes unusual abilities in art or music. There is actually a disproportionate regularity with which the triad of blindness, mental disability and musical genius occurs in savant syndrome. Examples include Derek Paravicini who has severe learning disability but can remember every song he has ever heard.

Others with savant syndrome are not autistic, but develop these abilities later on in life usually as a result of some accident, illness or trauma. For example Alonzo Clemons was a regular child until he suffered brain damage as a result of a fall. Afterwards he learned to create accurate animal sculptures from clay using his photographic memory. Some scientists thus believe that the potential to be a genius is latent in all people but is obscured by normal functioning intellect. In the case of savants, the damage to the brain has somehow disrupted normal functioning and has allowed the brain to access these latent skills. Savants are generally viewed as having exceptional spatial intelligence but verbal defects.

USE IN EDUCATION

Traditionally, schools have emphasized the development of logical intelligence and linguistic intelligence (mainly reading and writing). While many students function well in this environment, there are those who do not. Gardner's theory argues that students will be better served by a broader vision of education, wherein teachers use different methodologies, exercises and activities to reach all students, not just those who excel at linguistic and logical intelligence. Many teachers see the theory as simple common sense. Some say that it validates what they already know: that students learn in different ways. On the other hand, James Traub's article in *The New Republic* notes that Gardner's system has not been accepted by most academics in intelligence or teaching.

George Miller, the esteemed psychologist credited with discovering the mechanisms by which short term memory operates, wrote in *The New York Times Book Review* that Gardner's argument boiled down to "hunch and opinion". And Gardner's subsequent work has done very little to shift the balance of opinion. A recent issue of *Psychology, Public Policy, and Law* devoted to the study of intelligence contained virtually no reference to Gardner's work. Most people who study intelligence view M.I. theory as rhetoric rather than science, and they're divided on the virtues of the rhetoric. The application of the theory of multiple intelligences varies widely. It runs the gamut from a teacher who, when confronted with a student having difficulties, uses a different approach to teach the material, to an entire school using MI as a framework. In general, those who subscribe to the theory strive to provide opportunities for their students to use and develop all the different intelligences, not just the few at which they naturally excel.

A Harvard-led study of 41 schools using the theory came to the conclusion that in these schools there was "a culture of hard work, respect, and caring; a faculty that collaborated and learned from each other; classrooms that engaged students through constrained but meaningful choices, and a sharp focus on enabling students to produce high-quality work." Of the schools implementing Gardner's theory, the most well-known is New City School, in St. Louis, Missouri, which has been using the theory since 1988.

The school's teachers have produced two books for teachers, *Celebrating Multiple Intelligences* and *Succeeding With Multiple Intelligences* and the principal, Thomas Hoerr, has written *Becoming a Multiple Intelligences School* as well as many articles on the practical applications of the theory. The school has also hosted four conferences, each attracting over 200 educators from around the world and remains a valuable resource for teachers interested in implementing the theory in their own classrooms. Thomas Armstrong considers that Waldorf education organically engages all of Gardner's seven intelligences.

CRITICISM

Criticisms of the theory's application in schools come in four major forms. First, opponents argue that the theory may lead to a sort of intellectual relativism, wherein students' failures are explained away as being an example of a different kind of intelligence, not a lesser one. As a result, there are those in the Gifted and Talented community who have criticized Gardner's theory, because any support of the idea that all children are equally gifted, just in different ways, might lead to the reduction or broadening of Gifted and Talented programs. Gardner himself has said that he does not believe his theory will have this type of consequence for gifted programs, and that he never intended his theory to affirm that all people are equally gifted, but rather that the definition of intelligence was too narrow to encompass all types of intelligence.

The second major problem with Gardener's theory is that in his denial that there is any real statistical factor (such as "g") contributing to many intellectual tasks, he does not account for that correlation in the empirical data. That is, every multiple domain IQ test ever normed has shown that all the areas tested are correlated [citation needed]. This trend is also shown in tests like the Graduate Record Examination, the SAT, the PSAT, the ACT, etc., on every one of which each section correlates to a high degree with the others; the correlation rarely drops below 0.6 on the -1 to 1 scale. In fact, Gardener has downplayed the correlation between his intelligences. The third major criticism of multiple intelligences as an application in schools is that there is a risk of teachers excusing students from doing well in an area in which they are weak. Students who may not "naturally" learn to read and write well nevertheless need to read and write well. Similarly, the goal is for students to succeed in all areas defined as intelligence by Gardner, and not default to their strengths.

There is an inherent risk of students developing a sense of inferiority in given areas. Students who are identified as not being "musical" learners may have less incentive to become musical learners. A methodological criticism is that the assessment of one's form of intelligence is usually determined via a self-administered test. The usual form asks the respondent 40-60 questions such as "Do you prefer to stand when working?" This sort of question leaves much room for assessment error, and does not conform to survey techniques and methodology such as double-blind testing.

Another criticism is that the distinction between developmental stage and "intelligence" is not sufficiently well accounted for. For example, the average five-year-old is more likely to answer "yes" to the question "Do you like to move about a lot?" than the average forty-year-old. Conversely, the older person is more likely to seem to have interpersonal "intelligence," which might be better labeled as a developed skill — solving problems with others or speaking in public, for example.

OPPOSING VIEWS

The Definition of Intelligence

As one would expect from a theory that redefines intelligence, one of the major criticisms of the theory is that it is ad hoc. The criticism is that Gardner is not expanding the definition of the word "intelligence"; rather, he denies the existence of intelligence, as is traditionally understood, and instead uses the word "intelligence" whenever other people have traditionally used words like "ability". This practice has been criticized by Robert J. Sternberg (1983, 1991), Eysenck (1994), and Scarr (1985). Defenders of MI theory argue that the traditional definition of intelligence is too narrow, and thus broader definition more accurately reflects the differing ways in which humans think and learn. They would state that the traditional interpretation of intelligence collapses under the weight of its own logic and definition, noting that intelligence is usually defined as the cognitive or mental capacity of an individual, which by logical necessity would include all forms of mental qualities, not simply the ones most transparent to standardized I.Q. tests.

Some of these criticisms arise from the fact that Gardner has not settled on a single definition of intelligence. He originally defined it as the ability to solve problems that have value in at least one culture, or as something that a student is interested in. However, he added a disclaimer that he has no fixed definition, and his classification is more of an artistic judgment than fact:

Ultimately, it would certainly be desirable to have an algorithm for the selection of an intelligence, such that any trained researcher could determine whether a candidate's intelligence met the appropriate criteria. At present, however, it must be admitted that the selection (or rejection) of a candidate's intelligence is reminiscent more of an artistic judgment than of a scientific assessment.

Gardner argues that by calling linguistic and logical-mathematical abilities intelligences, but not artistic, musical, athletic, etc. abilities, the former are needlessly aggrandized. Many critics balk at this widening of the definition, saying that it ignores "the connotation of intelligence...[which] has always connoted the kind of thinking skills that makes one successful in school."

Gardner writes "I balk at the unwarranted assumption that certain human abilities can be arbitrarily singled out as intelligence while others cannot" Critics hold that given this statement, any interest or ability is now redefined as "intelligence". Thus, by adopting this theory, studying intelligence becomes difficult, because it diffuses into the broader concept of ability or talent. Gardner's addition of the naturalistic intelligence and conceptions of the existential and moral intelligences are seen as fruits of this diffusion. Defenders of the MI theory would argue that this is simply a recognition of the broad scope of inherent mental abilities, and that such an exhaustive scope by nature defies a simple, one-dimensional classification such as an assigned IQ value. They would claim that such one-dimensional values are typically of limited value in predicting the real world application of unique mental abilities.

INTELLECTUAL RELATIVISM

Many critics argue that the theory's definition of intelligence leads to the belief that all human beings are equally intelligent, but in large part this is based on misunderstanding. Gardner argues that there are many different kinds of intelligence and that none is better or more important. However, people have differing abilities within these types of intelligences. Albert Einstein and a person who is good at mathematics both display logical-mathematical intelligence, but at no point does the theory say that all people with the logical-mathematical intelligence are equally intelligent.

LACK OF EMPIRICAL EVIDENCE

Some critics argue that many of Gardner's "intelligences" actually correlate with the *g* factor, supporting the idea of single dominant type of intelligence. For example, Carroll (1993) argued that verbal comprehension, auditory processing, visual perception and ability in logic and mathematics all correlate with each other and are actually subsets of global intelligence. This gives further support for a theory of a single type intelligence.

A critical review of MI theory argues that there is little empirical evidence to support it:

"To date there have been no published studies that offer evidence of the validity of the multiple intelligences. In 1994 Sternberg reported finding no empirical studies. In 2000 Allix reported finding no empirical validating studies, and at that time Gardner and Connell conceded that there was "little hard evidence for MI theory". In 2004 Sternberg and Grigerenko stated that there were no validating studies for multiple intelligences, and in 2004 Gardner asserted that he would be "delighted were such evidence to accrue", and he admitted that "MI theory has few enthusiasts among psychometricians or others of a traditional psychological background" because they require "psychometric or experimental evidence that allows one to prove the existence of the several intelligences"."

Supporters of the MI theory would counter that such dependency is to be expected as this point, as scientific methodology aimed at uncovering intelligence was created under the traditional theory of intelligence, thus leaving a new theory the necessity of initially having to utilize the methodology of the old theory until new modes of scientific inquiry can be developed. The same review presents evidence to demonstrate that cognitive neuroscience research does not support the theory of Multiple Intelligences:

"the human brain is unlikely to function via Gardner's multiple intelligences. Taken together the evidence for the intercorrelations of subskills of IQ measures, the evidence for a shared set of genes associated with mathematics, reading, and g, and the evidence for shared and overlapping "what is it?" and "where is it?" neural processing pathways, and shared neural pathways for language, music, motor skills, and emotions suggest that it is unlikely that that each of Gardner's intelligences could operate "via a different set of neural mechanisms" (1999, p. 99). Equally important, the evidence for the "what is it?" and "where is it?" processing pathways, for Kahneman's two decision-making systems, and for adapted cognition modules suggests that these cognitive brain specializations have evolved to address very specific problems in our environment. Because Gardner claimed that that the intelligences are innate potentialities related to a general content area, MI theory lacks a rationale for the phylogenetic emergence of the intelligences."

A number of articles have surveyed the use of Gardner's ideas and conclude that there is no evidence that his ideas work in practice. Steven A. Stahl found that most of the previous studies which claimed to show positive results had major flaws:

Among others, Marie Carbo claims that her learning styles work is based on research. {I discuss Carbo because she publishes extensively on her model and is very prominent in the workshop circuit...} But given the overwhelmingly negative findings in the published research, I wondered what she was citing, and about a decade ago, I thought it would be interesting to take a look. Reviewing her articles, I found that out of 17 studies she had cited, only one was published. Fifteen were doctoral dissertations and 13 of these came out of one university—St. John's University in New York, Carbo's alma mater. None of these had been in a peer-refereed journal. When I looked closely at the dissertations and other materials, I found that 13 of the 17 studies that supposedly support her claim had to do with learning styles based on something other than modality.

However, the continuing evolution of scientific understanding about the brain and its function suggest further insight into alternative neural pathways and cognitive sources will be likely.

STENBERG'S TRIARCHIC THEORY

Sternberg's Triarchic Theory of Human Intelligence (1977, 1985, 1995) subsumes both Spearman's *g* and underlying information processing components. His triarchic theory includes three facets or subtheories:

- Analytical (componential)
- Creative (experiential)
- Practical (contextual)

Sternberg's theory builds on his earlier componential approach to reasoning. His theory is mostly based on observing Yale graduate students. Sternberg believes that if intelligence is properly defined & measured it will translate to real-life success. Sternberg's Triarchic Theory is an important effort to synthesize the various theories of intelligence.

ANALYTICAL (COMPONENTIAL) FACET (OR SUBTHEORY)

Analytical Intelligence similar to the standard psychometric definition of intelligence e.g. as measured by Academic problem solving: analogies and puzzles, and corresponds to his earlier componential intelligence. Sternberg considers this reflects how an individual relates to his internal world. Sternberg believes that Analytical Intelligence (Academic problem-solving skills) is based on the joint operations of metacomponents and performance components and knowledge acquisition components of intelligence.

Metacomponents: control, monitor and evaluate cognitive processing. These are the *executive* functions to order and organise performance and knowledge acquisition components. They are the higher-order processes that order and organise the performance components. Used to analyze problems and pick a strategy for solving them. They decide what to do and the performance components actually do it.

Performance Components: execute strategies assembled

by the metacomponents. They are the basic operations involved in any cognitive act. They are the cognitive processes that enable us to encode stimuli, hold information in short-term memory, make calculations, perform mental calculations, mentally compare different stimuli, retrieve information from long-term memory.

Knowledge acquisition components: are the processes used in gaining and storing new knowledge - i.e. capacity for learning. The strategies you use to help memorize things exemplify the processes that fall into this category.

Sternberg feels that IDs in intelligence are related to IDs in the use of these cognitive processes. He feels that people with better reasoning ability generally spend more time understanding the problem but reach their solution faster than those who are less skilled at the task.

CREATIVE (EXPERIENTIAL) FACET (OR SUBTHEORY)

Creative Intelligence: this involves insights, synthesis and the ability to react to novel situations and stimuli. This he considers the Experiential aspect of intelligence and reflects how an individual connects the internal world to external reality. Sternberg considers the Creative facet to consist of the ability which allows people to think creatively and that which allows people to adjust creatively and effectively to new situations. Sternberg believes that more intelligent individuals will also move from consciously learning in a novel situation to automating the new learning so that they can attend to other tasks.

TWO-FACET SUBTHEORY (NOVELTY AND AUTOMATIZATION)

Basic assumption: That there are two broad classes of abilities associated with intelligence: novelty skills and automatization skills. A task measures intelligence if it requires the ability to deal with novel demands or the ability to automatize information processing (two ends of a continuum). Novel tasks or situations are good measures of intellectual ability because they assess an individual's ability to apply existing knowledge to new problems.

PRACTICAL (CONTEXTUAL) FACET (OR SUBTHEORY)

Practical Intelligence: this involves the ability to grasp, understand and deal with everyday tasks. This is the Contextual aspect of intelligence and reflects how the individual relates to the external world about him or her. Sternberg states that Intelligence is: "Purposive adaptation to, shaping of, and selection of real-world environments relevant to one's life". Purposive means that intelligence is directed towards goals, however vague or subconscious they may be. This means that intelligence is indicated by one's attempts to adapt to one's environment.

Practical Intelligence can be said to be intelligence that operates in the real world. People with this type of intelligence can adapt to, or shape their environment. It might also be called "Street-smarts". In measuring this facet, not only mental skills but attitudes and emotional factors that can influence intelligence are measured.

So this practical intelligence is a combination of:

- Adaptation to the environment in order to have goals met
- Changing the environment in order to have goals met
- or, if (a) and (b) don't work moving to a new environment in which goals can be met

Sternberg believes that individuals considered intelligent in one culture may be looked on as unintelligent in another. An important asset of this theory is to avoid defining intelligence in terms of intelligence tests rather than performance in the everyday world (which is, after all, what intelligence tests try to predict!).

Measuring practical intelligence:

- Sternberg Multidimensional Abilities Test measures all 3 intelligences, on separate scales
- Sternberg and Wagner's test of Practical Managerial Intelligence measures:

- Ability to write effective memos
- Ability to motivate people
- Knowledge of when to delegate
- Ability to "read" people

When measuring practical intelligence Sternberg looks at things such as how people decode nonverbal messages e.g. can you tell who are the real couples?

CATTELL'S THEORY OF FLUID AND CRYSTALLIZED INTELLIGENCE

In psychology, fluid and crystallized intelligence are factors of general intelligence originally identified by Raymond Cattell. *Fluid* intelligence is the ability to find meaning in confusion and solve new problems. It is the ability to draw inferences and understand the relationships of various concepts, independent of acquired knowledge. *Crystallized* intelligence is the ability to use skills, knowledge, and experience. It should not be equated with memory or knowledge, but it does rely on accessing information from long-term memory.

The terms are somewhat misleading because one is not a "crystallized" form of the other. Rather, they are believed to be separate neural and mental systems. Fluid and crystallized intelligence are correlated with each other, and most IQ tests attempt to measure both varieties. For example, the Wechsler Adult Intelligence Scale (WAIS) measures fluid intelligence on the performance scale and crystallized intelligence on the verbal scale. The overall IQ score is based on a combination of these two scales.

THEORETICAL DEVELOPMENT

Fluid and crystallized intelligence are discrete factors of general intelligence, or *g*. Although formally recognized by Cattell, the distinction was foreshadowed by Charles Spearman who originally developed the theory of *g* and made a similar observation regarding the difference between eductive and reproductive mental ability. According to Cattell, "...it is apparent that one of these powers... has the 'fluid' quality of being directable to almost any problem. By contrast, the other is invested in particular areas of crystallized skills which can be upset individually without affecting the others." Thus, his claim was that each type, or factor, was independent of the other, though many authors have noted an apparent interdependence of the two.

FLUID VERSUS CRYSTALLIZED

Fluid intelligence includes such abilities as problem-solving, learning, and pattern recognition. As evidence for its continuity, Cattell suggests that *gF* abilities are rarely affected by brain injuries. The Cattell Culture Fair IQ test, the Raven Progressive Matrices, and the performance subscale of the WAIS are measures of *gF*. Crystallized intelligence is possibly more amenable to change as it relies on specific, acquired knowledge. For example, a child who has just learned how to recite the fifty states of America now owns a new piece of crystallized intelligence; but his or her general ability to learn and understand *gF* has not been altered.

An example of the flexibility of, or ability to revise, crystallized intelligence can be seen in beliefs about Santa Claus. A five year-old child may believe that Santa Claus lives at the North Pole. Later, when the child is eight years old, he learns there is no Santa Claus. His belief that Santa lives at the North Pole were then invalidated and new knowledge is gained, there is no Santa Claus. The prior knowledge was revised in order to accommodate the new learning. Vocabulary tests and the verbal subscale of the WAIS are considered good measures of *gC*. Not surprisingly, people with a high capacity of *gF* tend to acquire more *gC* knowledge and at faster rates. This is sometimes called *investment*. Researchers have found that criminals have disproportionately low levels of crystallized intelligence. This may be a result of these people investing their ability into skills that are not measured on IQ tests.

FACTOR STRUCTURE

Fluid intelligence generally correlates with measures of

abstract reasoning and puzzle solving. Crystallized intelligence correlates with abilities that depend on knowledge and experience, such as vocabulary, general information, and analogies. Paul Kline identified a number of factors that shared a correlation of at least r=.60 with *gF* and *gC*. Factors with median loadings of greater than 0.6 on *gF* included induction, visualization, quantitative reasoning, and ideational fluency. Factors with median loadings of greater than 0.6 on *gC* included verbal ability, language development, reading comprehension, sequential reasoning, and general information.

It may be suggested that tests of intelligence may not be able to truly reflect levels of fluid intelligence. Some authors have suggested that unless an individual was truly interested in the problem presented, the cognitive work required may not be performed because of a lack of interest. These authors contend that low scores on tests that measure fluid intelligence may reflect more of a lack of interest in the tasks rather than the ability to complete the task successful.

DEVELOPMENT AND PHYSIOLOGY

Fluid intelligence, like reaction time, peaks in young adulthood and then steadily declines. This decline may be related to local atrophy of the brain in the right cerebellum. Other researchers have suggested that a lack of practice, along with age-related changes in the brain may contribute to the decline. Crystallized intelligence increases gradually, stays relatively stable across most of adulthood, and then begins to decline after age 65. Working memory capacity is closely related to fluid intelligence, and has been proposed to account for individual differences in *gF*. Furthermore, recent research suggests that cognitive exercise can increase working memory and also improve *gF*. Preliminary experiments found that healthy young adults who practiced a demanding working memory task (dual n-back) approximately 25 minutes per day for between 8 and 19 days had statistically significant increases in their scores on a matrix test of fluid intelligence taken before and after the training than a control group who did no not do any training at all.

As of now, it remains to be seen whether the results extend to other kinds of fluid intelligence tests, and if so, whether, after training, fluid intelligence measures retain their correlation with educational and occupational achievement or if the value of fluid intelligence for predicting performance on other tasks changes; it is also unclear whether the training is durable of extended periods of time. According to David Geary, *gF* and *gC* can be traced to two separate brain systems. Fluid intelligence involves the dorsolateral prefrontal cortex, the anterior cingulate cortex, and other systems related to attention and short-term memory. Crystallized intelligence appears to be a function of brain regions that involve the storage and usage of long-term memories, such as the hippocampus.

MEASURING INTELLIGENCE: THE WECHSLER SCALES

The Wechsler intelligence tests, which include the WAIS, the WISC, and the WPPSI (Wechsler preschool and primary scale of intelligence), are the most widely used intelligence assessments and among the most widely used neuropsychological assessments. Wechsler published the first version of the WAIS in 1939, initially called the Wechsler-Bellevue. The newest version is the WAIS-III. Since Wechsler's death in 1981, the Wechsler tests have been revised by the publisher, the Psychological Corporation. The theoretical basis for the WAIS and the other Wechlser scales came from Wechsler's belief that intelligence is a complex ability involving a variety of skills. Because intelligence is multifaceted, Wechsler believed, a test measuring intelligence must reflect this multitude of skills. After dividing intelligence into two major types of skills—verbal and performance—Wechsler utilized the statistical technique of factor analysis to determine specific skills within these two major domains. These more specific factors formed the basis of the Wechsler subtests.

The WAIS-III consists of 14 subtests and takes about 60–75 minutes to complete. The test is taken individually, with a test administrator present to give instructions. Each subtest is given separately, and proceeds from very easy items to very difficult ones. There is some flexibility in the administration of the WAIS—the administrator may end some subtests early if test takers seem to reach the limit of their capacity. Tasks on the WAIS include questions of general knowledge, traditional arithmetic problems, a test of vocabulary, completion of pictures with missing elements, arrangements of blocks and pictures, and assembly of objects. The WAIS is considered to be a valid and reliable measure of general intelligence. When undergoing reliability and validity studies, other intelligence tests are often compared to the Wechsler scales. It is regularly used by researchers in many areas of psychology as a measure of intelligence. Research has demonstrated correlations between WAIS IQ scores and a variety of socioeconomic, physiological, and environmental characteristics.

The WAIS has also been found to be a good measure of both fluid and crystallized intelligence. Fluid intelligence refers to inductive and deductive reasoning, skills considered to be largely influenced by neurological and biological factors. In the WAIS, fluid intelligence is reflected in the performance subtests. Crystallized intelligence refers to knowledge and skills that are primarily influenced by environmental and sociocultural factors. In the WAIS, crystallized intelligence is reflected in the verbal subtests. Wechsler himself did not divide overall intelligence into these two types. However, the consideration of fluid and crystallized intelligence as two major categories of cognitive ability has been a focus for many intelligence theorists. The Wechshler scales were originally developed and later revised using standardization samples. The samples were meant to be demographically representative of the United States population at the time of the standardization.

RESULTS

The WAIS elicits three intelligence quotient scores, based on an average of 100, as well as subtest and index scores. WAIS subtests measure specific verbal abilities and specific performance abilities. The WAIS elicits an overall intelligence quotient, called the full-scale IQ, as well as a verbal IQ and a performance IQ. The three IQ scores are standardized in such a way that the scores have a mean of 100 and a standard deviation of 15. Wechsler pioneered the use of deviation IQ scores, allowing test takers to be compared to others of different as well as the same age. WAIS scores are sometimes converted into percentile ranks. The verbal and performance IQ scores are based on scores on the 14 subtests. The 14 subtest scores have a mean of 10 and a standard deviation of three. The WAIS also elicits four indices, each based on a different set of subtests: verbal comprehension, perceptual organization, working memory, and processing speed.

The full-scale IQ is based on scores on all of the subtests and is a reflection of both verbal IQ and performance IQ. It is considered the single most reliable and valid score elicited by the WAIS. However, when an examinee's verbal and performance IQ scores differ significantly, the full-scale IQ should be interpreted cautiously.

THE VERBAL IQ

The verbal IQ is derived from scores on seven of the subtests: information, digit span, vocabulary, arithmetic, comprehension, similarities, and letter-number sequencing. Letter-number sequencing is a new subtest added to the most recent edition of the WAIS (WAIS-III).

The information subtest is a test of general knowledge, including questions about geography and literature. The digit span subtest requires test takers to repeat strings of digits. The vocabulary and arithmetic subtests are general measures of a person's vocabulary and arithmetic skills. The comprehension subtest requires test takers to solve practical problems and explain the meaning of proverbs. The similarities subtest requires test takers to indicate the similarities between pairs of things. The letter-number sequencing subtest involves ordering numbers and letters presented in an unordered sequence. Scores on the verbal subtests are based primarily on correct answers.

THE PERFORMANCE IQ

The performance IQ is derived from scores on the remaining seven subtests: picture completion, picture arrangement, block design, object assembly, digit symbol, matrix reasoning, and symbol search. Matrix reasoning and symbol search are new subtests and were added to the most recent edition of the WAIS (WAIS-III). In the picture completion subtest, the test taker is required to complete pictures with missing elements. The picture arrangement subtest entails arranging pictures in order to tell a story.

The block design subtest requires test takers to use blocks to make specific designs. The object assembly subtest requires people to assemble pieces in such a way that a whole object is built. In the digit symbol subtest, digits and symbols are presented as pairs and test takers then must pair additional digits and symbols. The matrix reasoning subtest requires test takers to identify geometric shapes. The symbol search subtest requires examinees to match symbols appearing in different groups. Scores on the performance subtests are based on both response speed and correct answers.

EMOTIONAL INTELLIGENCE

Emotional Intelligence (EI), often measured as an Emotional Intelligence Quotient (EQ), is a term that describes the ability, capacity, skill or (in the case of the trait EI model) a self-perceived ability, to identify, assess, and manage the emotions of one's self, of others, and of groups. Different models have been proposed for the definition of EI and disagreement exists as to how the term should be used. Despite these disagreements, which are often highly technical, the ability EI and trait EI models (but not the mixed models) are enjoying considerable support in the literature and have successful applications in many different domains. The most distant roots of emotional intelligence can be traced to Darwin's early work on the importance of emotional expression for survival and second adaptation.

In the 1900s, even though traditional definitions of intelligence emphasized cognitive aspects such as memory and problem-solving, several influential researchers in the intelligence field of study had begun to recognize the importance of the non-cognitive aspects. For instance, as early as 1920, E. L. Thorndike used the term social intelligence to describe the skill of understanding and managing other people. Similarly, in 1940 David Wechsler described the influence of non-intellective factors on intelligent behaviour, and further argued that our models of intelligence would not be complete until we can adequately describe these factors. In 1983, Howard Gardner's *Frames of Mind: The Theory of Multiple Intelligences* introduced the idea of Multiple Intelligences which included both *Interpersonal intelligence* (the capacity to understand the intentions, motivations and desires of other people) and *Intrapersonal intelligence* (the capacity to understand oneself, to appreciate one's feelings, fears and motivations).

In Gardner's view, traditional types of intelligence, such as IQ, fail to fully explain cognitive ability. Thus, even though the names given to the concept varied, there was a common belief that traditional definitions of intelligence are lacking in ability to fully explain performance outcomes. The first use of the term "Emotional Intelligence" is usually attributed to Wayne Payne's doctoral thesis, *A Study of Emotion: Developing Emotional Intelligence* from 1985. However, prior to this, the term "emotional intelligence" had appeared in Leuner (1966). Greenspan (1989) also put forward an EI model, followed by Salovey and Mayer (1990), and Goleman (1995).

As a result of the growing acknowledgement by professionals of the importance and relevance of emotions to work outcomes, the research on the topic continued to gain momentum, but it wasn't until the publication of Daniel Goleman's best seller *Emotional Intelligence: Why It Can Matter More Than IQ* that the term became widely popularized. Nancy Gibbs' 1995 Time magazine article highlighted Goleman's book and was the first in a string of mainstream media interest in EI. Thereafter, articles on EI began to appear with increasing frequency across a wide range of academic and popular outlets.

DEFINING EMOTIONAL INTELLIGENCE

Substantial disagreement exists regarding the definition of EI, with respect to both terminology and operationalizations. One attempt toward a definition was made by Salovey and Mayer (1990) who defined EI as "the ability to monitor one's own and others' feelings and emotions, to discriminate among them and to use this information to guide one's thinking and actions."

Despite this early definition, there has been confusion regarding the exact meaning of this construct. The definitions are so varied, and the field is growing so rapidly, that researchers are constantly amending even their own definitions of the construct. At the present time, there are three main models of EI:

- Ability EI models
- Mixed models of EI
- Trait EI model

THE ABILITY-BASED MODEL

Salovey and Mayer's conception of EI strives to define EI within the confines of the standard criteria for a new intelligence. Following their continuing research, their initial definition of EI was revised to: "The ability to perceive emotion, integrate emotion to facilitate thought, understand emotions and to regulate emotions to promote personal growth." The ability based model views emotions as useful sources of information that help one to make sense of and navigate the social environment. The model proposes that individuals vary in their ability to process information of an emotional nature and in their ability to relate emotional processing to a wider cognition. This ability is seen to manifest itself in certain adaptive behaviors.

The model proposes that EI includes 4 types of abilities:

- Perceiving emotions — the ability to detect and decipher emotions in faces, pictures, voices, and cultural artifacts- including the ability to identify one's own emotions. Perceiving emotions represents a basic aspect of emotional intelligence, as it makes all other processing of emotional information possible.

- Using emotions — the ability to harness emotions to facilitate various cognitive activities, such as thinking and problem solving. The emotionally intelligent person can capitalize fully upon his or her changing moods in order to best fit the task at hand.
- Understanding emotions — the ability to comprehend emotion language and to appreciate complicated relationships among emotions. For example, understanding emotions encompasses the ability to be sensitive to slight variations between emotions, and the ability to recognize and describe how emotions evolve over time.
- Managing emotions — the ability to regulate emotions in both ourselves and in others. Therefore, the emotionally intelligent person can harness emotions, even negative ones, and manage them to achieve intended goals.

The ability-based model has been criticized in the research for lacking face and predictive validity in the workplace.

MEASUREMENT OF THE ABILITY-BASED MODEL

Different models of EI have led to the development of various instruments for the assessment of the construct. While some of these measures may overlap, most researchers agree that they tap slightly different constructs. The current measure of Mayer and Salovey's model of EI, the Mayer-Salovey-Caruso Emotional Intelligence Test (MSCEIT) is based on a series of emotion-based problem-solving items. Consistent with the model's claim of EI as a type of intelligence, the test is modeled on ability-based IQ tests. By testing a person's abilities on each of the four branches of emotional intelligence, it generates scores for each of the branches as well as a total score.

Central to the four-branch model is the idea that EI requires attunement to social norms. Therefore, the MSCEIT is scored in a consensus fashion, with higher scores indicating higher overlap between an individual's answers and those provided by a worldwide sample of respondents. The MSCEIT can also be expert-scored, so that the amount of overlap is calculated between an individual's answers and those provided by a group of 21 emotion researchers. Although promoted as an ability test, the MSCEIT is most unlike standard IQ tests in that its items do not have objectively correct responses. Among other problems, the consensus scoring criterion means that it is impossible to create items (questions) that only a minority of respondents can solve, because, by definition, responses are deemed emotionally 'intelligent' only if the majority of the sample has endorsed them.

This and other similar problems have led cognitive ability experts to question the definition of EI as a genuine intelligence. In a study by Føllesdal the MSCEIT test results of 111 business leaders were compared with how their employees described their leader. It was found that there were no correlations between a leader's test results and how he or she was rated by the employees, with regard to empathy, ability to motivate, and leader effectiveness. Føllesdal also criticized the Canadian company Multi-Health Systems, which administers the MSCEIT test. The test contains 141 questions but it was found after publishing the test that 19 of these did not give the expected answers. This has led Multi-Health Systems to remove answers to these 19 questions before scoring, but without stating this officially.

MIXED MODELS OF EI

The Emotional Competencies (Goleman) Model

The model introduced by Daniel Goleman focuses on EI as a wide array of competencies and skills that drive leadership performance. Goleman's model outlines four main EI constructs:

- Self-awareness— the ability to read one's emotions and recognize their impact while using gut feelings to guide decisions.

- Self-management— involves controlling one's emotions and impulses and adapting to changing circumstances.
- Social awareness— the ability to sense, understand, and react to others' emotions while comprehending social networks.
- Relationship management — the ability to inspire, influence, and develop others while managing conflict.

Goleman includes a set of emotional competencies within each construct of EI. Emotional competencies are not innate talents, but rather learned capabilities that must be worked on and developed to achieve outstanding performance. Goleman posits that individuals are born with a general emotional intelligence that determines their potential for learning emotional competencies. Goleman's model of EI has been criticized in the research literature as mere "pop psychology".

MEASUREMENT OF THE EMOTIONAL COMPETENCIES (GOLEMAN) MODEL

Two measurement tools are based on the Goleman model:

- The Emotional Competency Inventory (ECI), which was created in 1999 and the Emotional and Social Competency Inventory (ESCI), which was created in 2007.
- The Emotional Intelligence Appraisal, which was created in 2001 and which can be taken as a self-report or 360-degree assessment.

THE BAR-ON MODEL OF EMOTIONAL-SOCIAL INTELLIGENCE (ESI)

Bar-On (2006) developed one of the first measures of EI that used the term *Emotion Quotient*. He defines emotional intelligence as being concerned with effectively understanding oneself and others, relating well to people, and adapting to and coping with the immediate surroundings to be more successful in dealing with environmental demands. Bar-On posits that EI develops over time and that it can be improved through training, programming, and therapy. Bar-On hypothesizes that those individuals with higher than average E.Q.'s are in general more successful in meeting environmental demands and pressures. He also notes that a deficiency in EI can mean a lack of success and the existence of emotional problems.

Problems in coping with one's environment are thought, by Bar-On, to be especially common among those individuals lacking in the subscales of reality testing, problem solving, stress tolerance, and impulse control. In general, Bar-On considers emotional intelligence and cognitive intelligence to contribute equally to a person's general intelligence, which then offers an indication of one's potential to succeed in life. However, doubts have been expressed about this model in the research literature (in particular about the validity of self-report as an index of emotional intelligence) and in scientific settings. it is being replaced by the trait EI model discussed below.

MEASUREMENT OF THE ESI MODEL

The Bar-On Emotion Quotient Inventory (EQ-i), is a self-report measure of EI developed as a measure of emotionally and socially competent behaviour that provides an estimate of one's emotional and social intelligence. The EQ-i is not meant to measure personality traits or cognitive capacity, but rather the mental ability to be successful in dealing with environmental demands and pressures. One hundred and thirty three items (questions or factors) are used to obtain a Total EQ (Total Emotional Quotient) and to produce five composite scale scores, corresponding to the five main components of the Bar-On model. A limitation of this model is that it claims to measure some kind of ability through self-report items. The EQ-i has been found to be highly susceptible to faking.

THE TRAIT EI MODEL

Petrides and colleagues proposed a conceptual distinction

between the ability based model and a trait based model of EI. Trait EI is "a constellation of emotion-related self-perceptions located at the lower levels of personality". In lay terms, trait EI refers to an individual's self-perceptions of their emotional abilities. This definition of EI encompasses behavioral dispositions and self perceived abilities and is measured by self report, as opposed to the ability based model which refers to actual abilities, which have proven highly resistant to scientific measurement. Trait EI should be investigated within a personality framework. An alternative label for the same construct is trait emotional self-efficacy.

The trait EI model is general and subsumes the Goleman and Bar-On models discussed above. The conceptualization of EI as a personality trait leads to a construct that lies outside the taxonomy of human cognitive ability. This is an important distinction in as much as it bears directly on the operationalization of the construct and the theories and hypotheses that are formulated about it.

MEASUREMENT OF THE TRAIT EI MODEL

There are many self-report measures of EI, including the EQi, the Swinburne University Emotional Intelligence Test (SUEIT), the Schutte Self-Report Emotional Intelligence Test (SSEIT), a measure by Tett, Fox, and Wang (2005). From the perspective of the trait EI model, none of these assess intelligence, abilities, or skills (as their authors often claim), but rather, they are limited measures of trait emotional intelligence. The Trait Emotional Intelligence Questionnaire (TEIQue) is an open-access measure that was specifically designed to measure the construct comprehensively and is currently available in 15 languages.

The TEIQue provides an operationalization for Petrides and colleagues' model that conceptualizes EI in terms of personality. The test encompasses 15 subscales organized under four factors: Well-Being, Self-Control, Emotionality, and Sociability. The psychometric properties of the TEIQue were investigated in a recent study on a French-Speaking Population, where it was reported that TEIQue scores were globally normally distributed and reliable. The researchers also found TEIQue scores were unrelated to nonverbal reasoning (Raven's matrices), which they interpreted as support for the personality trait view of EI (as opposed to a form of intelligence). As expected, TEIQue scores were positively related to some of the Big Five personality traits (extraversion, agreeableness, openness, conscientiousness) as well as inversely related to others (alexithymia, neuroticism).

ALEXITHYMIA AND EI

Alexithymia from the Greek words literally "lack of words for emotions") is a term coined by Peter Sifneos in 1973 to describe people who appeared to have deficiencies in understanding, processing, or describing their emotions. Viewed as a spectrum between high and low EI, the alexithymia construct is strongly inversely related to EI, representing its lower range. The individual's level of alexithymia can be measured with self-scored questionnaires such as the Toronto Alexithymia Scale (TAS-20) or the Bermond-Vorst Alexithymia Questionnaire (BVAQ) or by observer rated measures such as the Observer Alexithymia Scale (OAS).

CRITICISM OF THE THEORETICAL FOUNDATION OF EI

EI is Too Broadly Defined and the Definitions are Unstable

One of the arguments against the theoretical soundness of the concept suggests that the constant changing and broadening of its definition- which has come to encompass many unrelated elements— had rendered it an unintelligible concept. Arguing that EI is an invalid concept, Locke (2005) asked: "What is the common or integrating element in a concept that includes: introspection about emotions, Emotional expression, non-verbal communication with others, empathy, self-regulation, planning, creative thinking and the direction of attention?" He answered by saying: "There is none."

Commenting on the multiple factors that have been included in the definition, Locke asked rhetorically: "What does EI not include?" Other critics mention that without some stabilization of the concepts and the measurement instruments, meta-analyses are difficult to implement, and the theory coherence is likely to be adversely impacted by this instability.

EI CANNOT BE RECOGNIZED AS A FORM OF INTELLIGENCE

Goleman's early work has been criticized for assuming from the beginning that EI is a type of intelligence. Eysenck (2000) writes that Goleman's description of EI contains assumptions about intelligence in general, and that it even runs contrary to what researchers have come to expect when studying types of intelligence:

"Goleman exemplifies more clearly than most the fundamental absurdity of the tendency to class almost any type of behaviour as'intelligence'... If these five 'abilities' define 'emotional intelligence', we would expect some evidence that they are highly correlated; Goleman admits that they might be quite uncorrelated, and in any case if we cannot measure them, how do we know they are related?

So the whole theory is built on quicksand: there is no sound scientific basis".

Similarly, Locke (2005) claims that the concept of EI is in itself a misinterpretation of the intelligence construct, and he offers an alternative interpretation: it is not another form or type of intelligence, but intelligence—the ability to grasp abstractions—applied to a particular life domain: emotions. He suggests the concept should be re-labeled and referred to as a skill. The essence of this criticism is that scientific inquiry depends on valid and consistent construct utilization, and that in advance of the introduction of the term EI, psychologists had established theoretical distinctions between factors such as abilities and achievements, skills and habits, attitudes and values, and personality traits and emotional states. The term EI is viewed by some as having merged and conflated accepted concepts and definitions.

EI HAS NO SUBSTANTIAL PREDICTIVE VALUE

Landy (2005) has claimed that the few incremental validity studies conducted on EI have demonstrated that it adds little or nothing to the explanation or prediction of some common outcomes (most notably academic and work success). Landy proposes that the reason some studies have found a small increase in predictive validity is in fact a methodological fallacy — incomplete consideration of alternative explanations:

"EI is compared and contrasted with a measure of abstract intelligence but not with a personality measure, or with a personality measure but not with a measure of academic intelligence." Landy (2005)

In accordance with this suggestion, other researchers have raised concerns about the extent to which self-report EI measures correlate with established personality dimensions. Generally, self-report EI measures and personality measures have been said to converge because they both purport to measure traits, and because they are both measured in the self-report form. Specifically, there appear to be two dimensions of the Big Five that stand out as most related to self-report EI – neuroticism and extraversion. In particular, neuroticism has been said to relate to negative emotionality and anxiety. Intuitively, individuals scoring high on neuroticism, are likely to score low on self-report EI measures. The interpretations of the correlations between EI questionnaires and personality have been varied, with the trait EI view that re-intrprets EI as a collection of personality traits being prominent in the scientific literature.

CRITICISM ON MEASUREMENT ISSUES

Ability Based Measures are Measuring Conformity, not Ability

One criticism of the works of Mayer and Salovey comes from a study by Roberts et al. (2001), which suggests that the EI, as measured by the MSCEIT, may only be measuring conformity. This argument is rooted in the MSCEIT's use of consensus-based assessment, and in the fact that scores on the

MSCEIT are negatively distributed (meaning that its scores differentiate between people with low EI better than people with high EI).

Ability Based Measures are Measuring Knowledge (not Actual Ability)

Further criticism has been offered by Brody (2004), who claimed that unlike tests of cognitive ability, the MSCEIT "tests knowledge of emotions but not necessarily the ability to perform tasks that are related to the knowledge that is assessed". The main argument is that even though someone knows how he should behave in an emotionally laden situation, it doesn't necessarily follow that he could actually carry out the reported behaviour.

SELF REPORT MEASURES ARE SUSCEPTIBLE TO FAKING GOOD

More formally termed socially desirable responding (SDR), faking good is defined as a response pattern in which test-takers systematically represent themselves with an excessive positive bias. This bias has long been known to contaminate responses on personality inventories, acting as a mediator of the relationships between self-report measures.

It has been suggested that responding in a desirable way is a response set, which is a situational and temporary response pattern. This is contrasted with a response style, which is a more long-term trait-like quality. Considering the contexts some self-report EI inventories are used in (e.g., employment settings), the problems of response sets in high-stakes scenarios become clear.

There are a few methods to prevent socially desirable responding on behaviour inventories. Some researchers believe it is necessary to warn test-takers not to fake good before taking a personality test. Some inventories use validity scales in order to determine the likelihood or consistency of the responses across all items.

CLAIMS FOR THE PREDICTIVE POWER OF EI ARE TOO EXTREME

Landy distinguishes between the 'commercial wing' and 'the academic wing' of the EI movement, basing this distinction on the alleged predictive power of EI as seen by the two currents. According to Landy, the former makes expansive claims on the applied value of EI, while the later is trying to warn users against these claims. As an example, Goleman (1998) asserts that "the most effective leaders are alike in one crucial way: they all have a high degree of what has come to be known as emotional intelligence....emotional intelligence is the sine qua non of leadership".

In contrast, Mayer (1999) cautions "the popular literature's implication—that highly emotionally intelligent people possess an unqualified advantage in life—appears overly enthusiastic at present and unsubstantiated by reasonable scientific standards."

Landy further reinforces this argument by noting that the data upon which these claims are based are held in 'proprietary databases', which means they are unavailable to independent researchers for reanalysis, replication, or verification. Thus, the credibility of the findings cannot be substantiated in a scientific manner, unless those datasets are made public and available for independent analysis.

EI, IQ AND JOB PERFORMANCE

Research of EI and job performance show mixed results: a positive relation has been found in some of the studies, in others there was no relation or an inconsistent one. This led researchers Cote and Miners (2006) to offer a compensatory model between EI and IQ, that posits that the association between EI and job performance becomes more positive as cognitive intelligence decreases, an idea first proposed in the context of academic performance. The results of the former study supported the compensatory model: employees with low IQ get higher task performance and organizational citizenship behaviour directed at the organization, the higher their EI (Emotional Intelligence).

CREATIVITY: RESEARCH ON THE EVIDENCE FOR CONFLUENCE APPROACH

The concept of creativity has gained importance in recent years. For example, a vast amount of management literature has been increasingly focusing on how to enhance creativity in the workplace, in order to cope with constant changing environments.

Another sign of the importance of creativity is the decision of the European Union of making 2009 European Year of Creativity and Innovation. The objective of the year is "to promote creativity for all as a driver for innovation and as a key factor for the development of personal, occupational, entrepreneurial and social competences through lifelong learning". The year should raise public awareness and promote public debate on creativity; in addition, it should stimulate research into how to develop creativity and innovative attitudes.

The Commission will draw in different policy fields such as education and training, enterprise, media, cohesion, rural development and research, to add impact of the Year. In this context and within the overall Lisbon Strategy and its monitoring policies on education and training, the Commission is launching the debate on measuring creativity. This chapter aims at constructing a preliminary understanding of research on creativity and the possibilities of constructing a "creativity composite indicator" using large scale surveys and other existing statistical tools. Thus, the paper is mainly focused on exploring measurement possibilities of creativity in an international comparative manner.

The paper aims at answering (at least partially) the following questions:

- Is it possible to measure creativity in a comparative international manner?
- Is it possible to use existing large scale surveys to assess creativity?

It is clear that the phenomenon of creativity is extremely complex. The study of creativity has different perspectives and approaches. This chapter review some work on creativity in psychology, mainly through the extensive reviews of Sternberg and Lubart (1999) and Runco (2007). The paper also presents some other perspectives on creativity, not necessarily linked to psychology. Sternberg and Lubart (1999) present different lines in the study of creativity in psychology.

For them creativity research has been marginalized due to the lack of multi- disciplinary approaches and because of problems on providing a sound definition of the phenomena. They refer to Wehner, Csikszentmihalyi and Magyari-Beck (1991, 270) that maintained that the situation in creativity research is similar to the fable of the blind men trying to describe an elephant by touching different parts of the animal, where the one touching the tail says it is like a snail and other touching the flank says it is like a wall. In a later work, Sternberg (2006a) maintains that there are five commonalities in the research of creativity around the world. First, creativity "involves thinking that aims at producing ideas or products that are relatively novel and that are, in some respect, compelling".

Second, creativity has some domain-specific and domain-general elements. That is to say, it needs some specific knowledge, but there are certain elements of creativity that cut across different domains. Third, creativity is measureable, at least to some extent. Fourth, it can be developed and promoted. And fifth, "creativity is not highly rewarded in practice, as it is supposed to be in theory". Towards an understanding of what creativity is Sternberg and Lubart (1999) find the origin of creativity research on spirituality. In this way, research associated with creativity has not had the necessary scientific back-up: "many people seem to believe, as they do about love, that creativity is something just doesn't lend itself to scientific study, because it is a spiritual process". They also refer to psychodynamic studies on creativity where creativity arises from the tension between the conscious and un- conscious drives.

Later "pragmatic approaches on creativity" have been mainly concerned with the development of techniques to promote creative thinking in organizations. According to

Sternberg and Lubart (1999) these studies are lacking a theory of creativity, since they are mainly practical approaches to enhance creativity. Thus, they do not provide a clear idea of what are the characteristics of creativity. Studies on cognitive psychology have tried to understand the process of creative thinking. In many instances, this research assumed that creativity is just extraordinary results of ordinary processes, and in this way, there is no real need of studying it as a separate subject. In other cases some authors maintain that creativity is not much different from intelligence.

Spearman (1927, 187) defended that there was no such thing as "creativity power" for him "that which is usually attributed to such special imaginative or inventive operation can be simply resolved into a correlate education combine with mere reproduction". Later research seems to agree that intelligence and creativity are related, using the threshold theory. These theory assumes that there is a "minimum level of intelligence (the lower threshold) below which the person cannot be creative ... They [creativity and intelligence] are related, but only at certain level of ability. Other studies in cognitive psychology try to discover the process of creative thinking.

Here the debate is between if creative thinking can be or not delineated. Plsek (1997) presents an overview of some prominent models of creativity. Wallas (1926), for example, proposed a creative process that involves: (1) preparation., (2) incubation, (3) illumination and (4) verification. Rossman (1931) extended this model to seven steps: Observation of a need or difficulty, (2) analysis of the need, (3) a survey of all available information, (4) a formulation of all objective solutions, (5) a critical analysis of these solutions for their advantages and disadvantages, (6) the birth of the new idea (the invention) and (7) experimentation to test out the most promising solution, and the selection and perfection to final embodiment. Plsek (1997) has proposed the "directed creativity cycle", composed of Observation, analysis, generation, harvesting, enhancement, evaluation, implementation, and living with it.

These are grouped within: (1) preparation, (2) imagination, (3) development and (4) action. Sternberg and Lubart (1999) also refer to psychometric approaches to creativity. They have been mainly focused in developing tests to measure creativity. These will be treated in more detail in the next section. Plucker and Renzulli (1999) differentiate four areas where psychometric methods have been applied in creativity research: creative process, personality and behavioral correlates, characteristics of creative products, and attributes of creative fostering environments. The psychometric approach will be treated in more detailed later on. Definitions Sternberg and Lubart (1999, 3) maintains that "Creativity is the ability to produce work that is both novel (i.e. original, unexpected) and appropriate (i.e. useful concerning tasks constrains)".

Runco (2007) present several authors that define creativity as involving the creation of something new and useful. Runco (2007, 385) calls these "products definitions" of creativity. He calls these definitions "product bias". For him, product bias consists on assuming that all creativity requires a tangible product: "It would be more parsimonious to view creative products as inventions and the process leading up to them as creative or innovative". In the UK, the National Advisory Committee on Creative and Cultural Education (NACCCE) published in 1999 a report where they provided a more elaborated, but similar definition of creativity. They maintain that creativity processes have four characteristics:

- It is imaginatively, it always involves imagination, since it is the process of generating something original.
- It is purposeful: it is imagination put into action towards an end.
- It produces something original in relation to one's own previous work, to their peer group or to anyone's previous output in a particular field.
- And finally, it has value in respect to the objective it was applied for.

Creativity involves not only the generation of ideas, but

also the evaluation of them, and deciding which one is the most adequate one. The NACCCE maintain that they understand creativity in a "democratic" way: "one which recognizes the potential for creative achievement in all fields of human activity; and the capacity for such achievements in the many and not the few". The Department for Culture, Media and Sport (DCMS) in the UK, referred to this definition in their implementation of actions to enhance creativity in schools in 2006 (DCMS 2006).

NACCCE (1999) opposed their view on creativity to two other different views: An "elite", and a "sector" definition. An "elite" definition involves that creative people are those with "unusual talents", that are able to make their creative mark without special help and sometimes gain strength from educational failure. This refers to the differentiation usually maintained in the creativity research between eminent-level and non-eminent-level creativity. Richards (1999a) maintains that the former, eminent-level creativity, refers to discoveries that are of particular importance for society (for example, scientific discoveries), while, the later refers to everyday creativity, meaning the capacity of people to adapt to new situations. The later is in line with the "democratic" understanding of creativity defended by NACCCE (1999).

The "sector" definition maintains that creativity is something associated with the arts, and that it does not involve other sectors of production such as science or technology. An extended version of the sector definition could be found in the definition of creativity that KEA European Affairs (2006) propose. In a macro-level approach, they define creativity in a cross-sector and multidisciplinary way, mixing elements of 'artistic creativity', 'economic innovation' as well as 'technological innovation'. They consider creativity as "a process of interactions and spill-over effects between different innovative processes". They differentiate between: Scientific, technological, economic and cultural creativity.

Also from a more macro-level approach, Richard Florida's popular book "The rise of the creative class" provides a view of what creativity encompasses at a societal level. He maintains that we live in a "Creative Age". Florida's thesis is centered on three main areas: Technology, Talent and Tolerance (the three T's model). Florida is mainly interested in studying the concentration of "creative individuals" in different regions. For him, these three T's, as he calls them, constitute the main magnets for creative people to establish themselves in a city. It is this creative class the one that has strong influence in making a region prosper economically. He does not provide a specific definition for creativity, but from his description of what are the "main themes" in the body of literature about creativity, one can find a short of definition of creativity.

In his view, creativity is an essential feature of our life. He presents a "democratic" conception of creativity in line with that of NACCCE, where creativity is embodied in different areas of human life. For him, creativity is multidimensional and experiential. Creativity requires "work" to appear and is usually guided by intrinsic rewards. As next section will present, he proposed different ways of measuring these three T's in a composite indicator that he refers to as the "creativity index". There is, thus, certain consensus on some of the creativity characteristics. It seems clear that it is related to the production of something new and with some short of value.

It also seems that there is certain agreement that everybody can be creative to some extent. However, as Mayer (1999, 450) addresses in his review of Sternberg's handbook: "In spite of agreement on basic definition of creativity, there are several clarifying questions for which Handbook authors –reflecting the diversity of the field – have different answers". As Mayer (1999) noted, studies on creativity can refer to personal or social creativity. Personal creativity refers to creating something new in respect to the person that creates the product. Creativity that is social refers to something new and useful in respect to the social or cultural environment where it is produced.

NACCCE (1999) maintain that creativity involves originality in three possible ways: Individual, relative or historic. Individual creativity coincides with Mayer's definition of personal creativity. Relative refers to originality in relation to their peer group. Finally, historic, refers to original in terms of anyone's previous output in a particular field. Sternberg (1999b) categorizes creative contributions in science into eight different types that differ qualitatively in respect to the context where they are produced.

The eight types of contributions can be divided in three major categories: Contributions that (1) accept current paradigms, (2) reject current paradigms and (3) attempt to integrate multiple current paradigms. In addition, Mayer (1999) maintains that there is a need to clarify if creativity is a property of: (1) People, (2) Product or (3) Processes. He maintains that depending on this assumption, different approaches have been used to study creativity. Runco (2007) adds approaches to creativity related to place, persuasion, in studying how creative people change the way other people think, and potential emphasizing research on those that have potential for creativity but are not realizing it. All these issues have to be addressed in a measurement model for creativity.

An understanding of creativity will necessarily require reflection of the issues presented above. This will require a multi-disciplinary approach to creativity, most likely. The confluence approach Sternberg and Lubart (1999) conclude that "confluence approaches" would be advisable in creativity research. This line of research put together multiple views on creativity, where different components must converge for creativity to occur. They mention Amabile (1983); Gruber and Davis (1988) and Csikszentmihalyi (1996) as valuable contributions, and their own "investment theory of creativity".

The basic idea is that "creative people are the ones who are willing and able to 'buy low and sell high' in the realm of ideas". According to this theory creativity requires six distinct but interrelated resources: intellectual abilities, knowledge, styles of thinking, personality, motivation and environment. Sternberg and Lubart (1999) describe a complex system, where theses different resources have to have a proper balance. Just as an exemplification of the complexity and the difficulties in creating the right balance, it is noteworthy to present the case of "intellectual abilities". They emphasize three particularly important intellectual abilities: (a) the synthetic ability of being able to see problems in a new way, (b) the analytic ability to recognize what ideas are worth, and (c) the practical-contextual ability to know how to persuade the others that your ideas are valuable.

The three have to occur together, since one without the other will not yield creative results. Analytic ability without the other two will only produce critical but not creative thinking. Synthetic ability without the other two will lack the possibility to carry out the ideas. And the practical-contextual ability might produce results, but not because the ideas are creative but because they had a powerful way of interpreting. Another example of the complexity can be easily seen in the case of knowledge. Sternberg maintains: "On the one hand, one needs to know enough about a field to move it forward [...] On the other hand, knowledge about a field can result in a closed and entrenched perspective".

The rest of the six resources also require the right balance of attributes. A "confluence approach" will obviously present tremendous challenges, especially in the case of measurement. Since the interest of the paper is to assess the possibilities of measuring creativity, the following section reviews main approaches of creativity measurement. It expands beyond psychological references and looks into ways of measuring creativity at a societal level, mainly through an extended approach to that proposed by Florida (2002). The review does not claim to be exhaustive, nor comprehensive, but it aims at providing a general overview in the field. This section is divided into four sub-sections that refer to two different forms of measuring creativity.

In most of the cases the approach consists on developing tests to measure creativity. Haensly and Torrance (1990) identified more than 200 instruments for measuring different aspects of creativity. Houtz and Krug (1995) provide a review of several test developed for the assessment of creativity. They followed Hocevar (1981) classifications into: tests of divergent thinking, attitude and interest inventories, personality inventories, biographical measures, ratings by teachers, peers or supervisors, product judgments, self-reports of creative achievements, and eminence or the study of well-known and establish creative people.

A typical item to test divergent thinking would be to ask to name as many objects as they can fall in certain category. It is somehow based on the ideas from associative theories that maintain that original ideas tend to be remote; they come later in the process of thinking about associations. It is important to note, however, that creative thinking is not synonymous of divergent thinking. Creativity involves also sensitivity to problems as well as redefinition abilities, such as transformation of thoughts or freedom from functional fixedness.

The most widely used test on creativity is the Torrance Test of Creative Thinking (TTCT). It is also the one that has the most extended research on their reliability and validity. This test has been translated into more than 30 languages and it is used in different places as a tool to assess creative potential. It is based on Guilford (1962) Structure of the Intellect (SOI) battery that included some measures of divergent thinking. Thus, it measures creativity through divergent thinking. The TTCT was developed in 1966, and it has been re-normed four times: 1974, 1984, 1990 and 1998. There are two forms, TTCT-Verbal and –Figural with two parallel tests each (form A and B).

Each test pertain to measure:

- Fluency: (The number of ideas) Total n. of relevant responses
- Originality: (The rarity of ideas) N. of statistically infrequent ideas. The score is 0 if the idea is common, and 1 all the other valid responses.
- Elaboration: The number of added ideas
- Flexibility: Number of categories of the relevant responses

In 1990 Torrance deleted the flexibility scale, since it correlated highly with fluency, and added two norm-reference measures of creative potential: Abstractness of titles and resistance to premature closure. Abstractness of titles refers to the "degree beyond labeling... it measures the degree a title moves beyond concrete labeling of pictures drawn". Resistance to premature closure pertains to measure the degree of psychological openness. The test can be administered in around 30 minutes, but the process of scoring requires some training and specific country norms.

In 1998 the manual provides norms for the United States and includes both grade-related and age-related norms. Thus, there is some country specificity in the measurement of creativity. Kim (2006) reported some normative measures in other countries. These norms have usually been developed for research activities. Heausler and Thomson (1988) refer to four main criticisms regarding the TTCT: First, the response set might influence the results. Thus, different order in the presentation of the items leads to different results. Second, some research has shown that "creativity tests administered under different conditions lead to differences in performance".

Third, raters of the TTCT might differ considerably in their scores to a similar person. Rosenthal et al. (1983, 39) found that "two raters may agree that a particular student's performance is better than that of all other students, yet still assigned significantly different scores to describe this performance". This means as Heausler and Thomson have pointed out that "these differences might be of practical importance in studies testing mean differences across experimental or other groups". Finally, a fourth group of criticism refers to the structure of the test. Some studies with factor analysis have shown that the factors found in the TTCT described a task more than underlying constructs.

CREATIVE PERSONALITY

Another line of measuring creativity is related to study individual differences and personality attributes. Studies in this line have tried to find characteristics of creative people. They could be divided into psychometric, biographical and historiometric approaches. In psychometrics approaches, studies attempt "to measure facets of creativity associated with creative people". Tools in this area for studying creativity consist of lists of personality traits, self-report adjectives check-list, biographical surveys and interest and attitudes measures. A famous check list is the Gough's (1952) Adjective Check Lists (ACL).

It consists of 300 descriptor words that a person checks as being self-descriptive. Using this tool, a sample of people that were evaluated as creative by experts is compared to other non-creative sample of people. Domino (1970) identified 59 of those descriptors that formed a Creativity Scale. Other similar tests have been developed and tested with different professionals. Kathena and Torrance (1976) developed the Creative Perception Inventory, composed of the Something About Myself (SAM) and What Kind of Person Are You (WKOPAY) scales. SAM asks people to answer if they have engaged in specific activities with creative potential. It also asks individuals to "agree of disagree with certain self-descriptors, such as 'I am talented in many different ways'".

The WKOPAY ask people to check personality traits that they think characterized them. Biographical and historiometric approaches are mainly related to the study of creative individuals and their context. Biographical approaches involve case studies of eminent creators "using qualitative research methodologies". Gruber and Wallace (1999) maintain that case study approaches to creativity provide a holistic picture of the creator and his/her environment. They maintain that in a case study method, the investigator has two central roles: a phenomelogical one and a critical one. The first requires that the investigator "goes into" the creators mind and tries to reconstruct the meaning of the subject's experience.

"In this role, the investigator comes as close as possible to the case". The critical role consists on standing "outside" the case to appraise the data, explain and interpret them. It has been used to study eminent products or people. Historiometric is also mainly concerned with the study of eminent creators, names that have "gone down in history" as Simonton (1999) puts it. Through a quantitative analysis of the biographical and historical records related to these eminent creators, historiometrics attempt to measure creativity. Simonton defines historiometrics as a "scientific discipline in which nomothetic hypotheses about human behaviour are tested by applying quantitative analyses to data concerning historical individuals".

This definition can be broken down in three components: Historimetric approaches look for "nomothetic hypothesis", that is to say "the goal is the discovery of general laws or statistical relationships that transcend the particular of the historic records". It uses quantitative analyses. The researcher has to transform the usually rich, ambiguous, and qualitative facts of history into more precise, clear numerical measurements. In addition, the researcher should use statistical techniques, mainly multiple regressions, factor analysis and latent-variable models to understand the relationship between different aspects of creativity.

The subject of study in the historiometric approach is always a "historical individual". Runco (2007) maintains that creative personality encompasses: Autonomy, flexibility, preference for complexity, openness to experience, sensitivity, playfulness, tolerance of ambiguity, risk taking or risk tolerance, intrinsic motivation, psychological androgyny, self-efficacy and wide interest and curiosity. He also noted that creative personality varies from domain to domain, and perhaps, even from person to person: "there is no one creative personality". He however, maintains that certain characteristics depend on values, intentions and choice; thus, people have the possibility of trying to enhance their creativity or not. This is in line with what Sternberg affirms (2006b, 93) in his review of creativity research: "Creativity is as much a decision about and an attitude toward life as it is a matter of ability".

THE CREATIVE CLASS

From a rather different perspective, Richard Florida (2002, 2004) has been instrumental for popularizing the concept of creativity. He has created the "creativity index". He is not specifically interested in measuring creativity per se, but on the factors associated with urban economic growth. Florida's main thesis is that creativity is the "ultimate economic resource". He maintains that economic success of urban centers is associated with the amount of creative people they can attract. In this way, Florida maintains that creative people are attracted to places that are characterized by a "culture that's open-minded and diverse". In his view, "places provide ecosystems that harness human creativity and turn into economic value". Inspecting the characteristics of these places he presents his 3 T's model.

These stand for: Technology, Talent and Tolerance. Technology is mainly referring to the presence in the region of high-tech companies and their production of patents. Talent is mainly referring to the amount of people in the "creative class". The Tolerance index is mainly referring to the openness of a place to other ideas and making outsiders welcomed. The technology index is compounded by the innovation index and the high- tech index. Florida maintains: "Each is a necessary but by itself insufficient condition".

A place must have all three T's "to attract creative people, generate innovation and stimulates economic growth". Florida has created a composite indicator, the creativity index that unifies the three indexes referring to each of the T's Florida and Tinagli (2004) calculated a version of Florida's creative index in European countries. They used somehow different indicators than the original ones from Florida (2002). In their "European creativity index", they consider also the three T's: Talent, Technology and Tolerance. However, they expand each of the indexes, including some extra indicators. For example, the Talent index is compound of creative class, human capital and scientific talent sub-indexes, while in Florida's first book it only encompassed the creative class index.

In the Tolerance Index, Florida and Tinagli (2004) do not used the famous "gay index" but some indexes derived from the World Value survey (Values index and self-expression index), and an attitude index derived from a survey of the European Monitoring Centre on Racism and Xenophobia. Following Florida's framework, KEA European Affairs (2006) proposed the "EURO CREATIVITY SCOREBOARD". They propose four sub-indexes: Talent, Cultural, Technology and innovation, and Diversity. The focus is specifically in creative industries, and thus almost all indicators are related to art.

Boschma and Fritz (2007) applied Florida's conception of creative class to study employment growth in 450 regions of eight European countries. They found that creative class had a positive effect on employment growth and that creative class workers seem to be attracted to places characterized by tolerance and openness. Florida's work is not exempt of criticism. Peck (2005), for example, makes a vivid criticism of Florida's thesis. Malanga (2004) also has severely criticised Florida's for its impact in urban policy. Glaeser (2000) has also raised some concerns about Florida's theories.

Entrepreneurship and innovation as pointers of creative potential Florida's views on creativity open up the door to consider other type of measures of creativity far away from the psychological methods and constructs. In particular indicators pointing to innovation and entrepreneurship become possible measures of creativity levels. The Oslo manual defines innovation as "a new significant improved product (good or service), or process, a new marketing method, or a new organizational method, business practices, workplace organization or external relations". Defined in this way, innovation requires creativity since it implies something new significantly improved.

The Oslo manual differentiate between product, process, marketing and organizational innovation. This means that which is "new" does not necessarily have to be a market product, but something that is 'significantly" different from what was previously in use. The problem of "relativity" of what is new, as in the case of creativity, is addressed in the case of innovation. For the Oslo manual "the minimum entry level for an innovation is that must be new to the firm" (OECD and EUROSAT 2005, 57, emphasis in the original).

Innovation in this definition differs from invention in that it has been introduced into the market, either by using it (an organizational innovation that has been implemented) or by putting it into the market (a new product). In this way, innovation complies with the second characteristic of creativity of "usefulness" or "value". The innovation being implemented is, at least theoretically, a solution to a problem (the lack of certain product in the market, the absence of a marketing strategy, etc.). Indicators on innovation have been developed in Europe within the context of the Lisbon Strategy.

Celikel Esser et al. (2008) present an overview of the innovation metrics used in the European Union in the last 10 years. They identified five tools at a European level: European Trend Chart, the Community Innovation Survey (CIS), the Inno-barometer, the European Innovation Scoreboard (EIS) and the European Service Sector Innovation Scoreboard (SSIS). The European Trend Chart is mainly concerned with policy developments in the European Union. CIS is a statistical survey coordinated by EUROSTAT that collects information on innovation using the methodological basis of the Oslo manual.

The Inno-barometer is an opinion poll carried out under the auspices of the European Commission. It explores the opinions of managers in relation to some innovation issues. EIS is defined by Arundel and Hollanders (2008) as a collection of national and regional indicators relevant to innovation. The EIS "is the range of measures produced to benchmark the EU countries' innovation performance. Finally, the SSIS is a respond to the increasingly importance given in policy to services in general and innovation in service in particular. In addition, entrepreneurship is another area where the development of indicators is progressing. Indicators of entrepreneurship are not specifically considered by Florida in The Rise of the Creative Class.

However, in an article for Regional Studies the authors linked creativity and entrepreneurship. In their analysis they measure entrepreneurship in the U.S. as firm birth per 1000 people. In the measurement of entrepreneurship, the OECD and EUROSTAT are collaborating in a project started in 2006: The Entrepreneurship Indicator Programme (EIP). EIP defines entrepreneurs as "those persons (business owners) who seek to generate value, through the creation, expansion of economic activity, by identifying and exploiting new products, processes or markets".

The definition differs from innovation. While an innovation refers to a new significant improved product or process, entrepreneurship is mainly concern with generation of value from these sources. Value is understood in different ways, and it can be economic or social, although the EIP has mainly focused on economic value. Entrepreneurship, therefore involves also creativity, since it requires the capacity to purposefully exploiting new opportunities. Entrepreneurship requires thus, also one of the common characteristics defined under creativity, the capacity to move one's ideas forward (persuasion).

EIP has developed a framework and proposed a list of indicators related to entrepreneurship. Most of these indicators are pointing to creativity efforts, since they, by definition, are focus on something "new" and with "value". Interesting enough, Ahmad and Hoffman point out that "[F]irms do not need to be new to be entrepreneurial. Older firms can demonstrate entrepreneurship too". In this way, they include high-growth firms based on employment and turn-over as indicators of entrepreneurship, under the assumption that firms that have demonstrated rapid growth are doing something "significantly different".

The previous section has shown that despite having some measures of creativity, it seems clear that understandings of creativity differ depending on the approach chosen to study it. Tests of creativity at individual level require, mainly, either some type of divergent thinking (as opposed to convergent thinking) or some personality traits (that have been associated with creative behaviour). Existing large scale surveys, such as PISA or TIMMS, are mainly convergent thinking tests. This means that in all the items proposed there is only one correct answer. From the description above on creativity, it can be said that trying to measure creativity with items that have been design specifically to test knowledge in one area (mathematics, science or reading) will present several challenges.

First, the differentiation of creative thinking from

knowledge proficiency might be difficult to achieve. It could be argue that certain items in the PISA study would require more creativity than others. If it were possible to differentiate between more or less creative items in the PISA test, would it be possible to create a sub-scale of "creativity" using PISA data?

MEASURING CREATIVITY USING LARGE INTERNATIONAL SURVEYS

This type of measurement, however, opens another question: how could we say that those items have been correctly answered by the more creative pupil and not by the most knowledgeable? The items have been constructed not to measure creativity (can the students provide an original and adequate answer?) but to measure their proficiency level in one area (can the student provide one adequate answer?). How plausible is to separate the "proficiency" to the "creative" part of solving a problem in PISA? Another important issue that appears when measuring creativity refers to the conditions of the test.

It is interesting to note what Runco (2007, 3) has pointed out: if schools care about creativity and give children exercises and test for creativity potential, but if those are given in test-like academic atmosphere, the same children who always do well on test will excel, and the children who do moderately or poorly on traditional tests will again do only moderately or poorly. He noted in this way, while revising evidence from Wallach and Kogan (1965), that in order for test for creativity (using divergent thinking tests) to differ from regular IQ tests, the application of the creativity tests has to be in a "game like" or "permissive environment".

The tests were described as games rather than tests, where no grades would be given. Only in this way, tests on creativity were significantly different than test on intelligence. Thus, one might ask, would the measurement of creativity with large scale survey data differ at all from the regular tests scores? In addition, how to decide which items require more creativity than others might be complicated. A group of experts could explore items and decide on this issue, but the items selected as "creative", would have been selected more or less arbitrarily (by a group of experts).

Very likely, the resulting scales would have the low reliability, which will make very complicated any interpretation of the results. We will be measuring, not only a small fraction of what apparently (and according to some 30 or 20 experts, if not less) creativity entitles, but we will not be able to be sure that we are actually measuring what we are suppose to measure (e.g. creativity in solving mathematical problems). How could we overcome such an obstacle? Can we empirically find evidence that some items are more creative than others? Literature on creativity presents a rather complicated view of what creativity is.

The most plausible approach to creativity is a multidisciplinary approach, in which creative behaviour and thinking emerged from the combination of the right variety of elements in a very sophisticated (difficult to replicate) interrelationship (similar to the views of Sternberg and Lubart (1999) or Runco (2007). Thus, can existing international surveys provide a (very small) fraction of what creativity encompassed? More complicated is to think of creativity as a social construct, in the sense that creative products are determined by the culture the product has been produced. To put an extreme example: "using a lever to move a rock might be judge novel in a Cro-Magnon civilization, but not in a modern one". In this way, creativity would be context dependent and difficult to be compared across countries. What type of creativity could we measure that is comparable across cultures?

DEVELOPING A LARGE SCALE SURVEY ON CREATIVITY

From the arguments presented above, it seems costly and maybe not very effective to use PISA or other international scale as a measure of creativity. However, the development of an instrument to test creativity in all European Member States could be considered, although, there is little doubt that the process would be extremely challenging and difficult. New methods of assessment with computers allow for simulations and games to assess students capacities. This open up one door to measure complicated constructs such as creativity. Could the emergence of Computer Based Assessment open a door to make the measurement of creativity at an individual level plausible in an international comparative manner?

The first step would necessarily be to agree on a working definition of creativity. The definition would require the participation of as many stake holders as possible, in order to make it relevant to different policy areas. It would have to be adaptable to many different backgrounds and cultures that compound the European Union. An extended review of the literature, more complete than the one presented here would be necessary, as well as involvement of experts in the area. With this definition in mind, it would be advisable to conduct a feasibility study.

This will require some expert group in measurement issues in psychology (and creativity research specifically) that would assess the possibility of developing a test to measure creativity in an international manner. If the feasibility study yields a positive result, it would provide the "green light" to start the process of developing a tool to measure creativity. The instrument would have to be tested and adapted to the National contexts in the European Union. The tool would have to necessarily be pre-tested in a pilot way, in as many different countries as possible.

If the results of these pilot tests are satisfactory, and the tool is good enough, it would be possible to start a full scale process that would provide a picture of creative levels in society. Such a project would necessarily be a long term project that would require an important amount of investment and political will. The process might be aborted in the way for different reasons. And great difficulties could be expected in the measurement and adaptation of test items to specific cultural aspects. The results of such a project are difficult to predict, as well as the reactions that might cause in the public sphere.

Unit VII

Personality

MEANING - FREUD'S THEORY OF PERSONALITY

The Psychoanalytic Theory of personality has held the interest of psychologists and psychiatrists for a long time. Sigmund Freud, its formulator, was quite an influence. The psychoanalytic position is that early experiences influence all human behaviour. It attends to — emphasizes — three main issues: the *id*, the *ego* and the *superego*. Psychoanalysts say that all human personality is comprised of these closely integrated functions. The id is considered as mostly biological or physical in function — unfettered, compelling and lacking morality, selfish and intolerant of tension. It functions on the principle of pleasure before anything else. Psychoanalysts consider the id the basic psychic energy and the seat of instincts. It always functions on the unconscious level. Its main quirk is "pleasure before everything, and at any cost." The ego is the rationally functioning element of human personality.

It exerts conscious control, trying always to be the mediator between the id and the superego. Though the id seeks pleasure blindly, based on the pleasure principle, the ego seeks pleasure using rationality instead of irrationality. Its main quirk is rationality, and is always conscious. The superego represents our moral system. It strives to put a right or wrong tag on our behaviour, often triggering conflict among the three divisions. Its main quirk is morality. The ego is that aspect we present to the "outside" — it is our *persona* our *celebrity*. Psychoanalysts treat humanity as a dismal breed — irrational, materialistic and mechanistic. Human beings, according to

Freud and his ardent followers, are mere energy systems — and the summation of that energy is the psychic energy. Anxiety occurs when there is conflict among the three divisions. Humans use *defence mechanisms* to control the anxiety.

Many are listed. Psychoanalysts also put considerable importance on *their* defined stages through which each proceeds toward maturity — the oral stage, the anal stage and the phallic stage in particular — and later the latent stage. They also put much stock in two processes called positive and negative transference (and the "counter-transference" of each) — positive: likening it to love for the therapist as he/she represents or substitutes for one or the other parent (or other significant person — surrogate) in their patient's maturing life; negative: likening it to dislike/hate for the therapist as he/she represents or substitutes for one or the other parent (or other significant person in their patient's maturing life) whom the patient considers the cause of their problem(s). Complicating the psychoanalytic theory of personality, Freud introduced concepts such as the Oedipus complex and, to balance it with a feminine touch, the Electra complex (although, some who write of Freud's theory say that this wasn't of Freud's thinking.)

Despite these noble attempts to balance the genders, the psychoanalytic theory of personality is very chauvinistic, giving the male gender much more attention than the female. From my perspective, Freud's greatest contribution to understanding human personality was his exquisite development of his concepts of human conscious and unconscious (and conscience.) Although not being the first to make this division, his concepts make more sense. And his concepts remain the basis for most other theories of personality. Treating patients, using the psychoanalytic theory, is complex, time consuming and costly. And, however it is viewed, and by whoever views it, it must be considered a closed system. Its main energy is that of the id. It lacks concern for any other outside energy — outside the self, that is. It is a self-centered model, closed and lacking any interest in a spiritual part that is invested in each person. I take issue with Freud's theory for this reason.

Later in Freud's work, two of his most ardent followers bolted, Alfred Adler and Carl Gustov Jung. Jung developed a most interesting — and every bit as complex — a theory of personality as Freud; perhaps more complex. More modern theorists, Otto Rank (who emphasized separation anxiety as the main issue with which to deal in understanding human personality), and Karen Horney (who believed that Freud's theory was too mechanistic, which it is, and who further believed that to understand human personality, it was necessary to extend its study to include social pressures and stressors.)

She developed a long list of *needs* that each had to fulfill to feel comfortable with themselves as well as with society. Yet, no matter what additional theories were developed, using Freud's ideas as their basis — with the exception of Jung — they continued to exclude the spiritual part of each individual, adding to my belief, that being closed systems, none could possibly bring the wholeness and completeness that each individual seeks in his living and his life after he dies.

ERIKSON: DEVELOPMENTAL CRISIS IN PERSONALITY

Erikson is a Freudian ego-psychologist. This means that he accepts Freud's ideas as basically correct, including the more debatable ideas such as the Oedipal complex, and accepts as well the ideas about the ego that were added by other Freudian loyalists such as Heinz Hartmann and, of, course, Anna Freud. However, Erikson is much more society and culture-oriented than most Freudians, as you might expect from someone with his anthropological interests, and he often pushes the instincts and the unconscious practically out of the picture. Perhaps because of this, Erikson is popular among Freudians and non-Freudians alike!

THE EPIGENETIC PRINCIPLE

He is most famous for his work in refining and expanding

Freud's theory of stages. Development, he says, functions by the epigenetic principle. This principle says that we develop through a predetermined unfolding of our personalities in eight stages. Our progress through each stage is in part determined by our success, or lack of success, in all the previous stages. A little like the unfolding of a rose bud, each petal opens up at a certain time, in a certain order, which nature, through its genetics, has determined. If we interfere in the natural order of development by pulling a petal forward prematurely or out of order, we ruin the development of the entire flower. Each stage involves certain developmental tasks that are psychosocial in nature. Although he follows Freudian tradition by calling them crises, they are more drawn out and less specific than that term implies.

The child in grammar school, for example, has to learn to be industrious during that period of his or her life, and that industriousness is learned through the complex social interactions of school and family.

The various tasks are referred to by two terms. The infant's task, for example, is called "trust-mistrust." At first, it might seem obvious that the infant must learn trust and not mistrust. But Erikson made it clear that there it is a balance we must learn: Certainly, we need to learn mostly trust; but we also need to learn a little mistrust, so as not to grow up to become gullible fools!

Each stage has a certain optimal time as well. It is no use trying to rush children into adulthood, as is so common among people who are obsessed with success. Neither is it possible to slow the pace or to try to protect our children from the demands of life. There is a time for each task.

If a stage is managed well, we carry away a certain virtue or psychosocial strength which will help us through the rest of the stages of our lives. On the other hand, if we don't do so well, we may develop mal-adaptations and malignancies, as well as endanger all our future development. A malignancy is the worse of the two, and involves too little of the positive and too much of the negative aspect of the task, such as a person who can't trust others. A maladaptation is not quite as bad and involves too much of the positive and too little of the negative, such as a person who trusts too much.

CHILDREN AND ADULTS

Perhaps Erikson's greatest innovation was to postulate not five stages, as Freud had done, but eight. Erikson elaborated Freud's genital stage into adolescence plus three stages of adulthood. We certainly don't stop developing — especially psychologically — after our twelfth or thirteenth birthdays; it seems only right to extend any theory of stages to cover later development! Erikson also had some things to say about the interaction of generations, which he called mutuality. Freud had made it abundantly clear that a child's parents influence his or her development dramatically.

Erikson pointed out that children influence their parents' development as well. The arrival of children, for example, into a couple's life, changes that life considerably, and moves the new parents along their developmental paths. It is even appropriate to add a third (and in some cases, a fourth) generation to the picture: Many of us have been influenced by our grandparents, and they by us.

A particularly clear example of mutuality can be seen in the problems of the teenage mother. Although the mother and her child may have a fine life together, often the mother is still involved in the tasks of adolescence, that is, in finding out who she is and how she fits into the larger society.

The relationship she has or had with the child's father may have been immature on one or both sides, and if they don't marry, she will have to deal with the problems of finding and developing a relationship as well. The infant, on the other hand, has the simple, straight-forward needs that infants have, and the most important of these is a mother with the mature abilities and social support a mother should have. If the mother's parents step in to help, as one would expect, then they, too, are thrown off of their developmental tracks, back into a life-style they thought they had passed, and which they might find terribly demanding.

The ways in which our lives intermesh are terribly

complex and very frustrating to the theorist. But ignoring them is to ignore something vitally important about our development and our personalities.

THE FIRST STAGE

The first stage, infancy or the oral-sensory stage, is approximately the first year or year and a half of life. The task is to develop trust without completely eliminating the capacity for mistrust. If mom and dad can give the newborn a degree of familiarity, consistency, and continuity, then the child will develop the feeling that the world — especially the social world — is a safe place to be, that people are reliable and loving. Through the parents' responses, the child also learns to trust his or her own body and the biological urges that go with it. If the parents are unreliable and inadequate, if they reject the infant or harm it, if other interests cause both parents to turn away from the infants needs to satisfy their own instead, then the infant will develop mistrust. He or she will be apprehensive and suspicious around people.

Please understand that this doesn't mean that the parents have to be perfect. In fact, parents who are overly protective of the child, are there the minute the first cry comes out, will lead that child into the maladaptive tendency Erikson calls sensory maladjustment: Overly trusting, even gullible, this person cannot believe anyone would mean them harm, and will use all the defenses at their command to retain their pollyanna perspective. Worse, of course, is the child whose balance is tipped way over on the mistrust side: They will develop the malignant tendency of withdrawal, characterized by depression, paranoia, and possibly psychosis.

If the proper balance is achieved, the child will develop the virtue hope, the strong belief that, even when things are not going well, they will work out well in the end. One of the signs that a child is doing well in the first stage is when the child isn't overly upset by the need to wait a moment for the satisfaction of his or her needs: Mom or dad don't have to be perfect; I trust them enough to believe that, if they can't be here immediately, they will be here soon; Things may be tough now, but they will work out. This is the same ability that, in later life, gets us through disappointments in love, our careers, and many other domains of life.

STAGE TWO

The second stage is the anal-muscular stage of early childhood, from about eighteen months to three or four years old. The task is to achieve a degree of autonomy while minimizing shame and doubt. If mom and dad (and the other care-takers that often come into the picture at this point) permit the child, now a toddler, to explore and manipulate his or her environment, the child will develop a sense of autonomy or independence. The parents should not discourage the child, but neither should they push. A balance is required. People often advise new parents to be "firm but tolerant" at this stage, and the advice is good. This way, the child will develop both self-control and self-esteem.

On the other hand, it is rather easy for the child to develop instead a sense of shame and doubt. If the parents come down hard on any attempt to explore and be independent, the child will soon give up with the assumption that cannot and should not act on their own. We should keep in mind that even something as innocent as laughting at the toddler's efforts can lead the child to feel deeply ashamed, and to doubt his or her abilities. And there are other ways to lead children to shame and doubt: If you give children unrestricted freedom and no sense of limits, or if you try to help children do what they should learn to do for themselves, you will also give them the impression that they are not good for much. If you aren't patient enough to wait for your child to tie his or her shoe-laces, your child will never learn to tie them, and will assume that this is too difficult to learn!

Nevertheless, a little "shame and doubt" is not only inevitable, but beneficial. Without it, you will develop the maladaptive tendency Erikson calls impulsiveness, a sort of shameless willfulness that leads you, in later childhood and even adulthood, to jump into things without proper consideration of your abilities. Worse, of course, is too much shame and doubt, which leads to the malignancy Erikson calls compulsiveness. The compulsive person feels as if their entire being rides on everything they do, and so everything must be done perfectly. Following all the rules precisely keeps you from mistakes, and mistakes must be avoided at all costs. Many of you know how it feels to always be ashamed and always doubt yourself. A little more patience and tolerance with your own children may help them avoid your path. And give yourself a little slack, too!

If you get the proper, positive balance of autonomy and shame and doubt, you will develop the virtue of willpower or determination. One of the most admirable — and frustrating — thing about two- and three-year-olds is their determination. "Can do" is their motto. If we can preserve that "can do" attitude (with appropriate modesty to balance it) we are much better off as adults.

STAGE THREE

Stage three is the genital-locomotor stage or play age. From three or four to five or six, the task confronting every child is to learn initiative without too much guilt. Initiative means a positive response to the world's challenges, taking on responsibilities, learning new skills, feeling purposeful. Parents can encourage initiative by encouraging children to try out their ideas. We should accept and encourage fantasy and curiosity and imagination. This is a time for play, not for formal education. The child is now capable, as never before, of imagining a future situation, one that isn't a reality right now. Initiative is the attempt to make that non-reality a reality.

But if children can imagine the future, if they can plan, then they can be responsible as well, and guilty. If my two-year-old flushes my watch down the toilet, I can safely assume that there were no "evil intentions." It was just a matter of a shiny object going round and round and down. What fun! But if my five year old does the same thing... well, she should know what's going to happen to the watch, what's going to happen to daddy's temper, and what's going to happen to her! She can be guilty of the act, and she can begin to feel guilty as well. The capacity for moral judgement has arrived. Erikson is, of course, a Freudian, and as such, he includes the Oedipal experience in this stage.

From his perspective, the Oedipal crisis involves the reluctance a child feels in relinquishing his or her closeness to the opposite sex parent. A parent has the responsibility, socially, to enourage the child to "grow up — you're not a baby anymore!" But if this process is done too harshly and too abruptly, the child learns to feel guilty about his or her feelings. Too much initiative and too little guilt means a maladaptive tendency Erikson calls ruthlessness. The ruthless person takes the initiative alright; They have their plans, whether it's a matter of school or romance or politics or career. It's just that they don't care who they step on to achieve their goals. The goals are everything, and guilty feelings are for the weak. The extreme form of ruthlessess is sociopathy.

Ruthlessness is bad for others, but actually relatively easy on the ruthless person. Harder on the person is the malignancy of too much guilt, which Erikson calls inhibition. The inhibited person will not try things because "nothing ventured, nothing lost" and, particularly, nothing to feel guilty about. On the sexual, Oedipal, side, the inhibited person may be impotent or frigid. A good balance leads to the psychosocial strength of purpose. A sense of purpose is something many people crave in their lives, yet many do not realise that they themselves make their purposes, through imagination and initiative. I think an even better word for this virtue would have been courage, the capacity for action despite a clear understanding of your limitations and past failings.

STAGE FOUR

Stage four is the latency stage, or the school-age child from about six to twelve. The task is to develop a capacity for industry while avoiding an excessive sense of inferiority. Children must "tame the imagination" and dedicate themselves to education and to learning the social skills their society requires of them. There is a much broader social·sphere at work now: The parents and other family members are joined by teachers and peers and other members of he community at large. They all contribute: Parents must encourage, teachers must care, peers must accept. Children must learn that there is pleasure not only in conceiving a plan, but in carrying it out. They must learn the feeling of success, whether it is in school or on the playground, academic or social.

A good way to tell the difference between a child in the third stage and one in the fourth stage is to look at the way they play games. Four-year-olds may love games, but they will have only a vague understanding of the rules, may change them several times during the course of the game, and be very unlikely to actually finish the game, unless it is by throwing the pieces at their opponents. A seven-year-old, on the other hand, is dedicated to the rules, considers them pretty much sacred, and is more likely to get upset if the game is not allowed to come to its required conclusion.

If the child is allowed too little success, because of harsh teachers or rejecting peers, for example, then he or she will develop instead a sense of inferiority or incompetence. An additional source of inferiority Erikson mentions is racism, sexism, and other forms of discrimination: If a child believes that success is related to who you are rather than to how hard you try, then why try? Too much industry leads to the maladaptive tendency called narrow virtuosity. We see this in children who aren't allowed to "be children," the ones that parents or teachers push into one area of competence, without allowing the development of broader interests. These are the kids without a life: child actors, child athletes, child musicians, child prodigies of all sorts. We all admire their industry, but if we look a little closer, it's all that stands in the way of an empty life. Much more common is the malignancy called inertia.

This includes all of us who suffer from the "inferiority complexes" Alfred Adler talked about. If at first you don't succeed, don't ever try again! Many of us didn't do well in mathematics, for example, so we'd die before we took another math class. Others were humiliated instead in the gym class, so we never try out for a sport or play a game of raquetball.

Others never developed social skills — the most important skills of all — and so we never go out in public. We become inert. A happier thing is to develop the right balance of industry and inferiority — that is, mostly industry with just a touch of inferiority to keep us sensibly humble. Then we have the virtue called competency.

STAGE FIVE

Stage five is adolescence, beginning with puberty and ending around 18 or 20 years old. The task during adolescence is to achieve ego identity and avoid role confusion. It was adolescence that interested Erikson first and most, and the patterns he saw here were the bases for his thinking about all the other stages. Ego identity means knowing who you are and how you fit in to the rest of society. It requires that you take all you've learned about life and yourself and mold it into a unified self-image, one that your community finds meaningful. There are a number of things that make things easier: First, we should have a mainstream adult culture that is worthy of the adolescent's respect, one with good adult role models and open lines of communication.

Further, society should provide clear rites of passage, certain accomplishments and rituals that help to distinguish the adult from the child. In primitive and traditional societies, an adolescent boy may be asked to leave the village for a period of time to live on his own, hunt some symbolic animal, or seek an inspirational vision. Boys and girls may be required to go through certain tests of endurance, symbolic ceremonies, or educational events. In one way or another, the distinction between the powerless, but irresponsible, time of childhood and the powerful and responsbile time of adulthood, is made clear. Without these things, we are likely to see role confusion, meaning an uncertainty about one's place in society and the world. When an adolescent is confronted by role confusion, Erikson say he or she is suffering from an identity crisis. In fact, a common question adolescents in our society ask is a straight-forward question of identity: "Who am I?"

One of Erikson's suggestions for adolescence in our society

is the psychosocial moratorium. He suggests you take a little "time out." If you have money, go to Europe. If you don't, bum around the U.S.

Quit school and get a job. Quit your job and go to school. Take a break, smell the roses, get to know yourself. We tend to want to get to "success" as fast as possible, and yet few of us have ever taken the time to figure out what success means to us.

A little like the young Oglala Lakota, perhaps we need to dream a little. There is such a thing as too much "ego identity," where a person is so involved in a particular role in a particular society or subculture that there is no room left for tolerance. Erikson calls this maladaptive tendency fanaticism.

A fanatic believes that his way is the only way. Adolescents are, of course, known for their idealism, and for their tendency to see things in black-and-white. These people will gather others around them and promote their beliefs and life-styles without regard to others' rights to disagree. The lack of identity is perhaps more difficult still, and Erikson refers to the malignant tendency here as repudiation.

They repudiate their membership in the world of adults and, even more, they repudiate their need for an identity. Some adolescents allow themselves to "fuse" with a group, especially the kind of group that is particularly eager to provide the details of your identity: religious cults, militaristic organizations, groups founded on hatred, groups that have divorced themselves from the painful demands of mainstream society. They may become involved in destructive activities, drugs, or alcohol, or you may withdraw into their own psychotic fantasies.

After all, being "bad" or being "nobody" is better than not knowing who you are! If you successfully negotiate this stage, you will have the virtue Erikson called fidelity. Fidelity means loyalty, the ability to live by societies standards despite their imperfections and incompleteness and inconsistencies. We are not talking about blind loyalty, and we are not talking about accepting the imperfections. After all, if you love your community, you will want to see it become the best it can be.

But fidelity means that you have found a place in that community, a place that will allow you to contribute.

STAGE SIX

If you have made it this far, you are in the stage of young adulthood, which lasts from about 18 to about 30. The ages in the adult stages are much fuzzier than in the childhood stages, and people may differ dramatically. The task is to achieve some degree of intimacy, as opposed to remaining in isolation. Intimacy is the ability to be close to others, as a lover, a friend, and as a participant in society. Because you have a clear sense of who you are, you no longer need to fear "losing" yourself, as many adolescents do.

The "fear of commitment" some people seem to exhibit is an example of immaturity in this stage. This fear isn't always so obvious. Many people today are always putting off the progress of their relationships: I'll get married (or have a family, or get involved in important social issues) as soon as I finish school, as soon as I have a job, as soon as I have a house, as soon as.... If you've been engaged for the last ten years, what's holding you back?

Neither should the young adult need to prove him- or herself anymore. A teenage relationship is often a matter of trying to establish identity through "couple-hood." Who am I? I'm her boy-friend. The young adult relationship should be a matter of two independent egos wanting to create something larger than themselves. We intuitively recognize this when we frown on a relationship between a young adult and a teenager: We see the potential for manipulation of the younger member of the party by the older. Our society hasn't done much for young adults, either.

The emphasis on careers, the isolation of urban living, the splitting apart of relationships because of our need for mobility, and the general impersonal nature of modern life prevent people from naturally developing their intimate relationships. I am typical of many people in having moved dozens of times in my life. I haven't the faintest idea what has happened to the kids I grew up with, or even my college buddies. My oldest friend lives a thousand miles away. I live where I do out of career necessity and, until recently, have felt no real sense of community.

Before I get too depressing, let me mention that many of you may not have had these experiences. If you grew up and stayed in your community, and especially if your community is a rural one, you are much more likely to have deep, long-lasting friendships, to have married your high school sweetheart, and to feel a great love for your community. But this style of life is quickly becoming an anachronism. Erikson calls the maladaptive form promiscuity, refering particularly to the tendency to become intimate too freely, too easily, and without any depth to your intimacy. This can be true of your relationships with friends and neighbors and your whole community as well as with lovers. The malignancy he calls exclusion, which refers to the tendency to isolate oneself from love, friendship, and community, and to develop a certain hatefulness in compensation for one's loneliness.

If you successfully negotiate this stage, you will instead carry with you for the rest of your life the virtue or psychosocial strength Erikson calls love. Love, in the context of his theory, means being able to put aside differences and antagonisms through "mutuality of devotion." It includes not only the love we find in a good marriage, but the love between friends and the love of one's neighbour, co-worker, and compatriot as well.

STAGE SEVEN

The seventh stage is that of middle adulthood. It is hard to pin a time to it, but it would include the period during which we are actively involved in raising children. For most people in our society, this would put it somewhere between the middle twenties and the late fifties. The task here is to cultivate the proper balance of generativity and stagnation.

Generativity is an extension of love into the future. It is a concern for the next generation and all future generations. As such, it is considerably less "selfish" than the intimacy of the previous stage: Intimacy, the love between lovers or friends, is a love between equals, and it is necessarily reciprocal. Oh, of course we love each other unselfishly, but the reality is such that, if the love is not returned, we don't consider it a true love. With generativity, that implicit expectation of reciprocity isn't there, at least not as strongly. Few parents expect a "return on their investment" from their children; If they do, we don't think of them as very good parents!

Although the majority of people practice generativity by having and raising children, there are many other ways as well. Erikson considers teaching, writing, invention, the arts and sciences, social activism, and generally contributing to the welfare of future generations to be generativity as well — anything, in fact, that satisfies that old "need to be needed."

Stagnation, on the other hand, is self-absorption, caring for no-one. The stagnant person ceases to be a productive member of society. It is perhaps hard to imagine that we should have any "stagnation" in our lives, but the maladaptive tendency Erikson calls overextension illustrates the problem: Some people try to be so generative that they no longer allow time for themselves, for rest and relaxation. The person who is overextended no longer contributes well. I'm sure we all know someone who belongs to so many clubs, or is devoted to so many causes, or tries to take so many classes or hold so many jobs that they no longer have time for any of them!

More obvious, of course, is the malignant tendency of rejectivity. Too little generativity and too much stagnation and you are no longer participating in or contributing to society. And much of what we call "the meaning of life" is a matter of how we participate and what we contribute.

This is the stage of the "midlife crisis." Sometimes men and women take a look at their lives and ask that big, bad question "what am I doing all this for?" Notice the question carefully: Because their focus is on themselves, they ask what, rather than whom, they are doing it for. In their panic at getting older and not having experienced or accomplished what they imagined they would when they were younger, they try to recapture their youth. Men are often the most flambouyant examples: They leave their long-suffering wives, quit their humdrum jobs, buy some "hip" new clothes, and start hanging around singles bars. Of course, they seldom find what they are looking for, because they are looking for the wrong thing! But if you are successful at this stage, you will have a capacity for caring that will serve you through the rest of your life.

STAGE EIGHT

This last stage, referred to delicately as late adulthood or maturity, or less delicately as old age, begins sometime around retirement, after the kids have gone, say somewhere around 60. Some older folks will protest and say it only starts when you feel old and so on, but that's an effect of our youth-worshipping culture, which has even old people avoiding any acknowledgement of age. In Erikson's theory, reaching this stage is a good thing, and not reaching it suggests that earlier problems retarded your development!

The task is to develop ego integrity with a minimal amount of despair. This stage, especially from the perspective of youth, seems like the most difficult of all. First comes a detachment from society, from a sense of usefulness, for most people in our culture. Some retire from jobs they've held for years; others find their duties as parents coming to a close; most find that their input is no longer requested or required.

Then there is a sense of biological uselessness, as the body no longer does everything it used to. Women go through a sometimes dramatic menopause; Men often find they can no longer "rise to the occasion." Then there are the illnesses of old age, such as arthritis, diabetes, heart problems, concerns about breast and ovarian and prostrate cancers. There come fears about things that one was never afraid of before — the flu, for example, or just falling down. Along with the illnesses come concerns of death. Friends die. Relatives die. One's spouse dies. It is, of course, certain that you, too, will have your turn. Faced with all this, it might seem like everyone would feel despair.

In response to this despair, some older people become preoccupied with the past. After all, that's where things were better. Some become preoccupied with their failures, the bad decisions they made, and regret that (unlike some in the previous stage) they really don't have the time or energy to reverse them. We find some older people become depressed, spiteful, paranoid, hypochondriacal, or developing the patterns of senility with or without physical bases.

Ego integrity means coming to terms with your life, and thereby coming to terms with the end of life. If you are able to look back and accept the course of events, the choices made, your life as you lived it, as being necessary, then you needn't fear death. Although most of you are not at this point in life, perhaps you can still sympathize by considering your life up to now. We've all made mistakes, some of them pretty nasty ones; Yet, if you hadn't made these mistakes, you wouldn't be who you are. If you had been very fortunate, or if you had played it safe and made very few mistakes, your life would not have been as rich as is. The maladaptive tendency in stage eight is called presumption. This is what happens when a person "presumes" ego integrity without actually facing the difficulties of old age. The malignant tendency is called disdain, by which Erikson means a contempt of life, one's own or anyone's.

Someone who approaches death without fear has the strength Erikson calls wisdom. He calls it a gift to children, because "healthy children will not fear life if their elders have integrity enough not to fear death." He suggests that a person must be somewhat gifted to be truly wise, but I would like to suggest that you understand "gifted" in as broad a fashion as possible: I have found that there are people of very modest gifts who have taught me a great deal, not by their wise words, but by their simple and gentle approach to life and death, by their "generosity of spirit."

MASLOW AND THE STUDY OF SELF-ACTUALIZING PEOPLE

Self-actualization is a term that has been used in various psychology theories, often in slightly different ways (e.g., Goldstein, Maslow, Rogers). The term was originally introduced by the organismic theorist Kurt Goldstein for the motive to realise all of one's potentialities. In his view, it is the master motive—indeed, the only real motive a person has, all others being merely manifestations of it. However, the concept was brought to prominence in Abraham Maslow's hierarchy of needs theory as the final level of psychological development that can be achieved when all basic and mental needs are fulfilled and the "actualisation" of the full personal potential takes place.

SELF-ACTUALIZATION IN GOLDSTEIN'S THEORY

According to Kurt Goldstein's book *The Organism: A Holistic Approach to Biology Derived from Pathological Data in Man*, self-actualization is "the tendency to actualize, as much as possible, [the organism's] individual capacities" in the world. The tendency to self-actualization is "the only drive by which the life of an organism is determined." Goldstein defined self-actualization as a driving life force that will ultimately lead to maximizing one's abilities and determine the path of one's life; compare will to power.

SELF-ACTUALIZATION AND MASLOW'S HIERARCHY

The term was later used by Abraham Maslow in his article, *A Theory of Human Motivation*. Maslow explicitly defines self-actualization to be "the desire for self-fulfillment, namely the tendency for him [the individual] to become actualized in what he is potentially. This tendency might be phrased as the desire to become more and more what one is, to become everything that one is capable of becoming." Maslow used the term self-actualization to describe a desire, not a driving force, that could lead to realizing one's capabilities. Maslow did not feel that self-actualization determined one's life; rather, he felt that it gave the individual a desire, or motivation to achieve budding ambitions. Maslow's usage of the term is now popular in modern psychology when discussing personality from the humanistic approach.

A basic definition from a typical college text book defines self-actualization according to Maslow simply as "the full realization of one's potential" without any mention of antiquated Goldstein. A more explicit definition of self-actualization according to Maslow is "intrinsic growth of what is already in the organism, or more accurately of what is the organism itself...self-actualization is growth-motivated rather than deficiency-motivated."

This explanation emphasizes the fact that self-actualization can not normally be reached until other lower order necessities of Maslow's hierarchy of needs are satisfied. While Goldstein defined self-actualization as a driving force, Maslow uses the term to describe personal growth that takes place once lower order needs have been met.

People that have reached self-actualization are characterized by certain behaviors. Common traits amongst people that have reached self-actualization are as follows:

- They embrace reality and facts rather than denying truth.
- They are spontaneous.
- They are interested in solving problems.
- They are accepting of themselves and also others and lack prejudice.

For Goldstein it was a motive and for Maslow it was a level of development; for both, however, roughly the same kinds of qualities were expressed: independence, autonomy, a tendency to form few but deep friendships, a "philosophical" sense of humour, a tendency to resist outside pressures and a general transcendence of the environment rather than a simple "coping" with it. Self-actualisation has been discussed by Schott in connection with Transpersonal business studies.

SELF ACTUALIZATION IN PSYCHOLOGY

Self actualization resides at the top of Maslow's hierarchy of needs and is considered a part of the humanistic approach to personality. The humanistic approach is one of several methods used in psychology for studying, understanding, and evaluating personality. The humanistic approach was developed because other approaches, such as the psychodynamic approach made famous by Sigmund Freud, focused on unhealthy individuals that exhibited disturbed behaviour.

The humanistic approach focuses on healthy, motivated people and tries to determine how they define the self while maximizing their potential. Stemming from this branch of psychology is Maslow's hierarchy of needs. According to Maslow, people have lower order needs that in general must be fulfilled before high order needs can be satisfied. As a person moves up Maslow's hierarchy of needs, eventually they will reach the summit—self actualization. Maslow's hierarchy of needs begins with the most basic necessities deemed "the physiological needs" in which the individual will seek out items like food and water, and must be able to perform basic functions such as breathing and sleeping. Once these needs have been met, a person can move on to fulfilling the "the safety needs", where they will attempt to obtain a sense of security, physical comforts and shelter, employment, and property.

The next level is "the belongingness and love needs", where people will strive for social acceptance, affiliations, a sense of belongingness and being welcome, sexual intimacy, and perhaps a family. Next are "the esteem needs", where the individual will desire a sense of competence, recognition of achievement by peers, and respect from others. Some argue that once these needs are met, an individual is primed for self actualization. Others argue that there are two more phases an individual must progress through before self actualization can take place. These include "the cognitive needs", where a person will desire knowledge and an understanding of the world around them, and "the aesthetic needs" which include a need for "symmetry, order, and beauty". Once all these needs have been satisfied, the final stage of Maslow's hierarchy—self actualization—can take place.

STUDYING THE SELF CONCEPT

Self concept, an ignored and neglected area in psychology and education for long, has now been recognised to play a vital role in personality development. It has been established by contemporary researches that the way an individual perceives himself goes to shape his behaviour patterns. According to Combs and Snygg (1949) and Rogers (1951), people behave in a manner which is consistent with the way they view themselves. Festinger (1962) says the ways we react to people, tasks,... etc. are those which seem to us most consistent with our self image.

To illustrate the influence of self concept on performance, Lowry (1961) narrates a story of *The mouse and Henry Carson,* in which he describes how a mouse ran into the office of the Educational Testing Service and accidentally triggered a delicate point in the apparatus just as the College Entrance Examination Board's data on one Henry Carson was being scored. Henry was an average high-school student who was unsure of himself and his abilities. Had it not been for the mouse, Henry's scores would have been average or less, but the mouse changed all that, for the scores which emerged from the computer were amazingly high. When the scores reached Henry's school, the word of his giftedness spread like wild fire.

Teachers began to re-evaluate their gross underestimation of this fine lad, counsellors felt guilty of having neglected such talent, and even College Admissions Officers began to recruit Henry for their institutions. Once Henry became aware of his potentialities and began to be treated differently by the significant people in his life, a form of self-fulfilling prophecy took place. Henry gained in confidence and began "to put his mind in the way of great things". Henry became one of the best men of his generation. Self concept has been defined by several authors.

William James(1890) holds it to be all that a person is tempted to call by the name *me* or mine. Murphy (1947) defines it as the individual as known to the individual. According to Symonds (1951), it is the way or manner in which the individual reacts to himself. He spells out four aspects of self: i. how a person perceives himself; ii. what he thinks of himself; iii. how he values himself; and iv. how he attempts through various actions to enhance or defend himself.

Carl Rogers (1951) views the self as a differentiated portion of the phenomenal field, consisting of a pattern of conscious perceptions and values of the "I" or "me". He spells out some of the properties of self: a) the self develops out of the organism's interaction with the environment; b) it may introject the values of other people and perceive them in a distorted fashion; c) it strives for consistency; d) the organism behaves in ways that are consistent with the self; e) experiences that are not consistent with the self-structure are perceived as threats; f) the self may change as a result of maturation and learning. Sherif & Cantril (1947) use the term "ego" and define it as the constellation of attitudes of the type "what I think of myself, what I value, what is mine, and what I identify with." According to them, these attitudes, when activated, energise, direct and control the person's behaviour.

As self concept seems to play a significant role in the growth and development of a person, a detailed knowledge about its nature and its relation to other important factors of personality will provide an objective and encouraging basis for the educators and counsellors to work on. Torrance (1954) vouches for the practical uses of knowledge of the self concept in counselling and guidance. With such educational and counselling ends in mind, numerous studies have been undertaken on the subject in different parts of the world. Indian studies on the subject have dealt with: factors contributing to changes in self concept; implementation of self concept in occupational choices; differences in self concepts of achievers and nonachievers in school; etc.

Adjustment is a state of "harmonious relation to the environment wherein one is able to obtain satisfaction for most of one's needs and to meet fairly well the demands, physical and social, put upon one" (English & English). One could distinguish between adjustment within oneself (intrapersonal) and with others (interpersonal). Achievement refers to bringing an effort to the desired end or the end gained. Since adjustment and achievement are two cardinal dimensions of a person's behaviour and since self concept is acceptedly a significant influencer of behaviour, it was felt that a knowledge of the relationship between self concept and the other two variables would be very enriching and useful.

METHOD AND MEASURES

On the basis of the available knowledge on self concept and its role in behaviour, the following specific hypothetical issues were raised with a view to testing them out empirically:

- Self concept correlates positively with adjustment.
- Self concept correlates positively with achievement.
- Some areas of self concept correlate more with personal adjustment than do other areas.
- Some areas of self concept correlate more with social adjustment than do other areas.
- Some areas of self concept correlate more with achievement than do other areas.

Following a discussion with the guide, it was decided to carry out the investigation among the students of the M.S. University studying in the preparatory class. A sample of two hundred and twenty-five was selected in a stratified random style to represent the various disciplines of the students. A self concept inventory and an adjustment inventory that suited our purpose were procured and data were collected by means of these instruments. The self concept inventory measured self concepts in six areas, such as the physical appearance, intellectual ability, sociability, temperament, morality, and position in the family. Two dimensions of adjustment, namely, personal and social, were measured by the adjustment inventory. These instruments had been standardised in the relevant population. Examination marks of the students were taken to indicate their academic achievement level. Thus scores on self concept, adjustment, and achievement were obtained.

ANALYSIS AND RESULTS

Pearson's product-moment correlations were computed for the total self-concept score with overall adjustment and achievement scores. Correlations were also computed for the six subself-concept scores with personal adjustment score, social adjustment score, and achievement score. All the six areal self concepts correlated positively with personal, social and overall adjustments. Many of these correlations were significant and a few of them were not: self concepts of physical appearance, intelligence and temperament did not correlate significantly with personal adjustment. Self concept on status in the family did not show a statistically significant relationship with social adjustment.

The present study corroborates the tenet that one's personal and social adjustment in life is positively related to one's overall self concept. IntrApersonal adjustment or one's being at peace with oneself does not seem to be related to what one thinks of one's physical appearance, intelligence or temperament. IntErpersonal adjustment or being adjusted in society, however, was found to be related to these conceptions.

The study did not bear out the prediction that achievement would be related to self concept. How shall we interpret this finding? Maybe, achievement is independent of self concept and Henry Carsons are nothing more than a fairy tale! Or, could it be that examination marks are no *achievement*?

REMARKS

The instruments, though they had been standardised on the population, were verbal and direct. In personal areas like self concept and adjustment, indirect approaches would be more effective. It is also desirable to obtain multiple measures of self concept, adjustment and achievement through means of more than one instrument for each of them, so as to enhance the robustness of the measures. Gender could be introduced as a variable to examine any differences between male and female respondents.

MEASURING PERSONALITY: SELF-REPORT TESTS LIKE QUESTIONNAIRES AND INVENTORIES

A self-report inventory is a type of psychological test often used in personality assessment. This type of test is often presented in a paper-and-pencil format or may even be administered on a computer. A typical self report inventory presents a number of questions or statements that may or may not describe certain qualities or characteristics of the test subject. Chances are good that you have taken a self-report inventory at some time the past. Such questionnaires are often seen in doctors' offices, in on-line personality tests and in market research surveys. This type of survey can be used to look at your current behaviors, past behaviors and possible behaviors in hypothetical situations.

Examples of Self-Report Inventories:

- The MMPI-2

Perhaps the most famous self-report inventory is the Minnesota Multiphasic Personality Inventory (MMPI). This personality test was first published in the 1940s, later revised in the 1980s and is today known as the MMPI-2. The test contains more than 500 statements that assess a wide variety of topics including interpersonal relationships, abnormal behaviors and psychological health as well as political, social, religious and sexual attitudes.

- The 16 Personality Factor Questionnaire

Another well known example of a self-report inventory is the questionnaire developed by Raymond Cattell to assess individuals based on his trait theory of personality. This test is used to generate personality profile of the individual and is often used to evaluate employees to help people select a career.

- California Personality Inventory

California personality inventory is based on the MMPI, from which nearly half questions are drawn. The test is designed to measure such characteristic as self control, empathy and independence.

STRENGTHS AND WEAKNESSES OF SELF-REPORT INVENTORIES

Self-report inventories are often an good solution when researchers need to administer a large number of tests in relatively short space of time. Many self report inventories can be completed very quickly, often in as little as 15 minutes. This type of questionnaire is an affordable option for researchers faced with tight budgets. Another strength is that the results of self report inventories are generally much more reliable and valid than projective tests. Scoring of the tests a standardized and based on norms that have been previously established.

However, self report inventories to have their weaknesses. For example, while many tests implement strategies to prevent "faking good" or "faking bad," research has shown that people are able to exercise deception while taking a self report test.

Another weakness is that some tests are very long and tedious. For example, the MMPI takes approximately 3 hours to complete. In some cases, a test respondent may simply lose interest and not answer questions accurately. Additionally, people are sometimes not the best judges of their own behaviour. Some individuals may try to hide their own feelings, thoughts and attitudes. A personality test aims to describe aspects of a person's character that remain stable throughout that person's lifetime, the individual's character pattern of behaviour, thoughts, and feelings. An early model of personality was posited by Greek philosopher/physician Hippocrates.

The 20th century heralded a new interest in defining and identifying separate personality types, in close correlation with the emergence of the field of psychology. As such, several distinct tests emerged; some attempt to identify specific characteristics, while others attempt to identify personality as a whole. There are many different types of personality tests. Common personality tests consist of a large number of items, where respondents must rate the applicability of each item to themselves. Projective tests, such as the TAT and Ink Blots are another form of personality test which attempt to assess personality indirectly.

SCORING

Personality tests can be scored using a dimensional (normative) or a typological (ipsative) approach. Dimensional approaches such as the Big 5 describe personality as a set of continuous dimensions on which individuals differ. Typological approaches such as the Myers-Briggs Type Indicator (r) describe opposing categories of functioning where individuals differ. Normative responses for each category can be graphed as bell curves (normal curves), implying that some aspects of personality are better than others. Ipsative test responses offer two equally "good" responses between which an individual must choose. Such responses (e.g., on the MBTI) would result in bi-modal graphs for each category, rather than bell curves.

Personality tests such as the Strength Deployment Inventory (r), which assesses motivation, or purpose, of behaviour, rather than the behaviour itself, combine a dimensional and typological approach as described here. Three continuums of motivation are combined to yield 7 distinct types. Many, but by no means all, psychological researchers believe that the dimensional approach is more accurate, although as judged by the popularity of the Myers-Briggs tool, typological approaches have substantial appeal as a self-development tool.

Few personality tests accurately predict behaviour in a specific context. For example, with some of the five factor model tests, only one of the five factors is significantly correlated with job performance. Emotive tests can become prey to unreliable results as most people strive to pick the answer they feel the best fitting of an ideal character and therefore not their personal response.

NORMS

The meaning of personality test scores are difficult to interpret in a direct sense. For this reason substantial effort is made by producers of personality tests to produce norms to provide a comparative basis for interpreting a respondent's test scores. Common formats for these norms include percentile ranks, z scores, sten scores, and other forms of standardised scores.

TEST DEVELOPMENT

A substantial amount of research and thinking has gone into the topic of personality test development. Development of personality tests tends to be an iterative process whereby a test is progressively refined. Test development can proceed on theoretical or statistical grounds. Theoretical strategies can involve taking psychological or other theory to define the content domain and then developing test items that should in principle measure the domain of interest. This can then be accompanied by assessment by experts of the developed items to the defined construct. Statistical strategies are varied. Common strategies involve the use of exploratory factor analysis and confirmatory factor analysis to verify that items that are proposed to group together into factors actually do group together empirically. Reliability analysis and Item Response Theory are additional complimentary approaches.

TEST EVALUATION

There are several criteria for evaluating a personality test. Fundamentally, a personality test is expected to demonstrate reliability and validity.

CRITICISM AND CONTROVERSY

Biased Test Taker Interpretation

One problem of a personality test is that the users of the test could only find it accurate because of the subjective validation involved. This is where the person only acknowledges the information that applies to them. This is related to what is called in psychology as the Forer effect

Application to Non-clinical Samples

Critics have raised issues about the ethics of administering personality tests, especially for non-clinical uses. By the 1960s, tests like the MMPI were being given by companies to employees and applicants as often as to psychiatric patients. Sociologist William H. Whyte was among those who saw the tests as helping to create and perpetuate the oppressive groupthink of the "organization man" mid-20th century corporate capitalistic mentality.

PERSONALITY VERSUS SOCIAL FACTORS

In the 60s and 70s some psychologists dismissed the whole

idea of personality, considering much behaviour to be content specific.

This idea was supported by the fact that personality often does not predict behaviour in specific contexts. However, more extensive research has showed than when behaviour is aggregated across contexts, that personality can be a modest to good predictor of behaviour.

Almost all psychologists now acknowledge that both social and individual difference factors (i.e., personality) influence behaviour. The debate is currently more around the relative importance of each of these factors and how these factors interact.

RESPONDENT FAKING

One problem with self-report measures of personality is that respondents are often able to distort their responses. This is particularly problematic in employment contexts and other contexts where important decisions are being made and there is an incentive to present oneself in a favourable manner. Work in experimental settings has clearly shown that when student samples have been asked to deliberately fake on a personality test, they clearly demonstrated that they are capable of doing so.

Several strategies have been adopted for reducing respondent faking. One strategy involves providing a warning on the test that methods exist for detecting faking and that detection will result in negative consequences for the respondent (e.g., not being considered for the job).

Forced choice item formats (ipsative testing) have been adopted which require respondents to choose between alternatives of equal social desirability.

Social desirability and lie scales are often included which detect certain patterns of responses, although these are often confounded by true variability in social desirability. More recently, Item Response Theory approaches have been adopted with some success in identifying item response profiles that flag fakers. Other researchers are looking at the timing of responses on electronically administered tests to assess faking.

PSYCHOLOGICAL RESEARCH

Personality testing is frequently used in psychological research to test various theories of personality. Research published by David Dunning of Cornell University, Chip Heath of Stanford University and Jerry M. Suls of the University of Iowa reveals that observers who are not involved in any type of relationship with an individual are better judges of the individual's relationships and abilities. These workers have studied a large body of investigations into self-evaluation, indicating that individuals may have flawed views about themselves and their social relationships, sometimes leading to decisions that can impact negatively on other persons' lives and/or their own.

ADDITIONAL APPLICATIONS

A study by American Management Association reveals that 39 percent of companies surveyed use personality testing as part of their hiring process. However, ipsative personality tests are often misused in recruitment and selection, where they are mistakenly treated as if they are normative measures. More people are using personality testing to evaluate their business partners, their dates and their spouses. Salespeople are using personality testing to better understand the needs of their customers and to gain a competitive edge in the closing of deals. College students have started to use personality testing to evaluate their roommates. Lawyers are beginning to use personality testing for criminal behaviour analysis, litigation profiling, witness examination and jury selection.

DANGERS OF SUCH PRACTICES

It is easy for personality test participants to become complacent about their own personal uniqueness and instead become dependent on the description associated with them. This can be potentially dangerous with persons who are already suffering from a form of identity disorder or may be a catalyst to instigate particular behaviours in a person who was previously believed to be of sound mental health.

The severity of the damage that individuals can sustain

to their personal identity was made clear during the case Wilson v Johnson &Johnson in which the plaintiff (Wilson) sued his former employer for irreperable damages that resulted from the over abundance of personality tests being administered in the worksplace. Wilson argued that repeated questioning and scrutiny of his personality was a cause of strain and eventually breakdown. In this historic case, Wilson was awarded $4.7 million after jurors agreed that excessive testing caused strain and led to unnecessary scrutiny resulting in personal grief. Similar cases have been tried since and won, but none with such a magnitude as this first monumental case that won mental health rights for employees.

Examples of personality tests:

- The first modern personality test was the Woodworth Personal data sheet, which was first used in 1919. It was designed to help the United States Army screen out recruits who might be susceptible to shell shock.
- The Rorschach inkblot test was introduced in 1921 as a way to determine personality by the interpretation of abstract inkblots.
- The Thematic Apperception Test was commissioned by the Office of Strategic Services (O.S.S.) in the 1930s to identify personalities that might be susceptible to being turned by enemy intelligence.
- The Minnesota Multiphasic Personality Inventory was published in 1942 as a way to aid in assessing psychopathology in a clinical setting.
- Myers-Briggs Type Indicator is a 16-type indicator based on Carl Jung's *Psychological Types,* developed during World War II by Isabel Myers and Katherine Briggs.
- Keirsey Temperament Sorter developed by David Keirsey is influenced by Isabel Myers sixteen types and Ernest Kretschmer's four types.
- The 16PF Questionnaire (16PF) was developed by Raymond Cattell and his colleagues in the 1940's and 1950's in a search to try to discover the basic traits of human personality using scientific methodology.

The test was first published in 1949, and is now in its 5th edition, published in 1994. It is used in a wide variety of settings for individual and marital counseling, career counseling and employee development, in educational settings, and for basic research.

- The EQSQ Test developed by Professor Simon Baron-Cohen, Sally Wheelwright, and their team at the University of Cambridge, England, centers on the Empathizing-Systemizing theory of the male versus the female brain types.
- The Personal Style Indicator (PSI) is a self administered, self scoring assessment, it is not a test that can be passed or failed. The PSI classifies four aspects of innate behaviour by testing a person's preferences in word associations.
- The Strength Deployment Inventory, developed by Elias Porter, Ph.D. in 1971 and is based on his theory of Relationship Awareness. Porter was the first known psychometrician to use colors (Red, Green and Blue) as shortcuts to communicate the results of a personality test.
- Other personality tests include the NEO PI-R, Millon Clinical Multiaxial Inventory, Eysenck Personality Questionnaire, and Swedish Universities Scales of Personality.

PROJECTIVE MEASURES OF PERSONALITY

Psychological testing is a field characterized by the use of samples of behaviour in order to infer generalizations about a given individual. The technical term for the science behind psychological testing is psychometrics. By *samples of behaviour*, one means observations over time of an individual performing tasks that have usually been prescribed beforehand, which often means scores on a test. These responses are often compiled into statistical tables that allow the evaluator to compare the behaviour of the individual being tested to the responses of a norm group. Psychological assessment is similar to psychological testing but usually involves a more comprehensive assessment of the individual.

Psychological assessment is a process that involves the integration of information from multiple sources, such as tests of normal and abnormal personality, tests of ability or intelligence, tests of interests or attitudes, as well as information from personal interviews. Collateral information is also collected about personal, occupational, or medical history, such as from records or from interviews with parents, spouses, teachers, or previous therapists or physicians. A *psychological test* is one of the sources of data used within the process of assessment; usually more than one test is used. Many psychologists do some level of assessment when providing services to clients or patients, and may use for example, simple checklists to assess some traits or symptoms, but psychological assessment is a more complex, detailed, in-depth process.

Typical types of focus for psychological assessment are to provide a diagnosis for treatment settings; to assess a particular area of functioning or disability often for school settings; to help select type of treatment or to assess treatment outcomes; to help courts decide issues such as child custody or competency to stand trial; or to help assess job applicants or employees and provide career development counseling or training. A useful psychological measure must be both valid (i.e., there is evidence to support the specified interpretation of the test results) and reliable (i.e., internally consistent or give consistent results over time, across raters, etc.).

Psychological tests, like many measurements of human characteristics, can be interpreted in a *norm-referenced* or *criterion-referenced* manner. Norms are statistical representations of a population. A norm-referenced score interpretation compares an individual's results on the test with the statistical representation of the population. In practice, rather than testing a population, a representative sample or group is tested. This provides a group norm or set of norms. One representation of norms is the Bell curve (also called "normal curve"). Norms are available for standardized psychological tests, allowing for an understanding of how an individual's scores compare with the group norms. Norm referenced scores are typically reported on the standard score (z) scale or a rescaling of it.

A criterion-referenced interpretation of a test score compares an individual's performance to some criterion other than performance of other individuals. For example, the generic school test typically provides a score in reference to a subject domain; a student might score 80% on a geography test. Criterion-referenced score interpretations are generally more applicable to achievement tests rather than psychological tests. Often, test scores can be interpreted in both ways; a score of 80% on a geography test could place a student at the 84th percentile, or a standard score of 1.0 or even 2.0.

TYPES OF PSYCHOLOGICAL TESTS

There are several broad categories of psychological tests:

IQ/Achievement Tests

IQ tests are measures of intelligence, while achievement tests are measures of the use and level of development of use of the ability. IQ (or cognitive) tests and achievement tests are common norm-referenced tests. In these types of tests, a series of tasks is presented to the person being evaluated, and the person's responses are graded according to carefully prescribed guidelines. After the test is completed, the results can be compiled and compared to the responses of a norm group, usually comprised of people at the same age or grade level as the person being evaluated. IQ tests which contain a series of tasks typically divide the tasks into verbal (relying on the use of language) and performance, or non-verbal (relying on eye-hand types of tasks, or use of symbols or objects). Examples of verbal IQ test tasks are vocabulary and information (answering general knowledge questions). Non-verbal examples are timed completion of puzzles (object assembly), making designs out of coloured blocks (block design).

IQ tests (e.g., WAIS-III, WISC-IV, Cattell Culture Fair III

and academic achievement tests (e.g. WIAT, WRAT) are designed to be administered to either an individual (by a trained evaluator) or to a group of people (paper and pencil tests). The individually-administered tests tend to be more comprehensive, more reliable, more valid and generally to have better psychometric characteristics than group-administered tests. However, individually-administered tests are more expensive to administer because of the need for a trained administrator (psychologist, school psychologist, or psychometrician) and because of the limitation of working with just one client at a time.

Neuropsychological Tests

These tests consist of specifically designed tasks used to measure a psychological function known to be linked to a particular brain structure or pathway. They are typically used to assess impairment after an injury or illness known to affect neurocognitive functioning, or when used in research, to contrast neuropsychological abilities across experimental groups.

Personality Tests

Psychological measures of personality are often described as either objective tests or projective tests. Some projective tests are used less often today because they are more time consuming to administer.

Objective Tests (Rating Scale)

Objective tests have a restricted response format, such as allowing for true or false answers or rating using an ordinal scale. Prominent examples of objective personality tests include the Minnesota Multiphasic Personality Inventory, Millon Clinical Multiaxial Inventory-III, Child Behaviour Checklist, and the Beck Depression Inventory. Objective personality tests can be designed for use in business for potential employees, such as the NEO-PI, the 16PF, and the Occupational Personality questionnaire, all of which are based on the Big Five taxonomy. The Big Five, or Five Factor Model of normal personality, has gained acceptance since the early 1990s when some influential meta-analyses (e.g., Barrick & Mount 1991) found consistent relationships between the Big Five personality factors and important criterion variables.

PROJECTIVE TESTS (FREE RESPONSE MEASURES)

Projective tests allow for a freer type of response. An example of this would be the Rorschach test, in which a person states what each of ten ink blots might be. The terms "objective test" and "projective test" have recently come under criticism in the *Journal of Personality Assessment*.

The more descriptive "rating scale or self-report measures" and "free response measures" are suggested, rather than the terms "objective tests" and "projective tests," respectively.

As improved sampling and statistical methods developed, much controversy regarding the utility and validity of projective testing has occurred. The use of clinical judgement rather than norms and statistics to evaluate people's characteristics has convinced many that projetives are deficient and unreliable (results are too dissimilar each time a test is given to the same person).

However, many practitioners continue to rely on projective testing, and some testing experts (e.g., Cohen, Anastasi) suggest that these measures can be useful in developing therapeutic rapport. They may also be useful in creating inferences to follow-up with other methods. Possibly they have lingered in usage because they have a mystical and fascinating reputation, and are more attractive to uninformed people than answering objective tests, e.g., true/false questionnaires.

The most widely used scoring system for the Rorschach is the Exner system of scoring. Another common projective test is the Thematic Apperception Test (TAT), which is often scored with Westen's Social Cognition and Object Relations Scales and Phebe Cramer's Defence Mechanisms Manual. Both "rating scale" and "free response" measures are used in contemporary clinical practice, with a trend toward the former.

Other projective tests include the House-Tree-Person Test, Robert's Apperception Test, and the Attachment Projective.

Sexological Tests

The number of tests specifically meant for the field of sexology is quite limited.

The field of sexology provides different psychological evaluation devices in order to examine the various aspects of the discomfort, problem or dysfunction, regardless of whether they are individual or relational ones.

Direct Observation Tests

Although most psychological tests are "rating scale" or "free response" measures, psychological assessment may also involve the observation of people as they complete activities. This type of assessment is usually conducted with families in a laboratory, home or with children in a classroom.

The purpose may be clinical, such as to establish a pre-intervention baseline of a child's hyperactive or aggressive classroom behaviors or to observe the nature of a parent-child interaction in order to understand a relational disorder. Direct observation procedures are also used in research, for example to study the relationship between intrapsychic variables and specific target behaviors, or to explore sequences of behavioral interaction.

The Parent-Child Interaction Assessment-II (PCIA) is an example of a direct observation procedure that is used with school-age children and parents.

The parents and children are video recorded playing at a make-believe zoo. The Parent-Child Early Relational Assessment (Clark, 1999) is used to study parents and young children and involves a feeding and a puzzle task. The MacArthur Story Stem Battery (MSSB) is used to elicit narratives from children. The Dyadic Parent-Child Interaction Coding System-II tracks the extent to which children follow the commands of parents and *vice versa* and is well suited to the study of children with Oppositional Defiant Disorders and their parents.

PERSONALITY AND HEALTH

PERSONALITY AND PERCEIVED STRESS

An individual must perceive a stressor in order for it to have an impact on them, and people's *personalities* determine how they will perceive something. Some people perceive certain events as more stressful as others. Also, the very same situation can be experienced differently depending on their personality. A shy person who is at a busy loud party will experience more stress in the situation than an outgoing person that thrives on that sort of experience.

PERSONALITY TYPES AND BEHAVIOUR PATTERNS

There are personality variables that are linked to certain *health* outcomes. Stress seems to be a factor in these personality types and specifically how a person responds to stress.

- Type-A Behaviour Pattern: This type of behaviour pattern occurs in individuals when they demonstrate: a) a competitive orientation towards achievement, b) a sense of urgency about time, and c) a strong tendency to feel anger and hostility. They tend to strive very hard and competitively towards certain goals, often without feeling much enjoyment in the process at all.
- Type-B Behaviour Pattern: This individual demonstrates low levels of competitiveness and urgency about time. They are more easygoing and relaxed and enjoy life.

Type A and Type B personalities react differently to stress. Type-A's respond more quickly and forcefully and tend to view sources of stress as threats to their personal self-control. They act in ways that increase the likelihood that they will encounter stress. They create their own stress, by seeking out demanding, competitive situations, and by creating artificial deadlines for themselves. A number of studies have found a link between Type-A behaviour and coronary heart disease. The three specific components of Type-A behaviour that contribute to heart disease include anger and hostility. Anger and hostility directed against the self may be especially damaging to health. Also, hostility characterized by suspiciousness, resentment, frequent anger and antagonism towards others seems to be bad for health.

Some reasons have been proposed as top why Type-A personalities experience more heart disease. As previously mentioned, these types of individuals experience more stress. One theory proposes that when people perceive stress, their bodies try to pump greater amounts of blood through narrower constricted blood vessels.

This may wear out the coronary arteries, lead to lesions and produce heart attack. Another theory suggests that hormones activated by stress may cause continual change in blood pressure and undermine resilient blood vessels. A third theory states that stress could cause lipids to release into the blood stream, which contributes to atherosclerosis, a disease that causes fatty deposits to constrict blood vessels.

Bibliography

Banks, J.A. (1993). Multicultural education: Development, dimensions, and challenges. Phi Delta Kappan, 75, 22-28.

Bigge, M. & Shermis, S.(1992). Learning Theories for Teachers. New York, 5th edition.

Fry, T.S. (2000). Multicultural perceptions held by preservice social studies teachers, Journal of Critical Inquiry into Curriculum and Instruction, vol. 2, No. 2.

Gardner, H. (1983). Frames of mind: The theory of multiple intelligences.

Grigorenko, E. L. (1998). Mastering tools of the mind in school—Trying out Vygotsky's ideas in classrooms. In Sternberg, R. & Williams, W. (Eds.) Intelligence, Instruction and Assessment—Theory into Practice, New Jersey.

Sadker, M. & Sadker, D. (1986). Sexism in the classroom: From grade school to graduate school. 68, 512.

Woolfolk, A. E. (1998). Educational Psychology, Allyn and Bacon 7th edition.

Bandura, A., & Walters, R. H. (1963). Social learning and personality development. New York.

Bjorn, D.W. (1993). B. F. Skinner; A life. New York.

Bloom, B. S. (1984). The 2 sigma problem. 13(6), 4-16.

Cameron, J. & Pierce, W.D. (1994). Reinforcement, reward and intrinsic motivation: A meta-analysis. Review of Educational Research, 64(3), 363-423. See also the Spring 1996 Review of Educational Research 66(1) for a number of articles following up on and challenging this Cameron and Pierce paper.

Keller, F. S. (1969). Learning: Reinforcement theory. New York.

Krumboltz, J. D., & Krumboltz, H. B. (1972). Changing children's behavior. Englewood Cliffs, NJ.

McGinnies, E. (1970). Social behavior: A functional analysis. Boston.

Morgan, M. (1984). Reward-induced decrements and increments in intrinsic motivation. 54(1), 5- 30.

Skinner, B. F. (1962). Walden two. New York.

Skinner, B. F. (1968). The technology of teaching. New York.

Skinner, B. F. (1972). Beyond freedom and dignity. New York.

Skinner, B. F. (1976). About behaviorism. New York.

Index

A

B

C

D

E

F

G

H

I

Q

R

S

T

V

W